Building Back Truth in an Age of Misinformation

Building Back Truth in an Age of Misinformation

Leslie F. Stebbins

Foreword by Ethan Zuckerman

ROWMAN & LITTLEFIELD
Lanham • Boulder • New York • London

Published by Rowman & Littlefield
An imprint of The Rowman & Littlefield Publishing Group, Inc.
4501 Forbes Boulevard, Suite 200, Lanham, Maryland 20706
www.rowman.com

86-90 Paul Street, London EC2A 4NE

British Library Cataloguing in Publication Information Available

Library of Congress Cataloging-in-Publication Data
Names: Stebbins, Leslie F., 1958- author. | Zuckerman, Ethan, writer of
   foreword.
Title: Building back truth in an age of misinformation / Leslie F. Stebbins
   ; foreword by Ethan Zuckerman.
Description: Lanham : Rowman & Littlefield, [2023] | Includes
   bibliographical references and index.
Identifiers: LCCN 2022033710 (print) | LCCN 2022033711 (ebook) | ISBN
   9781538163146 (cloth) | ISBN 9781538163153 (epub)
Subjects: LCSH: Social media. | Social media--Economic aspects. |
   Truthfulness and falsehood. | Misinformation.
Classification: LCC HM742 .S8329 2023 (print) | LCC HM742 (ebook) | DDC
   302.23/1--dc23/eng/20220729
LC record available at https://lccn.loc.gov/2022033710
LC ebook record available at https://lccn.loc.gov/2022033711

To Mang, Anna, and Chetra

Contents

Foreword

$\mathcal{O}$f all challenges to contemporary democracy, information disorder may be the most disturbing. Americans have grown used to the idea that we live in a deeply polarized society, that mistrust in government institutions is high, that debates about controversial issues seem intractable. But the rise of mis- and disinformation online and offline feels more viscerally destabilizing.

Democracy is based on the idea that citizens can evaluate the world they live in and decide how society should be governed and regulated, either by electing representatives or by voting directly on legislation. Democracy relies on deliberation—the process of discussing pressing issues with friends, neighbors, and ideological rivals—to identify solutions to civic problems.

Deliberation becomes impossible if we no longer have a shared reality of agreed-upon facts. For example, should schools require children to wear masks to prevent the spread of COVID? Meaningful deliberation is impossible between someone who believes COVID is a dangerous and highly contagious disease and one who believes COVID is mostly harmless and a ploy for increased government control. Our political tensions often stem not from rival interpretations of a common set of facts but from rival sets of "facts" marshaled by opposing sides.

Leslie Stebbins realizes the seriousness of this threat to democracy and responds with a challenging but comforting message: it is possible to fight information disorder, but it's certainly not easy. Simply identifying and correcting misinformation rarely works. Instead, confronting misinformation requires changing how we think and how systems function.

Stebbins leads the way through debates about misinformation, which span from the lofty heights of epistemology to the technical trenches of

Russian disinformation campaigns, following the paths she knows well from decades as a librarian. Her years helping others navigate information spaces before and after the advent of the World Wide Web mean that she is focused on answering concrete, practical questions: How do you avoid being misled by information? What is it possible for technology companies to do in fighting misinformation? What information resources do we need to build to be informed and engaged citizens at this moment in the history of democracy?

I've lived my entire adult life on the internet—from my first days as a college student in 1989 to teaching courses on internet architectures and politics at major universities—and I found new and helpful ideas from Stebbins for protecting myself against believing and sharing misinformation. Leveraging some of the ideas from Daniel Kahneman's *Thinking Fast and Slow*, Stebbins explains that cognitive heuristics that help us make split-second decisions are the same mental patterns that misinformation exploits and—not coincidentally—the same habits that platforms and the advertisers they serve seek to manipulate. We react emotionally to misinformation, and we can fight it by slowing down our thinking to react more analytically. Every time I have inadvertently shared misinformation, it's been something highly emotional or outrageous that I felt compelled to share. I need to slow down and think more analytically, and you probably do too.

But information disorder isn't a problem we can tackle individually, no matter how carefully we navigate online spaces. We need to rethink and rebuild the social media structures that have hastened the spread of misinformation in recent years. While Stebbins puts the blame squarely on the ad-based revenue model of social media platforms for turning online communities into amplifiers of misinformation, she explains that the solutions are far more complex than flipping a switch to "demonetize" misinformation. Artificial intelligence, embraced by tech companies as a solution to solving complex problems at scale, can't yet deal with the nuanced questions of whether a specific story is true or false. (Indeed, it's often a hard task for human readers.)

Recognizing the deep civic importance of online communities—our contemporary digital public sphere—and regulating them to ensure their social benefit are part of the solution. But so is choosing to imagine and build new social spaces that reject the surveillant commercial logic of Facebook and Twitter in favor of prosocial logics. Ultimately, the solution to combatting misinformation may be building an internet designed to help us be better citizens and neighbors rather than better consumers.

Combating information disorder is one of the hardest and most important challenges of our time. Stebbins gives us reason to hope we might navigate this complex landscape and, in the process, end up building something better than the internet we currently have.

Ethan Zuckerman
Associate Professor of Public Policy, Information and Communication
University of Massachusetts–Amherst
June 2022

Acknowledgments

$\mathcal{H}$elping connect people to reliable and trustworthy content has been a lifelong pursuit for me, first as an academic librarian and currently as an independent researcher. I have been disheartened to watch our online worlds degenerate from their early promise of connecting people to reliable information to the information disorder we find ourselves in today. What happened?

I'm so grateful to have had so many brilliant guides to help me understand the problem and to help point us all toward solutions. I am completely indebted to many scholars and activists. While there are far too many to list here, I did want to give a special shout-out to the work of Claire Wardle, Joan Donovan, Ethan Zuckerman, Barbara Fister, Renee Hobbs, Julia Angwin, Safiya Umoja Noble, Shoshana Zuboff, Israr Khan, danah boyd, Cass Sunstein, Miriam J. Metzger, Hossein Derakhshan, Martha Minow, Victor Pickard, Jonathan L. Zittrain, Eli Pariser, and Paul Mihailidis.

I would also like to acknowledge a few of the many heroes who have left their comfortable positions at large tech companies to work to build more humane online spaces: Frances Haugen, formerly a data engineer at Meta, who disclosed tens of thousands of Facebook's internal documents to the Securities and Exchange Commission and the *Wall Street Journal*; Tristan Harris, formerly a design ethicist at Google, who left to cofound, with Aza Raskin, the Center for Humane Technology; Tim Kendall, the former director for monetization at Facebook, who has testified before Congress and now helps fund humane technology projects; Timnit Gebru, a computer scientist who led an ethical AI team at Google and has now founded the Distributed Artificial Intelligence Research Institute (DAIR); and Jeff Allen and Sahar Massachi, former members of the integrity team at Facebook/Meta, who have now founded the independent Integrity Institute to advise policy makers, regulators, and the media about how to improve social media platforms. If you are interested in this type of work or study, please see my website for a curated list of organizations and programs (http://www.lesliestebbins.com).

More directly, I would like to express my special gratitude to the following people who played essential roles in the development of this book. Special thanks to my editor, Charles Harmon, senior executive editor at Rowman & Littlefield, for all of his support and feedback, to Jennifer Frakes for her brilliant proofreading skills, and to Doron Weber, vice president and program director at the Alfred P. Sloan Foundation, for his strong support. I would also like to give enormous thanks to John Richards, my mentor and coinvestigator, whose feedback was essential in helping me pull together and reenvision the structure of the book; Ethan Zuckerman, who quickly stepped in and wrote a wonderful foreword for the book; Anne Rodman, whose close reading of an early draft led to a much better book; and Chand Rajendra-Nicolucci, for his comprehensive editing—twice, no less—which was invaluable. I would also like to give a huge thank-you to Bella Ilievski, for her research assistance and careful attention to detail; to OnKee Min and Maggie Graham, for their helpful research assistance; to Erinn Slanina, associate editor at Rowman & Littlefield, for her help, and to Jessica Thwaite, who was brilliant at catching my mistakes and serving as my production editor.

Most crucially, extreme gratitude goes to my "psychological editor" and partner Tom "Mang" Blumenthal, who created a new category of editing that takes measure of the psychological undertones in a book and greatly improved it with comments such as, "I'm feeling lost and without hope here" and "You can't say that!" Finally, thanks go to my children, Anna and Chetra Blumenthal, for their support and love, once they both worked through the "Oh no! You're *not* writing another book!"

Introduction

$\mathscr{T}$he federal highway system transformed two million miles of poorly constructed and disconnected roads into a networked system of four million miles of paved roads. Moving away from a system that linked farms to markets, the federal system included limited-access expressways that connected city to city across the country. No other public policy shaped our physical environment more. Despite the vast efficiencies created, many urban planners today view the system as causing more harm than good. We are still working on repairing some of the damage.[1]

The infrastructure devised by engineers created winners and losers: some towns literally were "put on the map" due to their connection to an off-ramp and the rapid increase in the number of visitors who drove into town. The losers were those that were either left off the map or saw residents uprooted from their homes as the highway cut communities in half or dismantled them altogether. The negative impact on the environment, public health, communities of color, and low-income neighborhoods was substantial.[2]

Half a century later, urban planners are working to redress some of the damage done by the creation of the interstate. One project is investigating ways to repair some of the destruction caused by Interstate 10, which plowed through the historic Tremé district in New Orleans, a thriving Black community known as the "Main Street of New Orleans."[3] A highway deck was built in 1968 that ran over the town center, disrupting neighborhoods and local businesses, uprooting trees, and altering the quality of life for those living there. The planners are devising tools to help them collect community input on how best to remove a crumbling highway deck without causing further harm.

How were decisions made to roll out this highway system over the course of a handful of decades? The central players were a group of federal engineers who were viewed as neutral experts. They were seen as the best choice for becoming the arbiters of not just the technical decision-making but also the political and social decisions that needed to be made over the course of sixty years. In hindsight, we can see that this heavy reliance on engineers, rather than finding a healthy balance between democratic and community values and technical expertise, was an enormous mistake.

So what does all this have to do with misinformation?

Four years ago, I started looking into the problem of online misinformation. As a research librarian, my professional life has focused on connecting college students and faculty to reliable information. I have been stunned to watch as the rise in digital information that had initially held so much promise in providing people with abundant, diverse, and trustworthy content had instead spiraled into vast wastelands of clickbait, scams, advertising, false information, and toxic content, while at the same time, reliable information was often buried or behind a paywall.

Comedian Bo Burnham points out that "if you want to say a swear on television, you have to go in front of Congress, but if you want to change the neurochemistry of an entire generation, it can be, you know, nine people in Silicon Valley."[4] We have left the design of our online worlds, like the design of the federal highway system, in the hands of technical experts. And like the federal highway system, the internet has provided us with benefits for businesses, government, and citizens that were unthinkable a few decades ago. But just as the highway engineers overfocused on efficiencies, platform companies have focused too much on growth at all costs. A handful of people in Silicon Valley should not be left in charge of designing how we live our increasingly digital lives.

It's been said that Google "defines what we think" and Facebook "defines who we are."[5] Social media platforms and Google search did not set out with a business plan to spew misinformation out to users. Misinformation was an unintended by-product of their way of doing business.[6] Google's original purpose was to "organize all the world's information and make it available," and Facebook's early mission was to "help you connect and share with the people in your life."[7] But in their early days, tech companies were living hand to mouth, often in danger of going under. Companies such as Google were initially reluctant to embrace advertising, knowing that it would ultimately impact their mission. Once they started down that road, what followed was a transition from the goal of technology in service to people to technology in service to profit.[8]

Facebook and Google alone have scarfed up over half of all digital advertising throughout the world—70 billion and 135 billion dollars respectively—gutting the news industry that provided us with reliable information.[9] Their parent companies, Meta and Alphabet, control eight of the top ten sites online and are in the top five largest corporations in the world.[10] Google often points us to useful information, and Facebook supports lots of positive social interactions, but these platforms are not optimized for these purposes.

Social media platforms and Google search have caused significant damage because they are optimized for making money over providing value and serving the public. Platforms collect our behavioral data and sell it to advertisers, who can then create hyperpersonalized ads that are wrapped in engaging content to persuade us to spend more time and money online. In the quest to drive engagement, misinformation is incentivized and promoted because it is more exciting and keeps us online longer. And so it goes. For Google, the icing on the cake is that roughly half of its first-page search results push people toward companies that Google owns.[11]

We have made a grave error in who we put in charge of our digital worlds, and our democracy is in danger as a result. Access to reliable news is a cornerstone of democracy. As funding models for the news collapse, and information gatekeeping is in the hands of a few large tech platforms, this infringes on our right to accurate information that helps inform the choices we make and the leaders we elect. We have failed to apply moral standards to new technologies and instead have embraced innovation at all costs. We measure new tools by their efficiencies and growth potential and not by the degree to which they enhance our humanity.

When I started on my travels through the land of misinformation research, I came across Claire Wardle's work. Wardle, cofounder and director of First Draft—a nonprofit focused on misinformation—developed a useful metaphor for how misinformation was being studied and understood: "It's as though we are all home for the holidays and someone pulls out a 50,000 piece jigsaw puzzle. Everyone has gathered round, but our crazy uncle has lost the box cover. So far, we've identified a few of the most striking pieces, but we still haven't even found the four corner pieces, let alone the edges. No individual, no one conference, no one platform, no one research center, think tank, or non-profit, no one government or company can be responsible for 'solving' this complex and very wicked problem."[12]

I was intrigued. "Wicked problems" is a term that researchers use for hard-to-solve problems of indeterminate scope and scale. Wicked problems can't always be solved, but actions can be taken to mitigate their harmful effects. I waded into the different streams of research to see if I could help piece them together—to find the corner pieces and connect some edge pieces. Wardle was right: there are so many studies and reports out there from so many academic fields that one of the biggest challenges is to wrap our brains around all of it and figure out what is important. As I read, I focused on proposed strategies and solutions: Where were people seeing the most hope? Which solutions were showing the strongest evidence of potential impact? Was misinformation a problem of technology that had technological solutions? Was it a matter of education—that we just needed to learn more skills to avoid falling for misinformation? Or perhaps it was a legal problem: Could regulations fix it? Or were there deeper, less obvious solutions we needed to pursue?

The oft-cited parable of the blind men and the elephant illustrates the diversity of approaches by the many researchers working on this wicked problem. Like the blind men, each has a different view of what constitutes an "elephant" because each man is touching a different part of it—the "trunk," the "tail," and the "foot." Computer scientists are looking at technical solutions, psychologists and behavioral economists are investigating people's vulnerabilities, educators are moving beyond skills-based media literacy programs to address student agency, and ethicists and legal scholars are looking into questions of morality and regulatory solutions. The list goes on.

As I read across the disciplines, I also dove into the work of a rising group of activists—often disillusioned former Google and Facebook workers—who are now working on new approaches to technology development more aligned with values-driven goals. In-house programs, such as the Civic Integrity program at Facebook, paid lip service to curbing harmful misinformation and preventing election interference, but when push came to shove, revenue was prioritized over ethical action. Former Facebook engineer turned whistleblower Frances Haugen testified to Congress about a meeting where European political leaders told Facebook staff, "We've noticed now with the change in your algorithm . . . that if we don't have incendiary content, it gets no distribution. So you're forcing us to be more incendiary, to prey on people's fears and anger."[13]

The Hewlett Foundation sponsored a study that concluded that multidisciplinarity brings a richness to our understandings of the challenges of misinformation but that more work needs to be done to overcome siloed approaches and make stronger connections between different fields of study. Most importantly, we need to translate research findings into practical recommendations for use by policy makers, tech executives, activists, and citizens.[14] An Aspen Institute report stated that possibly the biggest lie being told about misinformation is that the misinformation crisis is uncontainable. It is not.[15]

This book is about making strong links between the different academic disciplines working on the problem of misinformation. It is about translating these potential solutions into a practical and realistic plan of attack. It's about understanding the mechanisms that create and incentivize misinformation and containing and addressing them.

This book is about hope.

The strength of this book is in explaining what we know about our current information disorder and what it will take to repair our broken digital spaces. We will never eradicate misinformation—it has been around since the beginning of time—but we can repair existing platforms and build better ones that are designed to strengthen community ties and promote access to reliable content. And we can stop incentivizing and promoting harmful information.

While the focus of this book is on the United States, it is important to note that more widespread harms are being caused outside of the United States. Misinformation is threatening democracy, public health, and general well-being around the globe. Facebook, for example, spends 87 percent of its global content moderation budget on trying to address misinformation impacting the United States, with only 13 percent left to address problems in the rest of the world, despite 90 percent of Facebook users living outside of the United States. The company has been found directly responsible for offline violence in India, Ethiopia, and Myanmar. In Myanmar, more than half the country rely on Facebook for news, and the platform was easily weaponized to spread political misinformation. UN human rights investigators concluded that Facebook was complicit in the Rohingya genocide in Myanmar.[16] In some countries, Facebook provides no content moderation staff who are fluent in the languages used by those countries, such as in India.[17]

This book seeks to shift our approach from a sole focus on going after misinformation from the top down—by picking it off piecemeal using AI and stronger content moderation—to attacking the problem from the bottom up. We need to go after the root causes of misinformation by requiring platforms to be redesigned to better serve the public interest. The core structures of social media platforms are built on a business model that prioritizes engagement over accuracy. We also need to support the creation and promotion of reliable content that is grounded in fact—the truth as we best know it—and to present a diversity of views to help us better understand our worlds. Our very democracy is at stake.

It's a big leap, but we need to change our mindset and start thinking of our digital spaces as more similar to public parks and libraries and less like shopping malls or roller derbies. We need to build an internet designed to help us be better citizens rather than better consumers. When creating the US National Park system, the goal was never to try to figure out how to get as many people as possible to visit and how to make as much money as possible. The planners focused on how to promote interactions and behaviors that would help people better understand and appreciate natural areas, treat the environment and each other with respect, be safe, not litter, and so on. Intentional, value-based design—whether offline or online—can promote healthier interactions and boost well-being.

Each national park has had its own local challenges, and what works for the least visited park, the Gates of the Arctic in Alaska, is not what works for Yellowstone. Yellowstone has had to make intentional design changes by piloting low-speed shuttles to reduce crowding, limiting parking and visitors, and creating best practices around wildlife jams to encourage safe interactions. The park engineers are focused on the visitor experience and safety while also balancing finite resources and the impact on stakeholders, including nearby communities. What would Yellowstone look like if the planners decided instead that they just wanted to make a lot of money? The same thinking—emphasizing public value over growth—can be applied to our digital spaces.

The mission of online public spaces needs to change course and start prioritizing technology in service to people rather than technology in service to profits. We need to build back truth online. Truth can be defined as beliefs that are in line with, and are supported by, the best available current evidence.[18] This is tricky: evidence shifts as our knowledge advances, which means our beliefs need to shift in response.

At the same time, we need to guard against bad actors that are now bending the truth for their own benefit. There have always been people seeking power who have spread lies to shape public opinion in service to their own goals. But we now have people who have been provided with megaphones who are not only bending the truth but also questioning whether such a notion as truth actually exists, whether science and empirical evidence matter, and whether the fourth estate—our independent news media—has value.[19]

A handful of social media platforms—"nine people in Silicon Valley"—now have enormous power over what information people see and what information is censored or buried. They are, despite their denials, the new "arbiters of truth."[20] Their business model has created a crisis in information that needs to be curtailed. Understanding what is happening and knowing that there are solutions—that the challenges of misinformation are not insurmountable—are the first steps we can take toward improving our digital public square.

Chapter 1 of this book explains the problem of misinformation within the larger context of what is being called information disorder. Chapters 2 through 7 provide a road map with six paths forward to help us better understand how the different puzzle pieces fit together so that we can move forward on all fronts, working together to improve our digital public spaces. The six paths forward are: to understand how platforms are designed to exploit us (chapter 2); to learn to embrace agency in our interactions with digital spaces (chapter 3); to build tools to reduce harmful practices (chapter 4); to require platform companies to prioritize the public good (chapter 5); to repair journalism and strengthen curation to promote trusted content (chapter 6); and to design new, healthier digital public squares to build back truth (chapter 7).

THE ROAD AHEAD . . .

The creation of new technologies is frequently followed by a combination of enthusiasm, concern, and the appearance of unintended consequences. When cars were first introduced into American life, the ability to travel and the freedom of the open road had a profound and permanent impact on society. But as the number of cars on the road increased, accidents and fatalities soon followed. Before the development of stop signs, seat belts, traffic lights, yellow lines dividing streets, rules and regulations on driving safety, and driver education and licensing tests, there was a free-for-all on city streets that resulted in tens of thousands of accidents and deaths.

As fatalities rose, competing interests argued over solutions. The auto industry, in an effort to avoid being regulated or held accountable, stated that cars themselves did not cause accidents if driven properly and that the focus should be on driver education.[21] Engineers pushed for technological solutions such as seat belts, and consumer groups argued that stronger driving laws would improve safety.

These disagreements over personal responsibility, technological solutions, and regulations played out over five decades with little progress made.[22] Seat belts, a technological solution, were introduced in the 1940s, but by the 1950s they were offered only as an accessory in some cars for an added cost. By 1967, laws were passed requiring seat belts in all cars, but this strategy failed. Few people chose to wear their seat belts.

Education campaigns followed but were scattered and had little impact. The National Highway Traffic Safety Board saw little hope in education, stating that these strategies created "unrealistic expectations of the American public."[23] New technological solutions were developed. The airbag and passive automatic belts, requiring no action on the part of the individual, made little traction, because manufacturers were wary about cost and because providing these safety features implied liability. Battles raged in courts and legislatures, with little accomplished. Seat belt wearing in the 1970s ranged from 3 percent to 10 percent.

Common ground was finally found when a third path was envisioned. Rather than pitting sides against each other, an integrated approach was created, and huge strides were made for improving safety. Airbags were rebranded as "supplemental systems" that needed to be used in combination with seat belts that required individual agency, addressing the fear companies had of taking sole responsibility for safety. This was combined with an accelerated effort in educating the public and with the passing of mandatory seat-belt-use laws. Seat belt use went from 14 percent in 1984 to over 90 percent today.[24] Seat belts have saved tens of thousands of lives in the past decade alone.[25]

The rise of social media platforms seems to be following a similar trajectory, with powerful companies prioritizing profits over safety, unrealistic expectations about educating users, and stalled legislation that will be difficult to move forward. The business philosophy that has pervaded Silicon Valley and spread to many tech companies is epitomized in PayPal's business plan: "Raise a boatload of money, expand quickly, and present lawmakers with a fait accompli. Here is the future, deal with it."[26] This needs to be called out, not celebrated.

This book provides six paths forward to create digital spaces that prioritize the public good. Drawing on many different fields, the book presents a comprehensive and connected strategy of how we can reduce misinformation online and build back truth. New, experimental models that are ethically designed to build community and promote trustworthy content are having some early successes. We know that human social networks—online and off—magnify whatever they are seeded with. They are not neutral. We also know that to repair our systems, we need to repair their design. We are being joined in the fight against misinformation by some of the best and brightest minds of the current generation as they flee big tech companies in search of vocations that value integrity and public values. The problem of misinformation is not insurmountable. We can fix this.

1

Understand the Problem

$\mathcal{N}$inety-five percent of people in the United States identify misinformation as a problem.[1] But what is the problem exactly? Misinformation has always been a challenge, but our new digital worlds have created an information crisis so severe that it threatens our democratic system of government. Social media platforms incentivize and promote misinformation, erode our shared understandings of the world, compromise our access to truth, and amplify polarizing, toxic, and racist content.

Frances Haugen, the data engineer turned whistleblower, was originally hired by Facebook to address issues related to misinformation. Frustrated with Facebook's lack of commitment to mitigating misinformation, Haugen left less than two years later with a trove of documents that provided Congress, and the public, with an inside look at what's been going on at one of the largest social media platforms.

Haugen testified to Congress about a meeting in which European political leaders said to Facebook staff, "We've noticed now with the change in your algorithm in 2018, that if we don't have incendiary content, it gets no distribution. So you're forcing us to be more incendiary, to prey on people's fears and anger."[2]

A year earlier, an internal presentation to Facebook leaders indicated that "64 percent of all extremist group joins are due to our recommendation tools. . . . Our recommendation systems grow the problem."[3] Former director for monetization at Facebook, Tim Kendall, testified before Congress that "the social media services that I and others have built . . . have served to tear people apart with alarming speed and intensity. . . . At the very least, we have eroded our collective understanding—at worst, I fear we are pushing ourselves to the brink of a civil war. . . . Social media preys on the most primal parts of your brain. The algorithm maximizes your attention by hitting you repeatedly with content that triggers your strongest emotions—it aims to provoke, shock, and enrage."[4]

And a few years ago, when Safiya Noble, faculty director of the UCLA Center for Critical Internet Inquiry (C2i2) googled "Black girls" to find some activities for her daughter and nieces, she was horrified when the search engine's top hits were racialized porn. The first recommended link was to a Black woman porn site with an obscene name, followed by unmoderated discussions including "why Black women are so angry" and "why Black women are so sassy." A search for White women showed much more positive results and no top links to porn.[5]

GOOD TECH GONE BAD

Social media platforms and Google search did not set out with a business plan to spew misinformation out to users. Spreading misinformation was an unintended by-product of their way of doing business.[6] Google's original purpose was to "organize all the world's information and make it available," and Facebook's early mission was to "help you connect and share with the people in your life."[7]

The early days of the internet were a time of great optimism and promise, when digital spaces were rapidly evolving with the vision of a new information age that would connect communities and instantly provide access to reliable content with just a few clicks. At that time, tech companies were living hand to mouth and were often in danger of going under. Government policies regulating tech companies were deliberately hands-off so as not to stifle innovation. Companies such as Google were reluctant to embrace advertising. Sergey Brin and Larry Page, the founders of Google, gave a presentation at the 1998 World Wide Web Conference, saying, "We expect that advertising funded search engines will be inherently biased toward the advertiser and away from the needs of the consumers. . . . It is crucial to have a competitive search engine that is transparent and in the academic realm."[8]

That same year Google transitioned from being housed on a Stanford University server to becoming a private company. And a dozen years later, Brin and Page found themselves pulling in $10 billion a year in ad revenue. Their mission shifted from one of technology in service to people to one of technology in service to profit.[9] Facebook and other platforms quickly followed suit. Advertising now provides 84 percent of Google's $135 billion annual revenue and 98 percent of Facebook's $70 billion annual revenue.[10]

What started as placing an ad on a page and making money on clicks evolved into a sophisticated engine that takes behavioral data—where we click, where we go online, what we buy, how we feel, and even where we are geographically—and turns this data into prediction products that are sold to retailers. This is called surveillance advertising.[11] Platforms have now collected vast amounts of behavioral data so that they can hyperpersonalize content and ads and persuade us to spend more time and money online. What does all of this have to do with misinformation? Misinformation tends to be more exciting and triggers stronger emotional reactions than reliable information does, keeping us online longer. The more time we spend online, the more behavioral data is collected and the more we click on ads means—in short—more money for platform companies.

While tech companies have said they are trying to address the issue, misinformation continues to be amplified over reliable news. Misinformation receives six times as much attention as reliable news on Facebook news feeds. Pages that post more misinformation regularly get more shares, likes, and comments.[12] This in turn has impacted what digital content is produced. As the European leaders told Facebook, "You're forcing us to be more incendiary," or, as former US president Barack Obama summed it up, the internet has a "demand for crazy."[13]

Platforms have sidestepped responsibilities in terms of moderating content except in extreme situations, such as the recent pandemic or the Russian invasion of Ukraine. Most tech companies point to their community guidelines and ask users not to violate these. Unlike traditional content providers such as news outlets, platforms are not held accountable as publishers. On Twitter, there are extensive guidelines with reassuring statements about keeping the community safe, but at the same time, Twitter states that it will not act as a publisher or censor. Banning content can create bad publicity for a platform.[14] When platforms do moderate content, they are not transparent in how it is done: we do not know what content is permitted or how it is promoted, demoted, or removed.

WHAT IS MISINFORMATION?

There are no agreed-upon definitions of mis- and disinformation. This book uses the more commonly used term "misinformation" to encompass content that includes mis- and disinformation, fake news, or propaganda. Researchers often define disinformation as false or misleading information *intentionally* created or strategically amplified to mislead for a purpose (e.g., political, financial, or social gain), whereas misinformation is defined as false or misleading information that is not necessarily intentional. But intention can be hard to parse and one piece of content can be both: the person selling capsules of bleach to "cure" COVID is spreading disinformation, but the person who shares this information may be unintentionally sharing misinformation.

Misinformation has been around in one form or another for centuries, but our current digital spaces have created a misinformation tsunami that promotes misinformation and sensationalized content over more reliable content. This in turn creates a market for the creation of content that gets the greatest number of eyeballs, content that, as Tim Kendall testified to Congress "aims to provoke, shock, and enrage." Like driving past a horrific car accident on the highway, we can't help ourselves, we slow down to look.

So why would social media companies want to design platforms that promote and reward harmful misinformation to users? This isn't their goal, but it is an unintended side effect—an externality—due to the way in which platform companies make money. Think of it as similar to a factory that is designed to manufacture goods but, in doing so, also unintentionally creates air pollution. Because the design of most of our digital spaces is focused on making money rather than serving the public interest, companies strive to generate compelling and addictive online content that is unregulated and unvetted. This content can also be easily weaponized.[15]

How Does Misinformation Work?

Social media platforms, interactive digital spaces that foster interaction and the sharing of content, collect streams of personal data about us: microdemographics and preferences. Advertisers and bad actors can harness this data to tailor messages and prey on our emotional vulnerabilities, biases, and weaknesses. This tactic can be used to sell soap or disrupt elections. Because platforms make more money the longer we stay online, they design algorithms to feed us highly engaging personalized content; for one person, that may be cat videos and for another, it may be conspiracy theories.

Algorithms used by social media feeds and search engines are a set of rules designed to calculate what content to recommend to us that will be most engaging based on our behavioral data. At first glance, this doesn't seem so terrible; for example, Netflix recommends a video based on our past viewing history. Though this tends to narrow our taste in films—my son stays in a bubble of anime, and I see a lot of films that have a "strong female lead"—it is not exactly dangerous.

But in addition to customizing our online experience, algorithms are only as good as the data they are trained on. In chemistry, for example, algorithms have been valuable for predicting properties such as toxicity or melting points by using large amounts of training data. But in many situations, the only training data available is flawed because it is data that replicates and reinforces societal biases. For example, when Amazon built a resume-screening tool to more efficiently screen job candidates, the algorithm it used was trained on a collection of resumes the company had collected for ten years, but the collection was dominated by male applicants. When the algorithm started screening new resumes, it discriminated against women by filtering out candidates with women's first names or who attended women's colleges.[16] And we see from Safiya Noble's example a stark reminder that societal racism is embedded in the Google algorithm, resulting in the search for "Black girls" recommending porn sites.

Researchers have determined that if an algorithm was trained by having it crawl through all the existing data on the internet, it would develop strong biases against people of color and women, because there is so much data online that is discriminatory.[17] On top of flawed training data, algorithms can be gamed by companies and individuals with enough money to pay for techniques like search engine optimization (SEO). This means that link recommendations—getting to the top of the list—are partly based on the ability to pay to manipulate the search engine. The implications are significant: a slight manipulation of a page rank could provide results that favor one political candidate over another, possibly impacting the outcome of an election.[18]

Algorithms are also intentionally designed to connect us with people who share our beliefs, because this keeps us online longer. This can be great, because it lets us connect to long-lost friends or people who enjoy the same hobbies as we do. But connecting to like-minded people can also create echo chambers, environments where we can hang out online with people who share our political beliefs and opinions. Echo chambers can serve to reinforce our opinions and move groups toward more extreme positions.[19] By pulling people into different streams of content, users can select what they want to believe is true and be targeted by advertisers or hate groups instead of being exposed to reliable, more balanced, fact-checked information.[20]

How Dangerous Is Misinformation?

Misinformation has played a significant role in mass shootings, impeded global efforts to get the COVID pandemic under control, interfered with elections, and buried content that explains the scientific evidence of climate change. The past few years provide us with many examples of the devasting impact of digital information systems that tap into our emotions and prioritize fear, anger, and toxicity over trustworthy information. While misinformation is not the only driver of the heightened polarization and extremism we are now seeing in the United States, it is a key player and is certainly fanning the flames.

Radicalization via Echo Chambers

When Dylann Roof first heard about the trial of Trayvon Martin's killer, George Zimmerman, he sided with Zimmerman and wanted to know more about violence between Black and White people. He then searched Google for "Black on White crime" and was quickly led down a rabbit hole connecting him to White supremacy sites and misinformation about racial violence. As he clicked on each link, Google's algorithm learned his preferences and embedded him in an echo chamber, encouraging him to join hate groups and providing him with racist and incendiary propaganda and new "friends" that gave him false information about brutal attacks on White people by Black people. Not everyone opts into echo chambers that are presented to them, but individuals with preexisting extreme views are more likely to head in this direction.[21]

Roof's lack of exposure to trustworthy sources or a diversity of opinions was baked into Google's search engine and the social media platforms he used. He quickly became radicalized. What was designed to be a "personalized ad experience" with engaging content aimed at selling products became a bubble that created isolation, polarization, and radicalization. Roof's next move was to "take it to the real world," he wrote in his manifesto, by murdering nine Black people who were holding Bible study in a church in South Carolina.[22]

Fanning the Flames of a Global Pandemic

During the first year of the COVID pandemic, the large volume of COVID misinformation online crowded out reliable information about the virus, prompting the World Health Organization to label the situation an "Infodemic."[23] False information about miracle cures and the dangers of vaccines and mask wearing were rapidly spread, while reliable but less exciting medical and news reports about COVID were buried.

By 2021, Facebook reported that it had removed eighteen million posts containing misinformation about COVID, but no information was provided about how many views and shares these posts had received before being removed. By not acting sooner, the damage was already done, as many people had already been convinced by misinformation about miracle health cures and false content about vaccine safety and mask wearing.[24]

Almost two years into the pandemic, when platforms promised they were addressing the issue, a video from a school board meeting in Indiana showed a man purporting to be a doctor making false claims about vaccines and masking. It was viewed more than ninety million times.[25] President Joe Biden went off script in exasperation about the harm Facebook was doing in spreading misinformation about COVID, saying, "They're killing people!," though he later backpedaled to say he was referring to leading misinformation spreaders on the platform rather than Facebook itself.[26]

Interfering with Election Integrity

During the 2016 US presidential election, Russian operatives engaged in an orchestrated campaign to spread disinformation on social media to sow discord and tilt the election against Hillary Rodham Clinton. Russians working for the Internet Research Agency (IRA) started buying digital ads on Facebook and other platforms that targeted groups that focused on religion and immigration. Using stolen identities to pose as American citizens, the IRA posted divisive and inflammatory ads and images to influence voters.[27]

More recently, misinformation about US election processes has been spread by domestic actors. Right-wing groups have been responsible for much of the misinformation spread about "stolen elections," mail-in voter fraud, and other false narratives about election security to try to undermine President Joe Biden's election victory.[28] In a similar vein, the QAnon conspiracy has continued to spread rumors that started with the Pizzagate conspiracy theory that claimed Hillary Clinton's campaign was running a pedophile ring out of the basement of a pizza parlor. In 2021, 15 percent of Americans agreed with the QAnon-endorsed statement that the US government, media, and financial worlds "are controlled by a group of Satan-worshipping pedophiles who run a global child sex trafficking operation."[29]

Other bad actors have been quick to pick up on the misinformation playbook. Tucker Carlson, a conservative political commentator on Fox News, is a master at using hatred and fear to drive up viewership. Carlson warns his cable TV viewers that the United States is under siege by violent Black Lives Matter protesters and diseased migrants from Mexico. His show is now the highest-rated cable news show in history.[30] Fox News has enjoyed a symbiotic relationship with social media platforms such as Facebook, where false narratives can be amplified back and forth between these two content providers.[31]

Feeding Climate Change Denial

A review of climate research has concluded that there is 97 percent consensus that humans are the predominant cause of global warming.[32] And yet only 12 percent of people in the United States are aware of this scientific consensus about climate change. Even more concerning is that this "consensus gap" is frequently found among science teachers and journalists. People in the United States are polarized over the issue of climate change, with Democrats more accepting and Republicans much less accepting of this scientific fact.

A major cause of the public's confusion and polarization around climate change is misinformation. Orchestrated campaigns are being carried out by the fossil fuel, coal, and automotive industries and conservative think tanks and politicians. Their strategies include denial that warming is taking place, denial that it is caused by humans, claims that the impact will not be that significant, and claims that there is not scientific consensus around the issue.[33] These campaigns have undermined public understanding of the climate crisis, making it difficult to move forward with policy measures to help address this serious issue.[34]

Deepfakes

Deepfakes are media in which a person in an existing image or video is replaced with someone else's likeness. They are now being used to deceive consumers and influence politics.[35] Deepfakes have been around for years, but with the advent of better machine-learning tools, it is now much easier to quickly and cheaply create convincing fake videos and images that are almost indistinguishable from real content. Deepfakes are being used for creating false news, hoaxes, financial fraud, and fake celebrity pornographic videos. Deepfakes can now provide realistic depictions of real people doing or saying things they have never said or done.

If nothing else, deepfakes could serve to undermine belief in historical events even when there is audio, video, or photographic proof. Some people already question whether the Holocaust or 9/11 occurred, despite clear verification from many media sources. Greater use of deepfakes could cause people to start questioning much of what they see online.

Fake People

Similar to deepfakes, new facial recognition software makes it possible to create fake people. An algorithm generates a composite headshot based on many real people combined; the "person" you are seeing as a result does not exist. Companies can use these fake images to create fake product reviews or to provide, for example, the illusion of a diverse workforce on their website. Fake faces can also be used to infiltrate online communities: Someone could don an attractive fake face or choose an ethnicity that differs from the person's own to more effectively influence people's behaviors.[36]

As personalized targeting grows more sophisticated, you may start to see models that look like slightly more attractive versions of you modeling a sweater that your past buying history suggests you might like. More concerning algorithms are also being developed that can influence our perception that more attention is being paid, or not paid, to particular social issues, exploiting our desire to conform. These types of manipulations can cause the views of a few bad actors to be misrepresented as being the majority view.

Posts on the web, such as on Reddit or TikTok, can manipulate social consensus intentionally or unintentionally. These manipulations can create information cascades where beliefs spread quickly regardless of their accuracy. The comments section on platforms can snowball in one direction or another (agreeing or disagreeing with the original post), and people tend to attach themselves quickly to trending content because it appears to be the popular opinion—whether it is true or not.[37]

Dark Patterns

Dark patterns, also known as deceptive design, are user interfaces that have been designed to trick users into doing things—for example, signing up for recurring bills or for insurance policies that are not needed. Dark patterns directly prioritize revenue over user value.[38] We've all experienced dark patterns online, such as when we have to search for ten minutes to figure out how to cancel a service or when we have to locate the unsubscribe button at the bottom of an email when it is in tiny, low-contrast text buried in three paragraphs of content. There are dozens of types of dark patterns regularly used on websites including, "privacy suckering" a pattern named after its pioneer, Mark Zuckerberg, which tricks users into publicly sharing more information than they intended to share.[39]

Malicious Bots

Malicious bots are automated programs designed to cause harm by impersonating social media users. They are difficult to detect and can have a significant impact on the spread of misinformation. Harmful bots artificially drive up user engagement by liking and sharing content and giving the false impression that a post is popular.[40] In some cases, bots can be easy to spot, such as the dozens of attractive, middle-aged, divorced men who keep trying to friend me on Facebook but suspiciously appear to have no friends or history of posts on the platform. But many bots are more clever.

We may not feel too concerned finding out that on Instagram, 48 percent of Ellen DeGeneres's followers are fake: They are bots. This isn't necessarily Ellen's fault. Her public relations people may have purchased some fake users, but chances are just as likely that these bots have attached themselves to Ellen in order to attract followers to the content they are trying to promote. Bots can do tremendous harm. Moving from Hollywood to the world stage, we see governments using social media bots as a tool to silence opposition and manipulate public opinion. Rodrigo Duterte's presidential campaign in the Philippines flooded the country's social networks with fake accounts, trolls, and bots, shifting public opinion in his favor, contributing to his successful election.[41]

Bots make up a significant amount of the misinformation landscape worldwide.[42] For example, researchers estimated that 33 percent of the one hundred most-followed political news accounts and 63 percent of a random sample of all accounts on Twitter during the US 2016 election were fake news accounts run by bots.[43] Take a moment to process these numbers: bots were controlling the information the majority of people got on Twitter related to the 2016 election. In 2017, Facebook estimated that bots and coordinated fake news campaigns run by Russia reached 126 million people.[44] And in 2020, researchers estimated that nearly half of the accounts tweeting about COVID were bots, leading to the vast spread of misinformation about potential cures, masks, and vaccines."[45]

MISINFORMATION WITHIN THE BROADER CONTEXT OF INFORMATION DISORDER

Misinformation is one piece of a larger digital ecosystem that is in crisis. The term "information disorder" helps us view misinformation within the context of a broader and dysfunctional digital information space. A report by the Aspen Institute states that information disorder is "a crisis that exacerbates all other crises. When bad information becomes as prevalent, persuasive, and persistent as good information, it creates a chain reaction of harm."[46] The report demonstrates how information disorder has made health crises like the COVID pandemic more deadly, has impacted our ability to respond effectively to climate change, and promotes an online culture where racial, ethnic, and gendered attacks have become the norm. The authors note that misinformation has "become a force multiplier for exacerbating our worst problems as a society. Hundreds of millions of people pay the price, every single day, for a world disordered by lies."

Our current online spaces have contributed to declining trust in institutions and the media, as the lines for what constitutes "news" blur. Social media taps into our gut responses that favor belief over evidence, and we can be easily swayed by platforms that elicit emotional responses over slower, more analytical thinking. Our doomscrolling, spending excessive amounts of time skimming images of natural disasters and extreme violence, can create compassion fatigue, apathy, and passivity.

The Decline in Trust and Truth Decay

In the United States, there has been a notable and steady decline of trust in institutions; it started during the Nixon administration and has continued to the present day. There have been significant declines in trust in the police, religious institutions, the medical system, the Supreme Court, public schools, banks, organized labor, the media, science, and big business.[47] The current pandemic has drawn attention to the loss of trust in science, medicine, and the government as millions of people have refused to get vaccinated.

For legacy media, the decline in trust has been especially pronounced: today, only 39 percent of people report having a "great deal" or "fair amount" of trust in the media.[48] Use of traditional media sources, such as the *New York Times*, has declined as people get information online from peers and news feeds that usually affirm their preexisting beliefs. Platforms and algorithms are in charge of what people see online, rather than editors and journalists who adhere to journalistic standards when curating the news to select fact-based, verified, and noteworthy stories.

"Truth decay" is a part of the growing climate of distrust that includes an increasing tendency to rely on personal beliefs over evidence to judge whether information is true. Truth decay encompasses an increase in disagreements about facts, the blurring of lines between opinions and facts in journalism, the increasing volume and influence of opinion and personal experience over fact, and a deterioration of trust in sources of information that were formerly respected.[49]

This epistemic phenomenon, prioritizing worldviews over facts, is not new, but the structure and strategies used by online platforms—by everyone from shoe companies, to politicians, to terrorist groups—are exacerbating it. Cueing fast, emotional thinking is key for targeting our psychological vulnerabilities to encourage greater engagement. As our emotions are tapped, we are pulled away from using analytical thinking. This, plus customized news feeds, results in increasingly polarized communities, disengagement from mainstream civic institutions, and the decline in shared cultural understandings.

Today, Facebook, YouTube, TikTok, and other platforms have taken over from legacy institutions such as the *New York Times* and CNN to control much of the media we consume. There is nonstop access to sensationalized content from around the world. Competition for "eyeballs" results in prioritizing negative, more graphic stories that spread more quickly. Each new disaster is framed to be even more shocking to grab our limited attention spans, while at the same time, we experience compassion fatigue with dramatic stories about global events but few meaningful opportunities to respond or help those in need.[50] TV news stations have taken part in this type of behavior for decades, but there was some accountability and pushback from regulators and sponsors when there were only a few channels to oversee rather than the thousands we have today.

On social media platforms, we are urged to "like," "share," or "review," and we tend to share more exciting and negative content, compounding the problem.[51] Deep discussions online are uncommon. People are wary of having meaningful discussions in "public" online, because discussions can quickly turn ugly, with reactionary responses and personal attacks. Platforms are designed for quick, superficial interactions with little time to slow down, explore, and discuss different points of view. We talk *at*, not with.[52] We leave comments on sites that rarely result in meaningful discussions but are instead simply voted up or down.

THE SILICON VALLEY MINDSET AND THE DEFICIT IN ETHICAL THINKING

Tech leaders have enormous visionary and analytic abilities; the digital spaces they have built are amazing and have connected people around the globe and provided us with many new efficiencies and opportunities. But like the engineers who built our interstate highway system, they have been given free rein to create these innovative new structures with little attention paid to how their designs cause harm. In addition, the competitive hyperfocus on profits over public value has resulted in the dramatic rise of misinformation and toxicity online. As technology rapidly changes so much about our lives, we have failed to figure out how to direct and govern Big Tech. Our communication policies are outdated and no longer focus on prioritizing the public good.[53]

There is nothing wrong with a company focusing on profits, but as we have learned from the tobacco and pharmaceutical industries, there need to be rules and consequences when company executives fail to act ethically and responsibly. Just a handful of tech companies control our digital spaces, and they are making billions of dollars tracking and manipulating user behavior with little accountability. Facebook and Google are now oligopolies that take in over half of all digital advertising throughout the world, and their power is almost unprecedented: they control eight of the top ten sites online and are in the top five largest corporations in the world.[54]

Analyses of leaders such as Mark Zuckerberg, Larry Page, and Elon Musk show us visionary thinkers who also have significant deficits in emotional intelligence, including a lack of empathy, self-awareness, and self-reflection.[55] Empathy helps us understand and share other people's feelings by being able to "walk in their shoes." Empathy is linked to prosocial and cooperative behaviors and is an essential component that helps ensure the healthy functioning of society. Self-awareness and self-reflection increase our understanding of the world around us and our responsibilities to others.

The Silicon Valley mindset includes a corporate culture built on insularity, a hierarchical structure, a lack of diversity, and the discouragement of feedback. This mindset also lacks an ethical framework built on values other than growth. Tech companies such as Facebook and Google have set up small ethics teams, but their work is not prioritized. When recommendations by internal ethics teams conflict with the bottom line, the recommendations are often ignored.[56]

MISINFORMATION AND THE THREAT TO DEMOCRACY

Essential to maintaining a healthy democracy is an independent press that provides us with access to reliable news and information. Social media platforms and Google search have disrupted the role of the press and now make decisions about much of the news the public views. The loss of local news outlets has been especially concerning and has been connected to declines in civic engagement. A few large tech companies have become our "arbiters of truth," deciding what information the public views, but they are not being held accountable for these decisions, and they are not beholden to journalistic standards. By giving platforms free rein, we are faced with a digital ecosystem that allows misinformation and poor quality content to flourish and has made it more challenging to access trustworthy information.

Media Capture by Big Tech

Media capture takes place when the news media is directly controlled by either the government or vested interests connected with politics.[57] Though not a new phenomenon, there is growing concern about media capture today for two reasons: news media have lost much of their advertising revenue and can be purchased cheaply, and platforms control much of the information we view. Capture can include owning the news or controlling what content the public views.

Initially, there was excitement with the transition to digital, because the barriers to publishing were now lowered and anyone could communicate out to the world. In some cases, this early enthusiasm was warranted. Social media has enabled people to directly broadcast first-person accounts without going through a news organization or paying to publish. This direct connection can be especially important in providing a voice to communities of color and other communities that have been marginalized by the mainstream press. Videos filmed by citizens of police brutality against Black people and reporting on other social injustices have resulted in a better-informed public and demands for greater accountability.

But these low barriers to entry also resulted in other players quickly jumping into the digital space, scarfing up advertising money and dominating news feeds. Independent and under-resourced voices quickly got downranked, as more powerful voices, ones that could afford large staffs to strategically exploit platforms' algorithms, were able to drown out other voices. Responsible news outlets also lost traction as ad agencies switched to funding more engaging, but often less reliable, content.

The transition from print to digital news accelerated the gutting of the traditional media industry that had—though imperfectly—upheld strong journalistic standards and employed teams of investigative reporters in service to reporting factual and verified information. Over $40 billion in annual ad revenues have now shifted to large online platforms such as Google and Facebook. The platforms have taken over much of the digital advertising market by selling highly valued user behavioral data to advertisers using the model of surveillance advertising, but they have not been held accountable for the content they publish, and unlike journalists, they do not adhere to a code of ethics.[58]

Struggling for revenue, some news outlets have lowered their standards and rely more on native advertising that blurs the line between news and ads. Native advertising uses ads that are designed to fit so closely with a publication's content and design that they appear to be part of a publication. This can undermine the trust of readers. The competition for ad revenue has given advertisers greater power to call the shots. In some cases, advertisers now dictate content creation, creating content just for the purpose of attaching ads to it. Writers once employed as journalists are now hired by ad agencies that pay them to mention specific products within their "news" stories.

An equally concerning trend is the "sponsoring" of news outlets by companies that then dictate what news is written, especially news coverage about their own companies. In the United Kingdom, multinationals such as Google and Uber, among others, that were receiving negative press "partnered" with the *Evening Standard* to help "support" the news. In fact, these companies were paying for influence over what "news" people would read. Capture and control over what is published via sponsorship are happening around the globe.[59]

Recent estimates are that Google and Facebook are the largest funders of journalism in the world.[60] Spikes in funds to support journalism have been traced to rises in potential regulatory activity directed at these companies. Cozy relationships between Big Tech and the news media are cause for concern. The news media should be investigating Big Tech, and accepting funding may make it harder to do so.

The idea of media capture is not new. Governments and wealthy industrialists have owned news outlets throughout history, and the degree to which they have exerted influence over the news varies but has always been cause for concern. Billionaire Michael Bloomberg barred *Bloomberg News* from writing about his unsuccessful run for president, and Rupert Murdoch and his son ensure that Fox News supports company interests and the Republican agenda. Jeff Bezos, one of the world's richest people, purchased the *Washington Post* and appears to, for the most part, keep his hands off the newsroom. But many people on the Left and the Right argue that Bezos's ownership of a major national newspaper in itself jeopardizes its independence.

While media capture is not new, what *is* new is the ability of tech platforms to control what news is viewed online. Google search, Facebook, and Apple news feeds make algorithmic decisions that impact what news is promoted and demoted. They are our new media gatekeepers, yet they are not subject to the accountability that other news publishers face. This consolidation of power in a few hands has created a distribution model for news embedded in a system primed for revenue growth over truth. Further, it is not much of a reach to see the potential these companies have to limit access to news that reflects badly on their companies or that jeopardizes their business model.

The Loss of Local News

Access to independent local news is the most serious challenge we now face with respect to news access. Metropolitan dailies and small-town weeklies—including ethnic and minority-owned newspapers—are rapidly disappearing. One in four newspapers—over two thousand—have shut down in the last few decades.[61] This has resulted in news deserts throughout much of the country. Two-thirds of counties in the United States no longer have a local daily newspaper, and more than two hundred towns have no newspaper.[62] These local news outlets provided important coverage of town meetings and local issues and events.

"Ghost newspapers" are now owned by hedge funds and investment firms that have purchased these dying local papers at rock-bottom prices. These new owners often keep the original name of the local paper but use it to channel nationally produced news. With budget cuts and a decline in deep, nuanced reporting of local issues, these news sources have become shells of their former selves.

Investment groups such as New Media/GateHouse have also created ghost newspapers by taking over larger regional papers such as the *Denver Post* and the *Wichita Eagle*. These investment firms treat their news outlet purchases in the same way they treat the other properties they purchase—with extensive cost cutting and financial restructuring to prioritize revenue. The new owners lay off staff and prioritize engaging fluff pieces while reducing deeper analytical articles and labor-intensive, local investigative reporting.[63] Local TV news has faced less of a decline, but its coverage typically provides little depth, fewer investigative stories, and less coverage of local issues outside of crime, weather, and human-interest stories.

Without access to information about local news, there has been a decline in the functioning of local governments, as officials may be less frequently held accountable by community reporters.[64] Local news has been a more trusted source for liberals and conservatives alike, in part because local reporters are known to the community and can be held accountable. With the disappearance of local news sources, people have turned to more partisan national news sources and social media sites. Algorithms then reinforce habits by feeding people increasingly partisan sources to drive engagement. Not surprisingly, the rise in polarization is likely connected to the decline in local news sources.[65] The lack of local media has also been tied to less-informed voters and reduced civic engagement.[66]

The New Arbiters of Truth

Since the founding of the United States, there have been concerns about factionalism and the need for bringing people together through shared understandings and common interests. Our democracy rests on three branches of government that serve as checks and balances for each other so that no one arm of government wields too much power. Also essential to maintaining a healthy democracy are an independent press and an educated public, to ensure that elected leaders will represent the public's best interests.

The media provides citizens with a way of understanding the societal challenges we face and gives us accurate information about ways to address these challenges. Maintaining an independent press has always been a struggle, but current access to unbiased reliable reporting is facing significant and novel threats. Some news outlets are increasingly using sensationalism and poor quality content to stay competitive in a marketplace that rewards entertainment over substance. There has been a decline in journalistic standards, and some news outlets fan the flames to generate anger, increase viewership, and divide citizens against each other.

People are now consuming vastly different streams of information in the United States. One media channel, MSNBC, provides reports on our current understanding of COVID from Dr. Anthony Fauci, the head of the National Institute of Allergy and Infectious Diseases. On another media channel, Fox News is accusing Dr. Fauci of causing COVID.[67]

As Pulitzer Prize–winning critic Michiko Kakutani states in the last paragraph of her book, *The Death of Truth*: "Without commonly agreed-upon facts—not Republican facts and Democratic facts; not the alternative facts of today's silo-world—there can be no rational debate over policies, no substantive means of evaluating candidates for political office, and no way to hold elected officials accountable to the people. Without truth, democracy is hobbled. The founders recognized this, and those seeking democracy's survival must recognize it today."[68]

Truth is an elusive concept. It can best be defined as the attempt to hold beliefs that can "serve as guides for making successful choices in the future" and that our expectation is that these beliefs "conform with and are supported by the available evidence."[69] This is tricky, because the "available evidence" shifts as our knowledge and evidence advances, and so our beliefs need to shift in response. There have always been people seeking power who have spread lies to shape public opinion, and we now find ourselves in a time of heightened threats from political actors willing to not only bend the truth but to question whether truth actually exists, whether science and empirical evidence matter, and whether the fourth estate has value.[70]

A handful of platforms now have enormous power over what information people see and what information is censored. They are, despite their denials, the new arbiters of truth and are referred to now as the "new governors" and even "net states."[71] Facebook's new independent advisory board is referred to as a "Supreme Court." Every day, over five billion searches are made on Google, and Google controls what information to promote or demote. Google devotes 41 percent to 63 percent of first-page search results to companies Google owns.[72] CEOs control the digital public square where we spend much of our time, but they are not held accountable.[73]

When Russia invaded Ukraine, it was Mark Zuckerberg who made the decision that people in Ukraine would be exempt from Facebook hate-speech policies: users would be allowed to call for the killing of Russian soldiers and of Putin but only in ways related to the invasion. So a single company is making decisions about free speech rights on the world stage: one group can be allowed to incite violence and call for the deaths of other people, and other groups are censored from doing this. Should we just hope that Meta makes wise decisions about what future wars the company will decide are worthy of supporting? Or should a company controlling the news we see have a responsibility to the public to uphold journalistic standards?

BUILDING BACK TRUTH

In just over thirty years, we have gone from a small number of people browsing a few websites to a world where many of us spend significant portions of our time online. The great migration to digital spaces—accelerated during the pandemic—has had an enormous impact on how we live, who we communicate with, how we work, and how we access information.

Many of our digital spaces are designed and run by a handful of companies in Silicon Valley whose business model has resulted in an information crisis. Information disorder has exacerbated the COVID pandemic, limited our ability to respond to climate change, and promoted an online culture where polarizing, toxic, racist, and hateful content rises to the top of our social media feeds.

The mission of digital public spaces needs to change course and start prioritizing technology in service to people rather than technology in service to profits. We need to build back truth online. Understanding what is happening and knowing that there are solutions—that the challenges of misinformation are not insurmountable—are the first steps we can take toward improving our digital public square. The following chapters provide six paths forward to help us understand and pursue strategies that can greatly improve our digital spaces. Our online worlds need to be designed to be more like public parks and libraries and not like shopping malls and roller derbies.

2

Learn to Protect Ourselves
from Misinformation

I've spent my career focused on helping people find reliable information. My job was to be Google before Google existed, and by that I mean early Google, before its mission succumbed to the lure of advertising revenue. Google has become our primary gateway for finding information, and social media has become our new daily news source. But Google and social media platforms are designed to focus on their bottom line, which prioritizes engaging content over trustworthy content. What they promote and demote has an enormous impact on our day-to-day lives. As an information expert, I consider myself able to navigate almost any information waters and come out on top, but this is no longer always true. Understanding my vulnerabilities and learning new strategies have helped me improve my odds.

When we think about misinformation online, we usually think of the extreme cases, such as misinformation during the pandemic that convinced people to drink bleach or blast hair dryers up their noses to "kill" the coronavirus. We think of Edgar Maddison Welch, who took an AR-15 semiautomatic rifle into a pizza parlor to put an end to Hillary Clinton's supposed pedophile ring operating out of the basement. We think of these extreme cases, but what we should really worry about are . . . kittens. I'll explain.

When we look at people like Edgar Maddison Welch, we think that we would never fall for such an obviously false claim. What was he *thinking*? But we all have a little Edgar inside of us in terms of being vulnerable to misinformation. It is how we are built. This was true long before the advent of social media. We all have a tendency to protect the sacred beliefs of our own social or political tribes, and we sometimes favor these beliefs instead of looking closely at hard evidence. We often fail to see things the way they actually are and instead see things the way we *want* to see them. We believe information that confirms our assumptions. We rely on fast thinking and using thinking shortcuts. It is much more challenging to slow down and verify or track down analyses of content, especially when our "friends" are there to let us know the score.

Getting back to kittens . . . a friend of mine who lives alone told me she would really like to get a kitten to keep her company. Kittens are hard to come by, so what good fortune when I read on our Nextdoor online community platform that "Cynthia" had two litters of kittens for sale. Was anyone interested? I immediately, and *without thinking*, messaged Cynthia and said "Yes!" Cynthia asked me to fill out an application listing my phone number, email, and other personal data and then, of course, came the request for a deposit. By now you probably know where this is going. Her scam was not overly sophisticated, and I quickly realized what was up.

What happened? I blame kittens. But really it was a combination of adaptive psychological processes that make us all vulnerable to scams and misinformation. We all have our kitten vulnerabilities, and though we may not bring an AR-15 into a pizza parlor, we are all exposed to social media that connects us with our Cynthias or, in the case of Edgar, his Breitbart News. Our job is to learn to quickly spot Cynthias. Unfortunately, Cynthias are getting more sophisticated in their approaches. They have our personal data, and they know how to use it to microtarget us. They can send us deepfake videos that have real people we trust and admire mouthing words they never said. They enter our online neighborhood platforms with ease and are served up to us as if they were a friendly neighbor who lives nearby. They know all about our kitten weaknesses.

This chapter explores our psychological vulnerabilities to misinformation and the ways in which content on social media can tap into our desires to belong and conform and persuade us that something is true even when it is clearly not. This chapter also looks at how certain personality traits can make some people much more susceptible to misinformation and conspiratorial thinking. Understanding our vulnerabilities is a powerful first step toward learning to protect ourselves. The remainder of the chapter takes the second step: helping us learn to develop new habits of mind that can make us less vulnerable and protect us from falling prey to misinformation.

SLOW DOWN, YOU THINK TOO FAST

Universal psychological processes, individual personality traits, and social group memberships greatly influence how we process and share information. These processes are highly adaptive and have helped us succeed as a species by relying on each other for knowledge and fostering collaboration. But these same processes also make us exceedingly vulnerable to believing false information.

Misinformation has always been a problem. The old adage that a lie travels halfway around the world while the truth is still putting on its shoes holds true for the online world. Misinformation spreads much more quickly than the truth online.[1] Not surprisingly, the false news that Hillary Clinton was running a pedophile ring out of a pizza parlor was more exciting to share than the mundane news of the day. Social media platforms provide us with great benefits, but also have increased the speed and capacity at which false information can spread and take root.

The degree to which platforms can harness the power of personal data has been a game changer in terms of influencing people's beliefs and behavior. Psychographics based on behavioral data move beyond classifying people based on general demographic data such as age or race. They dig more deeply to analyze people's emotional responses, motivations, and moral and political values, and they suss out people's attitudes and biases. Powerful microtargeting is then used to send personalized messages to specific people or groups.

Personalized messaging can be especially effective. In one study, beauty product ads were created to target two groups of people: extroverts and introverts. Extroverts were targeted with the message "Dance like nobody's watching," and introverts were targeted with "Beauty doesn't have to shout." The ads targeting extroverts or introverts were clicked on 40 percent more than ads that were not personalized.[2]

Based on the work of Daniel Kahneman, cognitive psychologists categorize thinking into two types. "Fast thinking" is an automatic intuitive process that requires little effort. For example, if we are driving and see a bird in the road, we quickly slam on the brakes. "Slow thinking" involves analytical and logical reasoning that requires much more time and effort.[3] We might use slow thinking when making a complex decision such as whether to make a career change.

There are dozens of mental shortcuts, called heuristics, that we rely on frequently when making judgments. Heuristics rely on our fast thinking processes. We use them daily, and they impact what we do, what we buy, and what we believe. We constantly have too much information to effectively process at any given time. This was true even before social media existed: the world provides us with a constant stream of stimuli. As a result of this onslaught of information, we rely on heuristics to give us efficient ways of making decisions. But these mental shortcuts can make us particularly susceptible to misinformation.

Our overreliance on fast thinking and related shortcuts is common across all groups regardless of education, income, or other differences. It has been instrumental to our success as humans. We rely on others for information and tend to trust that information. We are social animals dependent on fostering cooperation and adhering to shared belief systems that allow us to live successfully together. The rewards of fostering these shared beliefs—in part due to fast thinking—more than outweigh the deficits that occur when we sometimes fall prey to false information.

The following are some of the most common heuristics that can get us into trouble when we are exposed to misinformation.

The Fluency Heuristic: Easy + Familiar = True

When a politician uses a catchy sound bite to convey an idea—*Build the Wall!*—as opposed to a lengthy speech, the fluency heuristic holds that people will think the sound bite is more convincing than the speech because it is more accessible.[4]

Why does this happen?

The fluency heuristic is a mental shortcut that involves choosing the path that seems easiest when making a judgment. This perception of ease is based on how readily information can be retrieved from memory. We link statements that are easier to process as more likely to be true, more likable than the alternative, and more likely to come from a reliable source.[5] Often fluency benefits us by saving us time and energy while rendering a good decision. But we can rely too much on this shortcut, because we do not like to tax our brains if there is a seemingly easy solution right in front of us.

The fluency heuristic influences our judgment in many arenas: products with easy to pronounce names are purchased more often, and a statement is more likely to be judged as true when it is printed in an easier-to-read font, delivered in a more familiar accent, or presented in a rhyming format.[6] When a company goes public, stocks with easier-to-pronounce names consistently outperform stocks with harder-to-pronounce names. Stocks with easy names are judged to have higher value, which results in more people purchasing them.[7] A perception of ease cues our fluency heuristic, which taps our fast thinking to make a decision. Sometimes this is to our advantage, but sometimes misinformation is presented in a way that cues us to make a quick decision when we would be better off using more analytical thinking, such as when picking a successful stock.

The Availability Heuristic: The More I See It, the More I Believe It

During the winter holiday season, you may assume that *most* of your friends have traveled to warm places because you see many images on Instagram of friends sitting on beaches. In fact, only a small number of friends actually traveled during the holidays, but you draw the wrong conclusion because pictures of friends on the beach have a disproportionate influence on your perception. Your many friends who did not travel did not post any images.

The availability heuristic involves judging the probability or frequency of something occurring based on how easy it is to retrieve similar examples of it from memory, like seeing a number of friends on the beach. This leads to subjective decisions rather than decisions based on objective data.[8] Misinformation on social media platforms is often convincing because it is so widely shared and pervasive.

The Illusory Truth Effect: Repetition = Familiarity = Truth

In the early days of the pandemic, a Belgian newspaper article suggested that 5G, a global wireless standard, might be connected to catching the COVID virus. There was no evidence to support this, but multiple online sources picked up the story, and a few months later, a poll showed that 5 percent of UK residents believed that COVID symptoms were linked to 5G mobile network radiation. Within the next year, there were seventy-seven reported attacks on cell towers in the UK and forty attacks on cell repair workers.[9]

The illusory truth effect, similar to the availability heuristic, occurs through repeated exposure to a piece of information. This is easy to do online and can magnify a sense of familiarity, which can make us prone to believe misinformation that we see repeatedly. The illusory truth effect can occur even if a story is implausible, is labeled as untrue, or runs counter to someone's political beliefs.[10]

The Affect Heuristic: Tapping Our Emotions Makes Us Vulnerable

The inspiring image of Colin Kaepernick in a Nike ad with the words "Believe in something. Even if it means sacrificing everything. Just do it" tapped into our emotions and led to a surge in shoe sales, despite some organizations calling for a boycott of Nike because Kaepernick chose not to stand for the national anthem during NFL games to protest racial injustice.[11] The ad, which won an Emmy, was successful because it stirred up people's emotions: people loved it or people hated it; they bought Nikes or they burned Nikes. It tapped into people's raw feelings about sports, race, and patriotism. It successfully used the affect heuristic.

The affect heuristic is a mental shortcut in which people make decisions that are heavily influenced by their emotions. Emotions are important in helping us navigate the world, and in many cases, they help us make intuitive decisions that serve us well, but sometimes they can be prone to manipulation.

Advances in marketing strategies and clever misinformation campaigns have expanded our ability to influence people's behavior, often without their awareness. People respond more to the emotions generated by a piece of content than to the actual content itself. The most frequently shared posts are those that generate strong emotions.

Similar to other mental shortcuts, the affect heuristic can be cued when we are called on to make a quick, seemingly easy decision. When deciding to jump out of the way of an oncoming bus, emotions like fear are essential. But for other decisions, our emotions do not always serve our best interests. We often rely on them because they are immediately available to us and it would be more work to slow down and analyze information.[12]

The more sensational a story is, the more it taps into emotions and increases our attention. Even brief exposures to words or images can impact our judgments. Social media is especially good at playing to our emotions because it conveys a sense of time pressure so that we make quick judgments as we scan content. We are not always aware of emotional manipulations that can subtly cue our affect. We are more likely to recognize when someone is trying to persuade us with a logical argument, as this cues us to slow down and use analysis and reasoning.[13]

Emotionally laden stories appeal to our feelings and desires. Storytelling has many positive attributes, such as building a community with shared knowledge and culture. But a strong narrative can also be used as a powerful persuasion tool. Political advertisements that tap into patriotism, group membership, or an "us versus them" mindset can be effective by conjuring up strong emotions that get our attention and persuade us to think that something is true when it is not.

People who create misinformation often use emotional language and images, knowing that these appeals are more likely to go viral. Tapping into anger or anxiety cues our fast but faulty judgments about content. Tapping into fear has been especially effective in spreading false information about COVID. The more afraid people are of the virus, the more likely they are to believe in and share misinformation.[14] At the same time, advertisers, as in the Nike example, have found that appeals to our emotions can be effective tools to persuade us to do something we might not otherwise do.

The Self-Confirmation Bias: I Knew It!

A couple is having an argument about whether red wine is good or bad for your heart. One partner says it is, and she searches Google: Is red wine *good* for your heart? The answer: yes! The other partner says it is not, and she searches Google: Is red wine *bad* for your heart? The answer: yes!

The self-confirmation bias, another mental shortcut, is a tendency people have to believe information that confirms their preexisting beliefs and to view information as not credible if it goes against their beliefs. This bias is often unaffected by strong evidence that is contrary to a person's beliefs. This bias also influences the information that we seek out online. We tend to search, share, and view content more favorably that is consistent with our beliefs.

There are other common biases that interact with our self-confirmation bias. The false-consensus effect gives people the illusion that their own opinions are correct and are likely to be widely held.[15] Cognitive dissonance, which makes us feel uneasy when we run up against competing viewpoints, also activates our self-confirmation bias. The self-confirmation bias provides us with an easy way out by guiding us to make decisions that mesh with our existing beliefs, even when it is not in our best interest to do so.[16] We also have an aversion to ambiguous information: we are drawn to information that provides us with as much certainty as possible, regardless of the actual veracity of the information.[17]

Social media magnifies our tendency to believe information that confirms our existing beliefs by feeding us content that aligns with our thinking and by connecting us with users who share similar beliefs. Selective exposure— choosing to read and listen to media that agrees with our beliefs—helps us repeatedly confirm our beliefs and avoid being challenged by evidence that contradicts them.[18] These echo chambers that we choose, and that are created for us online, contribute to our increasing polarization from others around political and social issues.[19] People running misinformation campaigns take advantage of our echo chambers by personalizing their appeals and establishing trust by pretending to be one of our tribe. We are more susceptible to falling for misinformation shared by people who seem to be coming from our own like-minded group.

SOCIAL MEDIA TAPS INTO OUR DESIRES TO BELONG AND CONFORM

In addition to mental shortcuts, group dynamics can play an even stronger role in influencing our judgments and also make us vulnerable to misinformation.

We like to think that many of the decisions we make are rational and logical and stem from careful reasoning based on reliable evidence. Unfortunately, this is often not the case. Our desire to conform with majority views in our social group and to fit in with our peers greatly influences the decisions we make.

Every year, thousands of movies are released. How do we decide what to watch? It is unlikely that we would wade through thousands of titles blindly and choose for ourselves. We are social animals, and we benefit from our connections to groups. Groups help simplify our choices, and we rely on them to help us decide what to eat, where to live, what to believe, and what to watch. Our friends and social media feeds tell us what is "popular on Netflix now" or among the "top 10 shows watched today." Our groups and online feeds help us sort through an abundance of information.

While psychologists and behavioral economists study individual behaviors that make us prone to falling for misinformation, sociologists and anthropologists study the impact of social and cultural effects on how we come to form false beliefs. Much of what we believe is shaped by what other people tell us. It is rare that we rely on direct personal experience. This is often beneficial: doctors tell us what medicine to take, and meteorologists inform us about upcoming storms. We like to think most of our choices are rational and independent of manipulation, but they are highly subject to group influences.[20]

Social influences on our beliefs and decisions have always been with us. In recent history, the rugged Marlboro Man and the emancipated Virginia Slims Woman increased the already popular habit of smoking cigarettes at a time when scientific evidence clearly tied smoking to lung cancer. Today, social media rapidly multiplies the effects of social influence because information can be shared so rapidly by so many people. Katy Perry vaping at the Golden Globes was tweeted out by the company Juul to her twenty-seven million followers—#katyperry—within minutes of her appearance.

Social media can be easily manipulated to create misperceptions of group beliefs that can influence our thinking. Unreliable content can be broadcast by someone trying to sell a product or shared either by accident or with the aim of causing serious harm. We sometimes confuse popularity with truth, but popularity can be manipulated by those trying to drive up interest in a particular product or belief. People interpret the number of viewers of a video on YouTube, or the number of five-star reviews for a product on Amazon, as a signal of quality. But thousands of views and "likes" can be purchased cheaply to manipulate the perception of what is popular and then influence our behavior due to our desire to conform.[21]

Social Consensus

Social consensus has a powerful influence on shaping beliefs, particularly when people are uncertain about their own beliefs.[22] People pay a great deal of attention to social cues in their environment. This starts when we are young: three-year-old children show an awareness of consensus behaviors and tend to align themselves with the beliefs of the majority.[23] Social consensus is adaptive: it is often to our advantage to follow the majority. For example, when people see others running from a potential danger—such as a fire or avalanche—they, too, begin running, even before they know the nature of the danger. They assume the group is likely to be right, and their overreliance on fast thinking is an asset where there is sudden danger.

We tend to be more confident in our beliefs if they are shared by others, place more trust in something we remember if others remember it similarly, and are more likely to endorse something if we know many others have endorsed it.[24] We typically copy the beliefs of the majority in our group, and this tendency increases as the size of the majority increases.[25] We also think that most people's beliefs align with our own.[26] On the other hand, if we perceive that there is a controversy, or a great deal of dissent around a topic, we are much less likely to believe it.[27]

Fostering the illusion of consensus or dissent is a powerful tool for persuasion. People rely too often on the perception of consensus, and they do this even when the group is clearly wrong.[28] The pressure to conform plays a significant role in creating politically polarized groups. Bots—automated online programs—are used to create the illusion of consensus or to drive up popularity. Bots can be purchased cheaply and can aid in the spread of misinformation by driving up likes and view rates, and they can push the content to the top of our digital feeds. Nearly *half* of the Twitter accounts tweeting about the coronavirus in 2020 were bots designed to give the impression of popularity and consensus in order to persuade people to take actions or purchase products that would "cure" or "protect" them from the virus.[29]

Conformity Bias

Conformity bias occurs when people so strongly want to fit in with a group that they make decisions regardless of clear signals that there may be a better choice. Just call to mind stories about fraternity hazing that influenced pledges to engage in harmful behavior. Conformity bias differs from social consensus in that the prime motivation with conformity bias is the desire to fit in with the crowd, whereas the motivation in social consensus is to go with the majority behavior because it is perceived as likely to be the best choice.

These effects of conformity bias can be particularly strong in teenagers using social media. For example, the "Tide pod challenge" on YouTube resulted in many young people eating laundry detergent pellets that made them ill, because they wanted to fit in with the crowd. But conformity bias affects all of us. It even occurs with experienced scientists who can be strongly influenced by their network of peers. There have been numerous incidents in which a few early, but misleading, scientific results have been widely reported on and have then influenced how other scientists study a particular problem. Even when evidence begins to surface that these early results were not accurate, scientists have difficulty switching their beliefs.[30]

ARE SOME PEOPLE MORE SUSCEPTIBLE TO MISINFORMATION?

No one is immune from falling for a piece of misinformation. People exposed even briefly to a false news story, for example, can be influenced even when the information is inconsistent with their beliefs.[31] However, there are some individual personality differences that make some people more likely to fall for misinformation.

We all use fast, intuitive thinking and slower, more analytical thinking in making decisions every day, but some people are more likely to draw upon their analytical reasoning skills when making a decision, which helps them make better judgment calls when facing misinformation.[32] Personal deficits in using analytical thinking result in being more vulnerable to false information.[33] The ability to call on analytical reasoning when needed for a decision is not tied to education levels or political affiliation, but it does appear that some people have a greater tendency than others do toward using their analytical thinking skills.[34]

Deficits and Tendencies

People who have deficits in what is called "actively open-minded thinking" are much more likely to believe false information. These deficits are characterized by relying on fast thinking, not seeking out evidence that opposes one's own views, and not appropriately weighing different pieces of evidence when forming or revising one's beliefs.[35] Some people are more delusion-prone than others, and this causes them to be more willing to view an implausible idea as true, such as a wild conspiracy theory.[36] Delusion-prone people share some characteristics with people diagnosed with more serious psychoses. Delusion-prone people are also likely to have deficits in both analytical thinking and actively open-minded reasoning.[37]

Dogmatic thinking is also tied to deficits in both analytic reasoning skills and actively open-minded thinking. Dogmatic thinking is characterized by a deficit in the ability to view issues from another person's perspective. People with strong religious faith backgrounds tend to have higher levels of dogmatism. This suggests that they rely more on their intuitive fast thinking, whereas people with less strongly held religious beliefs are more likely to move back and forth between automatic and analytic thinking, choosing the appropriate way of thinking depending on the decision at hand.[38] Religious fundamentalists in particular tend to be less analytical and less actively open-minded thinkers, and they are more likely to engage in dogmatic thinking. This makes those drawn to fundamentalism more vulnerable to misinformation.[39]

Personality Traits Tied to Conspiratorial Thinking

Certain personality traits are linked to a tendency to believe in conspiracy theories. Not surprisingly, people who have high levels of anxiety, paranoia, and feelings of powerlessness are drawn to conspiratorial thinking.[40] People are also attracted to conspiracy theories when they have other needs that are not being met, including the need for knowledge and certainty, the need to feel safe and secure when feeling powerless, and—for those who rank high in narcissism—the need to feel unique.[41]

People who believe in conspiracies are more likely to have low levels of trust in others and believe that the world is a dangerous place full of bad people.[42] Early socialization into mainstream political systems can lay the groundwork for trust in government institutions; but for some people, that early socialization does not occur, and this can make them less trusting in institutions and more attracted to conspiratorial thinking.[43]

Belief in conspiracies is more likely when the theory is tied to a partisan issue. The predisposition toward conspiratorial thinking falls along a continuum, with some people rarely falling for conspiracies and others tending to fall for many.[44] Believing in conspiracy theories can have many negative consequences for people's health and safety, including making poor medical decisions and being more accepting of violent behavior.[45]

ANTIBODIES TO DECEPTION: DEVELOPING NEW HABITS OF MIND *AND* GUT

We will never be able to completely get rid of misinformation, but we can learn how to improve our emotional intelligence, tap into more sophisticated thinking strategies, and work to put the brakes on our emotional reactions so that we can rely more on analytical thinking skills when the situation demands it.

Researcher danah boyd has called for developing "antibodies to help people not be deceived. That's really tricky because most people like to follow their gut more than their mind. No one wants to hear that they're being tricked. Still, I think there might be some value in helping people understand their own psychology."[46]

Improving Our Emotional Intelligence

Developing greater emotional intelligence, intellectual empathy, and more open-minded analytical and reflective thinking are essential components to developing "antibodies" to misinformation. There has been increasing support for teaching emotional intelligence through social-emotional learning programs in kindergarten through twelfth grade, but there is less focus on this on the college level and beyond. As adults, we learn new skills all the time—cooking, car repair, pickleball—but there is less emphasis on developing emotional intelligence. Think of a world where more people were taught how to better understand and regulate their emotions. When we learn how to drive a car, we are taught the criminal penalties for road rage, but we are not taught how to reduce our own emotional reactions in response to a bad driving experience.

Emotional intelligence is a set of abilities that help us accurately perceive and understand emotions, access emotions to assist our thinking, and reflectively regulate emotions. Daniel Goleman has broken down emotional intelligence into five skills: self-awareness, emotional control, self-motivation, empathy, and relationship skills.[47] There is a great deal of variability in people's abilities to identify and regulate their own emotions, and this impacts their psychological health and academic and work success. Social-emotional learning is a broader skill set that incorporates emotional intelligence; it includes learning to make good decisions, care about others, and behave ethically. The need for these skills is obvious in today's climate, where school board meetings and children's sports events dissolve into screaming matches and fistfights.

Improving our emotional intelligence can also help us avoid falling for emotional appeals. High levels of emotional intelligence help us distinguish between real and fake content online. People who are *more* perceptive about their own emotions are much *less* likely to fall for fake information, because they are better at spotting emotionally charged content, prompting them to think more analytically.[48] Learning to recognize when our emotional reactions are being targeted—when we are feeling strong emotions in reaction to information—can help us switch over to drawing on more analytical thinking skills. This is connected to learning to slow down our thinking more generally: learning to spot when a situation calls for us to analyze information can help deter us from relying only on emotional, fast decision-making.

People with more highly developed reflective analytical thinking skills are less likely to fall for misinformation.[49] Some people tend to rely more on their analytical thinking, and others rely more on their emotions to process content. We can all probably think of people who overrely on one strategy or another. The ideal is being able to switch back and forth depending on what is called for in a specific situation. These are skills that can be taught and improved upon. Both types of thinking—fast and slow—are important.[50]

Developing a Scout Mindset

Julia Galef's work on developing a scout mindset shows that learning about our thinking shortcuts and biases alone is not sufficient for improving our decision-making. We need to proactively work to cultivate an attitude of curiosity and open-mindedness. We need to *want* to notice the things that we may be wrong about, *want* to understand the possible flaws in our decision-making, and *want* to improve. Galef contrasts having a scout mindset with having a soldier mindset. Thinking like a soldier leads us to defend our beliefs against outside threats, seek evidence to support our beliefs, and ignore evidence that goes against our beliefs. Soldiers resist admitting they are wrong because to do so would be to admit defeat.[51]

The scout mindset encourages seeing things as they are, not as we wish they were. It challenges the way we are built and the culture that surrounds us. Key characteristics of developing a scout mindset include the ability to accept criticism, know our own biases, and seek out critics who can help us verify or dispute our beliefs. We need to learn to tell others when they are right and reexamine the evidence to try to prove ourselves wrong.

In a similar vein, developing intellectual empathy helps people consider the viewpoints and experiences of others and better understand how social differences or the desire for status or belonging may influence our beliefs and how we evaluate information. This awareness can provide us with a more nuanced form of critical thinking that moves beyond using only logic and reason. Learning intellectual empathy encompasses developing a better understanding of our own and other people's worldviews and biases, while at the same time keeping the central focus on facts and evidence.

When people evaluate scientific information, they are much less likely to believe it if it contradicts their point of view, even when they are shown solid proof. Learning to be more open-minded can help people move outside of their own entrenched beliefs in order to evaluate information on its merits and evidence. Counterintuitively, people with higher levels of education can sometimes be worse at stepping outside of their worldviews to evaluate information more objectively. Motivated reasoning may, in some cases, cause people with more education to be more adept at interpreting information in ways that support their preexisting positions.[52]

The degree to which one is able to think open-mindedly—to be willing to judge one's own fallibility, to take risks to pursue knowledge despite the threat to one's worldview—improves the chances of not falling for misinformation.[53] Online spaces are not primed to support open-mindedness or persistence; instead, they cue fast thinking and the affirmation of existing worldviews. The onus is currently on us to be aware of the fast-thinking cues we are being fed, and try to slow down.

THE WAY FORWARD

Learning to develop more sophisticated analytical thinking abilities combined with improving our emotional intelligence can provide *some* protection against misinformation. At the same time, learning about these habits of mind can also inform the design of healthier digital spaces. Being aware that you are being emotionally manipulated does not mean you will always be able to resist it, but this understanding will help us advocate for changes to platforms that are currently designed to exploit our vulnerabilities. The work of psychologists, behavioral economists, and ethicists can play significant and exciting new roles in informing tool development and platform designs that can limit the reach of misinformation and prompt us to make better decisions when consuming content.

3

Teach Students to Play Offense against Misinformation

A media literacy lesson in Kentucky teaches students how to find and evaluate information online about vaping and health. It teaches them critical thinking skills and how to investigate the source of a piece of information. After school, students jump on social media and see images of Katy Perry sharing a vape pen with Orlando Bloom at the Golden Globe awards. Vape company Juul has grabbed the images from the award show and posted them to Twitter, tagging them #KatyPerry. Instantly her 27 million followers—mostly teens—see the images of Katy vaping.

Searching Google on vaping, one of the first hits is for "Top 5 Celebrities Who Love a Vape" by a vape shop marketing blog called the *Chief of Vapes*. It includes Katy: "Chart-topping celebrity sensation Katy Perry has made a very smart switch to vaping. The global superstar . . . began her little love in with vaping back in 2013, and she is certainly living a teenage dream by adding years onto her life."[1]

Vaping companies originally designed their product to help adults addicted to cigarettes reduce their consumption of nicotine with a safer alternative. But soon the drive for more customers led them to target the teen market by showing how cool it was to vape. For fourteen-year-olds, who were likely not already smokers, vaping was not going to add years onto their life but instead would get them hooked. The Kentucky media literacy lesson was left in the dust. It was no match against Katy Perry and a platform designed for fast engagement and hyperpersonalization.

Let's unpack this a little.

Ads pushing vaping to teenagers may not be what we typically think of when we think of misinformation. What comes to mind might be fake videos on TikTok of the Russian invasion of Ukraine or anti-vaxxer campaigns. But posts designed to entice young people to take up vaping can have a tremendous impact. Within a year of Juul launching its social media campaign targeting teenagers, teen vaping was considered an epidemic, with one in five high school students regularly vaping.[2]

In the age of social media, platforms control what content is promoted but incur no responsibility for that content. After years of promoting vaping to teenagers, Juul was sued and is now required to spend tens of millions of dollars to fund teen addiction treatment centers.[3] But social media companies have not been held accountable for the content they promote. Google pushed the *Chief of Vapes* article to the top of its recommended links and presented it as if it were a news article when it was, in fact, an advertisement.

Social media is now the primary way that more than half of all teenagers and adults get their news, and many of the sources consumed are not articles written and fact-checked by journalists. Increasingly, content is created that is designed to sell products rather than provide trustworthy content. We are now playing catchup and are struggling to address this dramatic shift in how we consume information.[4] Many people have migrated from a somewhat controlled and regulated information environment, limited to the morning newspaper and a few TV channels, to an avalanche of 24/7 social media feeds designed for maximum engagement. And while there is an appearance of greater choice in the information we consume, in fact, much of what we view is pushed at us and passively and superficially consumed. We leave it up to social media and Google search to determine what information is best for us.

Media literacy programs will not "fix" the problem of misinformation, but they can be a key component within a larger strategy that includes changing how platforms are designed. In a climate where there is rising distrust of all content online and an increasing tendency to favor belief over evidence, media literacy programs are expanding their focus from skill development to a broader approach that teaches students to have more agency. Students are learning that they can choose to play a role in how they interact with online spaces and that they can also have input into helping create healthier digital spaces. Media literacy programs are helping students learn to play offense, not just defense.

Education reformers—from John Dewey at the beginning of the twentieth century to David Buckingham and bell hooks in recent decades—have pushed for education to move beyond simply the passing on of current knowledge. Education should help students learn to question, explore alternatives, and demand change. What might it look like if students could learn about their digital spaces while at the same time working to improve them? What if students could help to build the kinds of online worlds they themselves want to live in? What if learning could include helping reform the underlying structures that are producing these unhealthy digital worlds?

Education generally needs to encompass support for stronger civic engagement to help improve society. The goals should include helping students develop a sense of responsibility and a passion for improving the world, not simply passing on knowledge from one generation to the next. Knowledge needs to be understood as something that evolves over time as we learn more about our worlds. Students need to learn to be flexible and open-minded thinkers to help us continue on the path of understanding our world more deeply and accurately.

MEDIA LITERACY: ONE PART OF A HOLISTIC STRATEGY

When I started digging into hundreds of research articles on misinformation, I found that the articles that focused on solutions often put education front and center. In part, this is likely because education is a less controversial option than going after the root causes of misinformation, which is more complex and challenging. New regulations are needed, but how do we balance those with free speech? Social media platforms need to be held accountable and stop incentivizing misinformation, but how can we scale and enforce that? Local journalism is on life support and needs to be resuscitated, but what kind of funding model could work when platforms have siphoned off much of the advertising revenue?

The research I reviewed on misinformation recommended that a key strategy should be stronger media literacy programs in schools. Students needed to be taught to spot and avoid misinformation and develop more robust critical thinking skills. Turning up the volume on media literacy is essential, but we also need to think strategically about how we can augment our current programs to address a rapidly changing and increasingly toxic digital environment. Turning up the volume will not be enough.

Focusing only on media literacy ignores the larger systemic challenges we face from platforms that are able to manipulate our psychological vulnerabilities and stream personalized content to keep us entertained and online. Learning to think more critically about the information we consume—whether we are five or fifty years old—is no match against sophisticated microtargeting, expertly doctored images, and sensationalized content. Equipping people with media literacy skills will not decrease the amount of misinformation online. Media literacy skills are important but can only have limited effectiveness against platforms that are prioritizing profits over serving the public.[5]

Social media platforms do not represent the first time that we have been outmaneuvered by advertising. In the past century alone, we have recognized the harms caused by sophisticated ad campaigns and we have clamped down on them. In the United States, we recognized the imbalance in power between advertising and consumers and attempted to right the balance. The United States created the Food and Drug Administration and the Federal Trade Commission in the early twentieth century to put up some guardrails.

When TVs entered the American home, we realized the massive scale at which companies could now speak directly to consumers, including children, and we designed laws regulating what companies could say on TV. We regulated ads for particularly harmful products such as cigarettes, alcohol, and pharmaceuticals. Cigarettes, for example, were banned from TV ads in 1971 and then later banned in magazines, newspapers, and on billboards.

But when the internet leaped onto the scene a few decades ago, we were so excited by all the possibilities. We didn't want to stifle innovation. We wanted to see where it could take us, and it has taken us to some incredible places, but at the same time it has created a great deal of harm. The internet is no longer new, and US communication policies have lagged far behind technological innovations. Online, we don't have basic protections from the harm and damage caused by manipulative advertising, misinformation, and toxic content. In particular, there is little protection for children and youth.

We have gone from a world where comedian George Carlin in 1972 ranted about the "seven words you can't say on TV"—which resulted in permission to use swear words on TV between the hours of 10:00 p.m. and 6:00 a.m., when children were presumably asleep—to a world where the majority of teenagers have viewed pornography long before the age of eighteen.[6] Online porn is so easy to access, it now serves as a child's first exposure to "sex education." Because more than half of all porn shows aggressive acts toward women, some high school sex education classes are now using porn to teach students what not to do.[7]

As our digital spaces became more central to our lives, while at the same time facing few restrictions on how they are designed, media literacy programs are switching gears to teach students more agency in how they interact with their online worlds.

FROM TEACHING SKILLS TO TEACHING AGENCY

Media literacy programs have had an uneven track record in schools and have fallen in and out of favor over the years. One innovative government-funded program called "Media Now," used a "learning by doing" approach designed to "improve students' knowledge of mass media terminology and techniques; demonstrate increased media production abilities; decrease students' susceptibility to persuasion by the mass media. . . . Students and teachers need to be prepared to evaluate and appreciate the proliferation of media activities that confront them in this technological age."[8]

The year was 1970.

The program used self-directed learning kits to teach film production skills in an experiential curriculum. The act of creating their own media helped students learn that they could "control whatever message they wanted to get across."[9] These kits were considered revolutionary at the time but, in fact, have deep roots in Dewey's experiential learning pedagogy that is called "learning by doing."

Support for media literacy plummeted eight years later, when Senator William Proxmire's Golden Fleece award—an award given for wasting taxpayer money—was given to a program for teaching college students "how to watch television."[10] Misunderstandings about the purpose of media literacy have continued to the present day as well as questions about how it should be taught, who should teach it, what discipline it should be housed in, and what content should be covered.

There are two main philosophies underpinning media literacy programs: protecting students from harm and teaching empowerment and agency through social and civic engagement. Media literacy has also straddled the line between being an educational approach and a social movement. One component found in most media literacy programs is a focus on skills that help students avoid falling prey to misinformation. Skills-based learning approaches help students learn to analyze and evaluate information and, over the years, have expanded to embrace more active inquiry and critical thinking.

At the college level, media and information literacy has been taught by librarians and media studies faculty, though teaching critical thinking is found within many disciplines. The Association of College and Research Libraries "Framework for Information Literacy for Higher Education" emphasizes the roles and responsibilities involved in producing and sharing information and encourages students to dive more deeply into understandings of expertise, authority, critical thinking, and the context in which information is being produced. The Framework also encourages students to develop strategies including self-reflection and a focus on ethics.

Since the release of the Framework, further work has been done to provide a stronger diversity, equity, and inclusion (DEI) lens as well as a focus on social justice. In a similar vein, K–12 educators are incorporating a DEI lens into teaching media literacy, though these new efforts vary across schools and often rely on the passions of individual teachers.

New programs expanding on these efforts teach critical disinformation studies—using a critical approach to understanding misinformation that takes into account history, inequality, power, and culture. This broader approach helps place misinformation within a wider context of the ways in which social inequalities—including race and ethnicity, gender, class, and sexual identity—can shape the dynamics of misinformation.[11] Critical disinformation studies are reaching across different disciplines and using a variety of approaches to improve our understandings of how online ecosystems impact people, communities, and social systems; how media manipulation works to spread misinformation; and how communities can come together to improve online spaces.

Media literacy programs are continuing to augment skills-based approaches with a stronger push toward helping students play a more active rather than passive role online. Educators understand that even broadening media literacy efforts to embrace skills such as critical thinking and understanding power and authority in relationship to information will not be sufficient. While most college students use social media as their primary source for news, research shows that only a small percentage of students can accurately gauge their ability to identify a false news story.[12] Even after receiving extensive instruction, most students make poor decisions about what information to trust and are unable to distinguish between advertisements and news stories or verify the authority of a website.[13]

This is not just a youth problem. Adults are unable to navigate an information space where corporate-funded sites are posing as grassroots organizations, extremist groups are camouflaged as professional societies, and lobbying efforts are designed to look like nonpartisan think tanks. Studies on interventions with adults to encourage stronger media literacy competencies have failed to show encouraging results. Adults are even more likely to share misinformation than young people are, even when they know it is untrue.[14]

There is also a growing recognition that skills taught in the context of writing a research paper in the constrained world of the classroom are less applicable outside of school, where the fast pace of social media discourages analyzing and evaluating sources. Teaching is now shifting to help students understand that they need to focus their thinking on how they interact with digital spaces: less passive scrolling and more strategic interactions to help people take ownership and not just rely on Google, TikTok, and Facebook to select their content. Media literacy programs are starting to incorporate discussions about the power that algorithms have over what information we view and the media manipulation tactics that target our emotions and cue us to think quickly rather than more analytically.[15]

Media literacy efforts are also starting to take into account the current climate of declining trust in institutions and, in particular, a lack of faith in the news media.[16] Information scientists have discovered that media literacy that focuses on teaching critical thinking and skepticism in the current environment has sometimes had the paradoxical effect of making students overly cynical and suspicious of *all* information, including legacy media. This then moves them further toward alternative news sources selected by algorithms.[17]

In a study of college students, Project Information Literacy found that "trust is dead for many students, and skepticism lives. Students who grew up with the internet had acquired . . . a certain cynicism about the reliability of the World Wide Web. Yet, most did not find the heuristics they learned in school and the critical thinking skills practiced in college either useful or relevant when trying to make sense of the volume of information they encounter in their daily lives."[18]

Educators are also trying to figure out how best to address what is being referred to as "truth decay": the growing climate of distrust combined with the overreliance on personal beliefs instead of using evidence and facts to judge whether information is true. While there has always been a tension between believing in facts versus being influenced by worldviews, social media platforms are now exacerbating this shift by cueing fast, emotion-based thinking and promoting sensationalized and low-credibility content.

Education as Action

John Dewey started the push over a century ago for education to be viewed as a "fundamental method of social progress and reform" rather than just a means for passing on existing knowledge. New educational initiatives to combat misinformation are starting to involve students as active participants in their online worlds. We can draw on the research and insights from many disciplines. Addressing misinformation is starting to augment current practices that focus on skills such as critical thinking and source evaluation to encourage students to play a participatory role in helping design better digital spaces.

Media literacies need to include helping students learn about, and design, the new online communities in which they want to live; civic media literacies to promote stewardship of our democracy; ethical frameworks for our digital spaces, including a personal code of ethics; and integrating tech ethics into computer science and other courses that can impact the design of our online spaces. Teaching students about the deficits in our current digital spaces can help promote agency and empowerment and can encourage learners to actively construct new online worlds rather than passively accept the designs laid out by Silicon Valley.

Agency by Design to Create Healthy Online Spaces

Agency by Design is a research-based approach developed by Harvard's Project Zero that uses maker-centered learning to empower people of all ages to actively build and reshape their worlds. "Maker-centered" means developing a sensitivity to how objects and systems are designed, combined with growing the capacity for people to shape their worlds through building, tinkering, and redesigning. This provides people with the opportunity to make improvements in order to make systems or objects more effective, efficient, ethical, and beautiful.[19]

Agency by Design is one of many maker-centered learning innovations that are being used in schools today. These ideas are not new, but they provide innovative tweaks to older learning theories, such as the work of educators Maria Montessori and Seymour Papert, that stress that learning should be authentic and student-centered. The important takeaway is the notion of learner agency. Students can explore and learn about existing digital spaces while at the same time creating ways to improve these spaces to reduce harm and help people thrive online.

The Agency by Design framework recommends three interrelated capacities that can help people develop greater sensitivity to design. They include:

1. Looking closely with sustained observation to cue what Daniel Kahneman refers to as slower, more analytical thinking. Looking closely moves beyond superficial understandings to more deeply notice the different parts of things and how these parts interact.
2. Exploring complexity, which involves investigating how things function in the world and how they interact and connect to larger systems. Exploring complexity can help us understand different worldviews, beliefs, and emotions and develop more open-minded thinking.
3. Finding opportunities by framing learning as a chance to envision new designs and inventions and imagine how systems can be reframed or reworked. This often takes the form of tinkering, prototyping, making, and revising plans.[20]

Applied to digital spaces, maker-centered learning as well as agency by design approaches can be used to help students reflect on, analyze, and explore the spaces' complexities while at the same time finding ways to design new digital worlds that can be of greater benefit to society. The key goal of maker-centered learning is to frame learning within the context of action and improvement, not passivity. Kindergartens might explore ideas about how kids should treat each other online and experiment with building or working within simple online spaces. For example, lesson plans for K–5 students are helping students learn about online bullying by creating their own app that is designed to prevent bullying.[21]

At the college level, students can be involved in creating more complex digital spaces. At Brown University, students have designed a new social media app that embraces the original mission of social media: to promote authentic and meaningful connections with people in their real-world spaces. Students at Brown created a new social media platform called Tagg, which is designed to focus on people rather than content, to prioritize social good over profit, and to help foster more genuine connections. With designs created by the nearby Rhode Island School of Design, the Tagg platform lets you link to your other social accounts, provides information about clubs and hobbies you are involved in, and helps you connect to potential friends, study partners, and dates. It is designed for inclusivity and with the goal of repairing the bad parts of the dominant social media platforms.[22]

Civic Media Literacies: More Rebels Needed

There is a need for a renewal of civic engagement at a time when so many people are caught up in a shallow loop of tweets, images, and videos online. In a new book encouraging us to reconnect to society and break free from our stupor-inducing "infinite browsing," civic advocate Pete Davis writes of "rebels" who live in defiance of the dominant online culture:

They're *citizens*—they feel responsible for what happens to society.

They're *patriots*—they love the places where they live and the neighbors who populate those places.

They're *builders*—they turn ideas into reality over the long haul.

They're *stewards*—they keep watch over institutions and communities.

They're *artisans*—they take pride in their craft.

And they're *companions*—they give time to people.[23]

Creating new civic media literacies can help address a climate of increased apathy, distrust, and cynicism emerging from our digital spaces. Rather than passive viewing and suspicion directed at all information online, civic media literacies can help students develop a sense of power through participation in changing digital systems while they learn about them.

Sustaining a healthy democracy requires education so that citizens can understand policy, communicate needs, and hold politicians accountable for improving society. Education should encourage people to become active in bettering our communities and institutions rather than being passive bystanders. Echoing the words of John Dewey, education should be viewed as a "fundamental method of social progress and reform," which should involve "learning by doing."[24]

Researchers and educators Eric Gordon and Paul Mihailidis are calling for civic media literacies that can inspire students to become active civic participants. They suggest moving beyond helping people understand how these structures work to taking intentional civic actions to reform and improve media's role in our communities.[25] They have called for new media literacies that would prioritize civic intentionality to help bring people together to solve social problems, to help create spaces that encourage meaningful engagement and positive dialog, and to develop a commitment toward working for the common good.[26] Mihailidis suggests five constructs that focus on renewing civic engagement through civic media literacy education.

The first construct is to cultivate a sense of agency and self-efficacy while participating in online communities to strengthen our capacity for understanding the power we have to impact our communities.[27] This includes asking people to understand and reflect on their place in society, the power they have as individuals and how this agency can impact society.

The second construct is to develop new literacies to help people become more open to learning about diverse views and create a caring ethic that places value on relationships, the practice of caring for others, and working to reduce polarization.

The third construct, stemming from the work of educators and activists Paulo Freire and bell hooks, is critical consciousness that teaches people that their social reality is something they can transform, that they have the "possibility of response"; that no matter their background, they can participate in shaping their own destiny and their community. The role of the individual is seen as "embracing transgression" and challenging the status quo.

The fourth construct is to promote perseverance and stamina without submitting to the distracting tendencies of the Web. This involves helping people learn to embrace complexity and recover from failure. Students need to learn to absorb issues deeply, persist in engaging with complex ideas, and work against a digital environment that encourages the scattered and shallow rapid digestion of small packets of information.

The fifth construct is emancipation, which requires developing new media systems that challenge the current platforms. Civic media literacies need to have an emphasis on reform and social justice. Creating new ways to form communities and exchange ideas online involves going against the grain and pushing back against powerful interests that do not want this to happen.[28] This last construct calls for emancipatory communication activism that challenges how power is distributed online, who has a voice, how messages are prioritized, and who should control personal data and algorithm design.[29]

What might this look like in practice? Teaching these new civic media literacies will only work in a model that provides opportunities for activism and participation in issues that directly impact students. Mihailidis describes a light bulb moment for him when his hometown of Chelmsford, Massachusetts, came together to actively use social media—in all its messiness—to fight to restore funding for a beloved high school librarian.[30] While students can learn about the powerful ways social media can influence global events—such as the Arab Spring—engaging them directly in a local issue that directly impacts their lives can resonate and result in a more deeply felt learning experience.

Tech Ethics

Organizations and academic institutions are working to address the role ethics should play in the design of online spaces and how we interact online. This starts with helping students learn that truth seeking adheres to facts over belief systems and that scholarship, science, journalism, medicine, and other areas work under established codes of ethics that safeguard the reliability of the information they communicate. People need to make distinctions between ethical research and viral personalities.

Librarian Barbara Fister recommends that students develop their own personal "code of ethics" when interacting online, comparable to other professional codes of conduct, such as that of the Society of Professional Journalists.[31] Communication researchers Phillips and Milner advocate for developing a network ethics, which centers on reciprocity, interdependence, and shared responsibility in how our digital spaces function. This network ethics should focus on strategic, day-to-day actions with awareness as to how these actions impact others.[32]

Online worlds have become so central to our daily lives—from interactive gaming and entertainment to Zoom church services or online town meetings—that we need to think about what behaviors and etiquette need to be called for when we interact with others online. Behaviors that would not be tolerated in the physical world—such as walking down the street and harassing or yelling at someone—take place frequently online. We need to work on clarifying what acceptable behavior should look like in our online public spaces.

Promising new educational initiatives are now taking place in the field of computer science, with new courses being taught in "deep tech ethics" to educate students about the large-scale social implications of their actions.[33] At Rice University, a pilot course on ethics and accountability in the field of computer science is teaching a deep ethics approach that seeks to counter some of the significant harms technology designs are imposing on society. At Harvard, Embedded EthiCS is a collaborative program run by philosophy and computer science faculty that uses a weekly teaching lab to incorporate ethical practices into developing new technologies. Integrating these new constructs into the design and planning of new technologies can help students develop a stronger sense of responsibility for their digital creations.

EDUCATION TO BUILD NEW DIGITAL SPACES

New media literacy initiatives are starting to expand their jurisdiction by fostering agency in addition to teaching skills. Successful initiatives should strive to be holistic, integrated, coordinated, and interdisciplinary.[34] We need to decide how we want to interact online, not continue to fall back on a blanket acceptance of the algorithms and data collection that are driving how we interact with information. We need to embrace action.[35]

Understanding how our current systems prey on our psychological vulnerabilities and helping students develop emotional intelligence, intellectual empathy, and open-minded, analytical and reflective thinking should also be a component of new media literacies. Education can help us focus on creating new communities online to foster deeper conversations, slower engagement, and a purposeful pulling together of our polarized world—online and offline—to better support democratic systems. We can all learn to start playing offense, not just defense.

4

Design Tools to Create Healthier Digital Communities

$\mathcal{N}$udges are an example of a tool that can be implemented to greatly improve the environment of our digital public spaces. They are tiny changes in the design of systems that affect user behavior. Nudges can be embedded in choice architecture—the different ways in which choices are presented to users—to alter people's behavior in predictable ways without forbidding any options.[1]

Nudges, under study by behavioral scientists for decades, have resulted in some creative solutions to what were once seen as insurmountable challenges. Take urinal accuracy, for example—if we must. In the 1990s, an airport in the Netherlands struggling with the problem of spillage around urinals in men's bathrooms printed an image of a housefly on the inside of the urinals to provide users with a target in hopes of improving their aim. Spillage on the bathroom floor declined by 80 percent as a result of this simple nudge that *targeted* the problem.[2]

Nudges exploit our cognitive biases—the thinking shortcuts that we commonly rely on—to influence our decisions and behaviors. In the "real world," there are nudges everywhere, both helpful and harmful. A helpful nudge would be to automatically enroll employees in a retirement plan and then ask them if they want to opt out rather than ask them if they want to opt in. This tiny design change results in significantly greater participation. A harmful nudge is when fast-food restaurants are located close to schools, which results in dramatic increases in children's obesity rates.[3]

Online, harmful nudges are common and effective. The alcohol industry has used harmful nudges, also called "dark nudges," to encourage changes in consumer behavior that go against consumers' best interests. In online "public service" announcements to educate people about "responsible drinking," the industry uses dark nudges in the form of social norming, by telling consumers that "most people" are drinking; priming, by showing images that cue people to drink while at the same time appearing to warn them about the harms of alcohol; and misinformation to undermine science and imply that nonalcohol causes may be responsible for harms that have, in fact, been clearly linked to alcohol.[4] Education and awareness of nudges do not have much of an impact on their ability to influence the choices we make. Policies and sanctions are needed to prevent companies and bad actors from making false claims and manipulating people.

Social media companies have voluntarily taken action in the case of some health misinformation and also during volatile political situations by demoting and putting labels on false content and dark nudges. In the case of the pandemic, it was too little too late, but we have seen evidence that these actions can be effective and can be used in many other areas to greatly reduce our exposure to misinformation. Sidestepping the question, for now, of how we could require social media platforms to deploy these new tools that would not enhance their bottom line, this chapter looks into what tools might be most effective in combatting misinformation.

CAN TECH FIX WHAT TECH CREATED?

If tech companies made it a top priority to fix social media platforms, could they do it? Could tech leaders effectively staunch the flow of misinformation if they made this their primary goal? Can the same algorithms that reward fake and sensationalized content be adjusted to favor reliable content? The answer is yes and no. Yes, tech companies could greatly reduce the amount of misinformation on their platforms if it was their primary goal, but no, algorithms would not be sufficient to fix the problem.

Despite a great deal of media hype, AI is not sophisticated enough to identify unreliable versus reliable content.[5] Heck, AI can't even tell the difference between illegal revenge porn and a nude by Titian.[6] Tech tools that focus on demoting or removing misinformation will need to be used in combination with human reviewers who are better able to evaluate content.

The good news is that there are some promising new tools under development that can help aid in the fight, sometimes working alone and sometimes combined with humans. Tools designed to limit our exposure to false information are far from perfect, but even small design modifications can have dramatic consequences. Behavioral psychologists are helping design nudges and boosts that encourage healthier interactions in digital spaces. Going after malicious bots—automated programs designed to mimic social media users— can take out a huge chunk of viral misinformation. And while corrections to misinformation after it has left the gate are not as effective as stopping exposure in the first place, they are essential, because we will never be able to eliminate all misinformation. How we design these corrections to misinformation can greatly increase their effectiveness.

AI + Humans: A One-Two Punch

The most obvious way to combat misinformation would be for platforms to use AI to identify and promote reliable information and to label and demote or remove misinformation.[7] Easier said than done. Promoting engaging viral content is much simpler; determining whether content is reliable or untrustworthy is a heavier lift. AI systems do not yet have the ability to make fine distinctions between reliable and unreliable information; they function more like a blunt force instrument and are prone to overblocking content.

Information is often nuanced and complex. One of the first newspaper articles on COVID in the United States was in February 2020. The reporter encouraged people not to worry, stating that early panic about the virus was unfounded: "'Based on the medical professionals, the risk [of contracting the coronavirus] is low in comparison to other things like the flu,' Chen said. 'I think that people are overly concerned.'"[8]

At the time, this was the best-known scientific advice about COVID. Accuracy and truth in news reporting are moving targets. As new information comes out, stories are changed to report the most recent understanding of events or scientific knowledge. Journalists and experts are needed to sort out what information and which sources are likely to be reliable and that reflect current understanding. While AI has developed sophisticated language processing models, most experts agree that AI is currently not sophisticated enough to parse the nuances in language use and meaning to identify a fake versus reliable news article or recognize a satirical piece.[9] Using the strengths and the scalability of AI combined with the wisdom of human reviewers is needed to combat misinformation: a one-two punch.

Tagging and Flagging

Automated systems are unable to determine truth in a granular way, but they can be a key component in the identification process by efficiently tagging millions of pieces of information and clustering this information into categories for humans to review. AI can be used to flag suspicious content and track spikes in network activity to indicate potential misinformation and also to suggest verifiable alternative sources.[10]

AI can also quickly remove glaring pieces of harmful content related to terrorism, graphic violence, and child sexual abuse material (often incorrectly referred to as "child porn"), but fake news or misinformation presents a more complex challenge.[11] No matter how sophisticated AI systems become, there will always be a need to keep humans in the loop, especially related to judgment calls that could threaten freedom of expression. The need for speed is paramount, because misinformation often goes viral, and the harm is already done before a post can be pulled down. Having human reviewers is a far from perfect solution, as it adds to the time it takes to remove content, can be subjective, and is also expensive, but humans will remain essential to the process for the foreseeable future.[12]

Some platforms currently give users the option to flag posts for review and fact-checking. Scalable algorithms are being developed to help flag articles and schedule a human-monitored fact-checking process.[13] Platforms have only instituted this on a small scale, so effectiveness has been limited. Even when extra efforts were made to address COVID misinformation, platforms did not devote sufficient resources to this process, and many posts were not identified; or if they were identified, they were not labeled or removed.[14]

Humans are expensive, but AI can't do it alone. Again, think blunt force instrument. AI is a rule follower, which can be a problem. When YouTube started relying more on AI during the pandemic lockdown, AI doubled the number of video takedowns compared to when human reviewers were part of the equation and could make more nuanced appraisals.[15]

In the late 1960s, *The Smothers Brothers Show* was repeatedly censored by CBS due to its anti-Vietnam and pro-drug culture and the show's satirizing of middle American values. CBS executives said that the program violated good taste and that they had an obligation to the public because they were an "invited guest" in peoples' homes. Tom Smothers lobbied the FCC and Congress to intervene against corporate censorship. The FCC said broadcasters, as private companies, could decide what content to censor and were not in violation of the First Amendment, but the FCC also ruled that broadcasters had a responsibility toward operating in the public interest.

Operating in the public interest is a moving target. The human component in making decisions about content that serves the public is necessary, as is having difficult conversations about what current social mores are and what type of content should be broadcast to the public. The Smothers Brothers' show helped push the needle and allowed for more open conversations about current news topics of the day. If AI alone had tagged and censored the Smothers Brothers' show, these conversations might not have taken place. AI is not able to understand satire, nor can it track evolving cultural norms. AI is trained on data that represents past decisions; it is not able to tap into the current and evolving social zeitgeist.

Tracking Provenance

Identifying the source of a piece of content can be automated by tracking the diffusion network for that piece of information. Social media influencers who have large groups of followers and have published misinformation in the past can be more carefully tracked, and their posts can be demoted or in some cases removed.[16] This process has already been implemented in a limited way in cases where national security was threatened, such as by QAnon influencers or Donald Trump.

Automated systems are good at spotting sudden viral spikes in activity, and these posts can be slowed down or pulled and verified if enough human reviewers are used. Identity verification can be used to filter out misinformation by known purveyors, while anonymity can still be maintained when essential for safety.

Collaboration on building tools is needed because designing them is expensive and because a diversity of views needs to be incorporated into the design. Collaborative automated systems are being set up, such as the Global Internet Forum to Counter Terrorism. This group has created a large database of terrorist content to identify and remove content quickly.[17] These collaborative activities could be broadened to work in other priority areas, including health and extremist recruitment. Most platforms are still not doing enough to prevent harmful content from going viral. Social media platforms failed to remove 95 percent of the vaccine misinformation reported to them, and over one hundred companies have pulled ads from Facebook because it has failed to remove hate speech.[18]

Taking Down Malicious Bots

Taking down malicious bots—automated programs designed to cause harm by impersonating social media users—can have a significant impact on the spread of misinformation. Bots are used to artificially drive up the appearance of user engagement by mimicking users through liking and sharing content and giving the false impression that a post is popular.[19] AI can be particularly effective at spotting bots based on networked sharing patterns, and regulations could ensure that going after bots is prioritized.[20]

Bots make up a significant amount of the misinformation landscape worldwide, so spotting and removing them could have a big impact.[21] It has been estimated that one-third of the one hundred most followed political news accounts on Twitter just before the US 2016 election were actually fake news accounts run by bots.[22] In 2017, Facebook estimated that bots and coordinated fake news campaigns run by Russia reached 126 million readers.[23] And, in 2020, researchers estimated that nearly half of the accounts tweeting about COVID were bots, leading to vast sharing of health misinformation.[24]

Behavioral Psychologists + Computers: Nudge, Boost, or Slow

The internet's potential for strengthening democratic societies is largely untapped and has not been prioritized by platform companies because it is not in their interest to do so. But if platform companies were required to promote trustworthy content over high-engagement content, we now have evidence that they could implement effective strategies to greatly reduce the amount of harmful content online.

Platform companies try to sidestep the issue of content moderation because they do not want to be held liable for the content on their platforms, but this distracts from the fact that these companies make hundreds of design choices that influence exactly what information we view online every day. Platform companies are, in fact, constantly moderating content by designing algorithms that select and recommend which content is promoted to users.[25] Small tweaks in recommender systems can result in significant changes in the behaviors of enormous numbers of people, and these tweaks could be designed to benefit the public.[26] Using research from the behavioral sciences, tech companies could design platforms that are better at recommending reliable information over false content to help inform health decisions, provide information about candidates running for office, and respond quickly and effectively to natural disasters. We already know a great deal about what types of nudges, boosts, and friction could be effective in pointing users toward choosing trustworthy content.

Nudge

Nudges—tiny changes in design that affect user behavior—may sound minor, but they can have a dramatic effect. Many behavioral nudges are designed to work to protect us from our overreliance on the shortcuts we take in analyzing and making decisions. For example, a nudge was devised to help protect us from using our availability heuristic, the thinking shortcut we take that causes us to judge the probability of an event happening based on how easy it is for us to recall examples of the event happening. One researcher redesigned the permission dialogue of the Google Play Store to include personalized scenarios of what could occur if users gave the app permission to view their data. The Google Play Store showed them images stored on their phone with the message "This app can see and delete your photos."[27] By being able to call to mind what might occur if the user gave the app permission, fewer people were willing to sign away their privacy rights.

Nudging interventions embedded in platform designs can promote the viewing and sharing of trustworthy information and the avoidance of viewing or sharing suspicious content. Without censoring content, educative nudging can inform users about when content is coming from an anonymous or questionable source, to encourage people to slow down and critically analyze the information.[28]

Fact-checking organizations such as PolitiFact and Snopes and trustworthy media sites such as the *Washington Post* can use nudges combined with fact-checking that provide verified information to help counter false information. Social media platforms are in the early stages of providing corrections and fact-checking for important topics such as health information, but these strategies are not yet commonplace.

Fact-checking and labeling an article using a tag such as "disputed" or "rated false" can have only a modest effect on counteracting belief, but it can result in people being less likely to share the content.[29] Even labeling information by type—such as ad, news, or opinion piece—can reduce the amount of poor-quality information shared online. Credibility scores are being developed to rate sources based on their overall accuracy, quality, and reliability. These scores can nudge people, and algorithms, toward more trusted content.[30]

Fact-checking and then labeling content have been shown to have less of an influence with volatile or heavily politicized issues, and there can sometimes be a "backfire effect" that causes people to become more entrenched in their original, though false, beliefs.[31] The research confirming backfire effects is mixed.[32] Providing fact-checking in real time can be more effective, perhaps because the formation of a strong belief is interrupted before it can take hold.[33]

New tools are being created that can authenticate text, images, and videos to verify their origins and certify that the content is real.[34] For example, a deceptively edited video of US House Speaker Nancy Pelosi showed her appearing to drunkenly slur her words during a speech. The video went viral and prompted questions about Pelosi's health but was later labeled as having been altered.[35] Creating systems that can watermark a video or image at the time it is created could establish provenance and confirm source legitimacy.[36]

Boost

Boosts are interventions that promote individual capabilities to make more informed choices. The objective of boosts is to foster people's competence to make their own choices and to give users greater control over their digital spaces. Whereas nudges are interventions designed to steer users in a particular direction, boosts facilitate people's agency to improve their online space and make their own decisions.[37] Boosts can let users customize their news feeds, or they can help make transparent what was previously shielded, such as cues about context and source. Sharing information about how many people have viewed a piece of content, dismantling the "like" system that implies agreement, putting a date stamp on information, and providing cues to trigger more analytical thinking and resistance to manipulation can help users make choices and avoid falling prey to misinformation.[38]

Boosting can be used to reduce filter bubbles. Currently, if people read an article stating that the world is flat, they are then provided with similar stories and "proof" based on their having clicked on the first article. Even if there are only one hundred people in the world who believe that the world is flat, suddenly the user that clicked on one article may become surrounded by people who believe the world is flat, and this becomes their reality online. Boosts can help motivate people to choose news feeds that provide a variety of opinions and research about a topic. If boosts had been in place at the time, would Dylann Roof have become radicalized so quickly?

Current work is underway at the Stanford Institute for Human-Centered Artificial Intelligence (HAI) to provide users with more control over what content they see online. One early project connected to HAI is being carried out by NewsGuard, which can be used as a browser plugin that rates the credibility of more than 7,500 news sources. Using NewsGuard could help boost a viewer's ability to select more reliable sources.[39] While NewsGuard uses AI, it is important to note that the company states: "Trust ratings for news—produced by humans, not AI."[40] Journalists have rated and reviewed all the news sources that account for 95 percent of online use, using several scales and apolitical criteria of journalistic practice.

It seems likely that many people will not take the time to opt in to installing and using NewsGuard. Perhaps a small number of highly rated and trusted independent public media news articles could be amplified on people's news feeds, and this is already occurring—though imperfectly—on some platform feeds. Algorithms combined with human curators could provide exposure to a diversity of viewpoints, especially for disputed topics. Transparency will be needed to make it clear that alternative viewpoints are being offered.[41] At the same time, equal "airtime" should not be given to opinions—such as those of the Flat Earth Society—over commonly agreed-upon and established scientific findings that the earth is, in fact, a sphere.

Slow

Some friction tools can be created by simply placing limits on sharing and mass forwarding of information to slow the spread. This can have a substantial impact on the rate at which misinformation can spread. In India, false rumors about child abductions were rapidly shared and spread over the WhatsApp chat program, resulting in dozens of people being lynched. Facebook then instituted limits on the number of texts that could be forwarded by individuals in India and also removed the "quick forward button" that appeared next to a text. These changes were able to quickly squelch a misinformation fire that had been stirring up angry mobs who were killing people.[42] Eliminating or reducing the prominence of a reshare button, or limiting how far reshares can move across a platform, can be surprisingly effective and requires no additional staffing and no difficult choices about censoring content.

Introducing friction can be simple but powerful. In 2022, Reddit opened up a blank canvas containing one million tiles in the form of pixels in one of its subreddit spaces. Users could create images on the blank canvas using XY coordinates to lay down colored tiles. Over six million people participated in creating stunning digital artwork on many different themes over the course of four days. One simple piece of friction prevented harmful images from being created: participants had to wait five minutes between each tile they placed, and this meant that any negative activity by one person or group could quickly be repaired by others.

Friction tools are being designed that are informed by behavioral psychology research to help prompt slower, more analytic thinking. Friction can be applied to low-credibility sources without having to censor content. Requiring people to pay a few cents to share content or asking them to stop and fill out a CAPTCHA form or provide phone confirmation before sharing would also cut down on the excessive amount of content online and make it easier to track. Often there are no costs for "publishing" and sharing content, and as a result, much of what is online is of poor quality created to generate attention. Restoring some type of "pay to play" in tiny amounts of time (CAPTCHAs) or money (small amounts, such as ten cents) could reduce the billions of pieces of useless, poor-quality information and misinformation posted online every day.[43]

Algorithms are being developed to slow down the spread of misinformation. These digital speed traps are good at tracking how information is spreading and can minimize the sharing of viral messages until they can be verified by humans.[44] Facebook and Twitter are experimenting with a process that identifies a source and its past history of issuing misinformation and then implants an integrity score, with a low score cueing a circuit breaker to slow down potential misinformation until it can be assessed.[45]

CREATE MORE EFFECTIVE CORRECTION TOOLS

Researchers stress that the key to mitigating the impact of misinformation is to focus on preventive efforts: keep misinformation from getting out in the first place and limit the sharing of misinformation.[46] But it will never be possible to eliminate all misinformation from online platforms, so providing corrections will be an important tool in the arsenal for combating misinformation.

Providing corrections is tricky, because once we have been exposed to a piece of misinformation, we are resistant to changing our views.[47] But if offered strategically, corrections can sometimes lead to changes in belief. Researchers are continually testing new ways of delivering more effective corrective information.[48] Understanding why beliefs are so hard to change, and understanding individual differences in how people respond to corrections, can help us design strategic corrections that take into account our resistance to change.

Why We Hold On to Beliefs: The Continued Influence Effect

After living in my house for ten years, I decided to make my kitchen more efficient. I moved my silverware drawer into the topmost accessible kitchen drawer and put my measuring spoons and cups one drawer below. Over the decade that followed, I have proceeded to open the measuring cup drawer almost every time I want a fork. Sigh. This is the continued-influence effect.

Once a piece of information, or misinformation, has been consumed, it takes a strong hold and is difficult to reverse.[49] Unlike computers, our memories can't just be deleted. Our memories retain original information even as we are exposed to competing information. I know I switched the two drawers, but the ten-year memory of "silverware second drawer" is resistant to change.

The continued-influence effect results in our being unable to let go of information once we have learned it, even after receiving clear and credible corrective information. We are resistant to changing our beliefs because we build resilient mental models about what we know, and we rely on automatic memory processes that easily recall the initially learned misinformation rather than use more analytic memory processes. We are pretty good at integrating small updates to our model as we learn new information, but when something comes along that completely reverses a belief we hold, we are not good at globally replacing our initial model. This can make it challenging for constantly evolving science and health information content to take hold, especially when later research completely contradicts earlier conclusions. I'm not ready to give up the idea that having a glass of wine every night is beneficial to my health, despite the new research findings.

We are especially poor at replacing our mental model if there is simply a negation of our belief with no alternative explanation provided.[50] For example, the misconception that vaccines are responsible for causing autism is appealing to people because it provides them with an explanation, and it is resistant to change because there is no alternative explanation offered for what causes autism.

The continued-influence effect is a result of our having two types of memory processes: automatic and strategic. We often rely on our automatic memory recall because it is easily accessible and fast.[51] There are individual differences in the degree to which we rely on automatic memory, including differences by age, motivation, and length of time the information has been stored in memory.[52] Overreliance on automatic retrieval of memory can result in believing something just because it is familiar, not because it is necessarily true. I still automatically believe my forks are in the second drawer, and millions of people still believe in Bigfoot because they saw images of him and are unable to replace those images of him with new information that the entire story was made up.

Using automatic memory processes can also decontextualize a memory, and a person can be more likely to remember the original piece of information but not a later retraction. For example, when a potential juror is exposed to false information about a defendant being guilty, the damage caused is viewed as irreversible and can result in being barred from serving on the jury. The power of the continued-influence effect makes it clear that our focus needs to remain on mitigating the false content people view in the first place.

Individual Differences in Responding to Corrections

Some people are more strongly tied to powerful worldviews that make them unlikely to respond to corrective information that contradicts these views. Ideological and religious beliefs sometimes fuel strong worldviews, provide people with a sense of identity and belonging, and make them resistant to changing their beliefs even when facing compelling factual evidence countering their beliefs.[53] In general, people are drawn toward information that affirms what they already believe. This has always been true, but social media platforms now further ensconce people in echo chambers with others who share and amplify their beliefs, making those beliefs more embedded and resistant to alteration.[54]

In times of social upheaval, while we like to think of ourselves as rational, our need for belonging often outweighs our ability to prioritize truth seeking. As social animals, we see security in our group, and we get reassurance by framing our ideas as against the ideas of our perceived enemies. As partisan divides grow in the United States, this feeds distrust of others and makes us more vulnerable to misinformation, especially when it confirms the beliefs of our group.

Conspiratorial beliefs are particularly "sticky" and resistant to corrective information.[55] Information that counters a conspiracy theory is often ineffective; that's because people drawn to conspiracies are not drawn by facts but by their predispositions toward believing in a conspiracy theory that matches their beliefs and provides them with a sense of belonging to a group. They are responding to the passions that these theories stir and to the affirmation of their feelings of resentment and disappointment with the world.[56]

Designing Effective Corrections

We now know a great deal about what works and what does not work in providing people with corrections after they have consumed false content. The big takeaway: simply supplying corrective information is rarely effective. Strategies such as keeping it simple and fast, using voices that are trusted by the viewer, and educating people about how they may be duped before it happens can help improve the effectiveness of corrections.

One of the problems with the COVID pandemic was that the truth, as we knew it at any given time, was simply not easy to understand. Vaccines are effective, but even vaccinated people can get COVID; everyone should get a vaccine to prevent spread, but even vaccinated people can spread the virus, and so on. Corrections need to be easy to digest to appeal to people's over-reliance on fast thinking, and they need to be provided quickly to decrease the degree to which the misinformation will become deeply rooted in memory. The greater the time lag between viewing misinformation and viewing a correction, and also the greater the number of times someone has been exposed to a piece of misinformation, the less effective the correction.[57] Corrections need to be coherent and give a clear, factual alternative explanation.[58] The truth needs to be presented in a simple, fluent, and easy to understand format; and when issuing a retraction, it is important to provide limited information about arguments that supported the original misinformation. It may be that being exposed to these incorrect details can call up mental models that make replacing the original misinformation more challenging.[59]

Corrections need to be provided, when possible, within the context of someone's existing social groups or from a source they trust; if Fox News or CNN relays information that is not true, it needs to issue a retraction.[60] The focus should be more on the honesty and integrity of the source giving corrections over source expertise.[61] For example, many people respond more favorably to corrections from someone they trust—such as Oprah, their minister, or a friend—over someone who has official credentials and expertise, such as Chief Medical Officer Anthony Fauci.[62]

When offering a correction, trying to appeal to people's respective worldviews and providing them with a narrative that resonates with their beliefs can be especially effective in helping them accept corrected information.[63] Conspiracy theories are particularly effective when they use powerful narratives that tap into deep fears; using a strong counternarrative to combat these strongly rooted beliefs can help.

It can be effective to provide an "inoculation" against, or "prebunking" of, misinformation prior to people viewing it, by exposing them to the way in which arguments they see will strategically try to mislead and persuade them.[64] If we could have explained to teenagers that they were about to be targeted by vaping companies showing them their favorite pop stars vaping and explained how these companies were going to convince them to smoke, this perhaps could have reduced the number of young people taking up vaping.

Educating people about their psychological vulnerabilities, such as the continued-influence effect, can provide some limited protection, but it is not as effective as we would hope.[65] Most of us believe that we are much better than others at identifying false information, so we tend to underestimate our own vulnerability.[66] Teaching people to be more skeptical of information also has limitations because it can sometimes backfire and cause people to distrust all information.[67] Also, engaging people in generating their own counterarguments when consuming information can help, but asking people to generate reasons why they initially supported the misinformation can cause them to continue to believe the misinformation.[68]

Surprisingly, images can backfire in correcting misinformation. In general, realistic images combined with text increase the chances that someone will believe false information, but using images—especially strong or disturbing images—is ineffective for changing people's minds *after* they have formed a belief.[69] Beliefs are *really* strong. We may think that a sad or powerfully disturbing image that upsets us will upset other people as well. But people who do not believe something—for example, the seriousness of the COVID pandemic—will not be moved by graphic images of patients on ventilators, because their underlying belief convinces them that these images are hyped up or inaccurate.[70]

We now know a great deal about what tools could be effective in reducing the viewing and spread of misinformation and harmful content without interfering with First Amendment rights to free speech. If platform companies were required to design and implement tools that focused on promoting reliable information and demoting poor-quality content, our current online spaces would be dramatically transformed. AI and algorithm design alone cannot solve these challenges, but combined with humans, we can greatly change our digital public squares.

5

Require Platforms to Serve
the Public Interest

In 2013, Tristan Harris was working as a product manager at Google when he spoke at a staff meeting about the company's moral responsibility to its users. He told his colleagues that they were making decisions about what content people were consuming and that this was going to have a huge impact on culture, relationships, and politics. They were shaping the attention of billions of people. It was important that they get this right. Harris saw it as an opportunity, but Google leaders had other priorities, and in those early days, they likely underestimated the scale of the impact they were starting to have.[1]

In 2018, Guillaume Chaslot, a Google engineer working with a team on YouTube's recommender engine, said that he realized that what they were designing was not being optimized for balance, truth, or useful content. Chaslot reported talking to friends at Google, but the general feeling was that if people didn't complain, they must be happy. He was later fired from the company.[2] Chaslot then designed a program to better understand how YouTube pushed content to users. His research found that engagement was prioritized above all else. One case he investigated found that videos by Alex Jones, the conspiracy theorist who spread misinformation that the Sandy Hook killings had been staged by "crisis actors," were recommended on YouTube fifteen billion times.

Newton Minow has had what he calls "a front-row seat" to the communication revolution that began when he was as a teenager in World War II and continued through more than seventy years working on communication policy in Republican and Democratic administrations, including serving as the chair of the Federal Communications Commission (FCC). Taking the long view, Minow notes that the rapid, unfettered development of social media platforms has run parallel to a disappearance of public protections. As technological innovations have barreled ahead, advances in policy have lagged far behind: "The basic concept that our communications systems are to serve the public—not private—interest is now missing in action," he writes. No "scientist, philosopher, or engineer has figured out how to program AI to serve the public interest."[3]

This lack of regulation has resulted in an information disorder so severe that it threatens our democratic system of government. Our old communications policies centered on viewing speech as scarce and audiences as plentiful. Today, we have the reverse: in an attention economy, there is a wealth of information that creates a poverty of attention. There is so much content online that no one can be heard. By incentivizing and promoting misinformation, healthy democratic discussions cannot take place.

Harris, Chaslot, and Minow have helped us connect the dots: our current information crisis can be tied directly to a handful of technology companies that dominate our communication channels and use a business model that fuels misinformation and creates information disorder. And while this was not their original intention, and they report that they are working to fix the problem through privacy features and labeling, they have little motivation to change the model that is providing them with billions of dollars in revenue.

Understanding how these platforms are built and that their core infrastructure is defective can help us focus on going after the root causes of misinformation and not just trying to pick off harmful content from the top down. Fixing the misinformation problem is not an issue of free speech, though that is often used as a red herring. By focusing on renovating the core structure of these platforms, we can make design choices that minimize misinformation without having to censor speech.

Updating our communication policies to focus on the public interest over the profits of a few companies is the clear path forward. Access to reliable information needs to be viewed as a human right, like clean water. Carrots have not worked so far in encouraging platform companies to do better; it is time to use sticks. Their business models rely on driving engagement. While some platforms seem to be more aggressively downgrading misinformation and policing hate speech, the problem is structural.

FOLLOW THE MONEY

"How do you sustain a business model in which users don't pay for your service?" Sen. Orrin Hatch (R-UT) asked Zuckerberg early on in the hearing.

"Senator, we run ads," Zuckerberg replied.[4]

Asking platforms to self-regulate and address the problem of misinformation is asking them to bite the hand that feeds them. Optimizing for money has been baked into the structure of platforms. Unless that underlying architecture is redesigned, platform companies will continue to pay lip service to reducing misinformation without any significant change taking place.

Who Is Getting a Slice of the Digital Advertising Pie?

The current digital advertising system is based on placing personalized ads in front of users based on their past online behavior. Billions of dollars are being made. While Senator Hatch was asking a rhetorical question, many people do not understand how this advertising system works and how it differs from our previous systems. Understanding digital advertising can be half the battle in moving to correct these systems that are incentivizing misinformation.

Here is a primer on how misinformation drives the money bus: there are four key players that all get a slice of the digital advertising pie: platform owners, ad servers, retailers, and publishers.[5]

Player 1: Social Media Platform Owners

Social media platforms, such as Facebook, YouTube, Instagram, and TikTok, are designed to keep users engaged. The more engaged users are, the more time they spend online and the more they click on ads. These clicks are a platform's primary source of income. Platform owners make more money by promoting enticing content. Misinformation is designed to be highly emotional and engaging, so misinformation is often ranked higher than more reliable information. At the same time, the more time a user spends on a platform, the more behavioral data the platform can collect on the user: a win-win for the platform. This data in turn is used to make better predictions about what types of ads a user is most likely to click on in the future.

Advertising sales account for almost all of Facebook and Google's annual revenue. Smaller platforms also make money, but they are not able to charge retailers as much, because they have less behavioral data and therefore provide less effective ad personalization. Less than a dozen large platforms receive a huge proportion of the digital advertising revenue.[6]

Platforms can also make money by allowing retailers to pay to promote their ads by boosting them to be put in front of users who would not otherwise see them.[7] Some platforms, such as Twitter and Facebook, allow users to opt out of personalized ads, but this does not change the number of ads that users see; nor does it stop the platform from tracking their activities.[8]

Player 2: Ad Servers

Ad servers[9] are modern-day advertising agencies that make money by placing programmatic ads on high-traffic sites. Programmatic ads are complex animals, but they essentially function like an automated auction. As the user hops on a website, retailers use ad servers to bid for the user's eyeballs based on personal data about the user. The website publisher—it could be the *Washington Post* or the *ScaryMommy* blog—has put the ad space on its website up for auction. The ad servers are paid by the retailers; platforms such as Facebook, and publishers such as *ScaryMommy*, also get a cut.

Google is the largest ad server operator, owning almost one-third of the market and funding 30 percent to 62 percent of all weighted ad traffic going to low-credibility news sites.[10] The Tech Transparency Project identified ninety-seven websites that regularly publish false information and are funded by Google. The Global Disinformation Index found 1,400 sites that earned $76 million from advertising by spreading COVID misinformation.[11] COVID misinformation is a hot commodity because users are quick to click on promises such as "Miracle Cure for COVID!"

Player 3: Retailers

Retailers[12] and their in-house or external advertising agencies have always preferred to choose where they place advertisements. Personalization has long been a part of that process. Betty Crocker Cake Mix was advertised in *Good Housekeeping* magazine, and Budweiser Beer commercials continue to be linked to National Football League (NFL) broadcasts. Brands want two things: to be able to target their audience and to be connected to media that is looked on favorably by consumers.

With the new auction and bidding process mediated by ad servers, retailers often do not know which sites their ads are being placed on. Other than being able to check off a few boxes, such as "don't list on porn sites," the relationship that used to exist between brands and the content they sponsor has been severed. Many retailers feel they have no choice over where their ads are placed, though 95 percent express concern that their association with misinformation could erode the trust consumers place in their brand.[13]

Ad servers have forced retailers to choose between buying digital ads that microtarget consumers using surveillance advertising versus maintaining strong relationships with content producers. Large brands, such as Nike and Pepsi, continue to have relationships with reputable media companies online, but many retailers choose microtargeting and give up control over where their ads will appear because they get more bang for their buck that way.[14]

Retailers play an integral role in funneling money via ad servers to purveyors of misinformation. Retailers in the top-ten-thousand-visited websites on the internet make up a quarter of all ad traffic on low-credibility news sites.[15] They are directly funding and incentivizing misinformation or low credibility information.

Depending on a company's consumer base, it is not always viewed as a negative to appear on a low-credibility news site, because that may be where their consumers are hanging out amid the cat videos and stories about Hillary Clinton being a cannibal. Ad space also tends to be less expensive on low-quality sites. Sometimes ad servers purchase ads on the more reliable media sites long enough to track and lure users toward visiting less reputable sites with cheaper ad rates. Once users get onto these low-credibility sites with more sensationalized "news," they may choose to remain there.[16]

Player 4: Publishers

Finally, about that publisher. . . . The online advertising ecosystem has created new, low-quality-content-producing scavengers by changing the incentive structure for media production.[17] Traditional reliable publishers, such as the *Chicago Tribune*, that fund expensive investigative journalism and news gathering have seen their ad revenue gutted by the new surveillance advertising model.[18] Low-credibility sites have been rewarded with more revenue because they can garner more clicks and engagement by using emotion-laden content. These fake news sites cost little to produce and maintain because they do not fund reporters, editors, and fact-checkers. At the same time, social media platforms continue to uprank this unreliable information and favor it over trustworthy content. This has turned our information world upside down.

Can We Demonetize Misinformation?

Removing the revenue stream that is funding misinformation and low-credibility news is unlikely to happen because of the billions of dollars to be made under the current structure. Platforms are also not optimized for identifying and funding reliable media sites. Without policy changes, little will shift in the current architecture designed for the attention economy.

Each of the players in the current marketplace could take steps to improve the situation. The largest ad servers provide 67 percent of the funds that go directly to misinformation providers.[19] If the largest ad servers pulled their money from misinformation providers, it would be a small loss for the ad servers but would result in defunding two-thirds of the current misinformation providers online.[20] Unfortunately, without regulations, ad servers have no motivation to pull their money.

Retailers could help demonetize misinformation by insisting on more transparency and control over where their ads appear. In the last few years, large brands, such as REI and CVS, have threatened to pull—or have temporarily pulled—their advertising agreements with ad servers because they do not want their brand associated with sketchy content.[21] Ad servers appear to be responsive when retailers demand action, but with no transparency, it is difficult to confirm exactly how much action has been taken. Collectively demanding change—either by associations of retailers or by consumers—might put enough pressure on ad servers to make some changes and allow outside verification that these changes have occurred.

Reputable news publishers may want to consider leaving the surveillance advertising space altogether. Surveillance advertising can influence how the news is covered by being too focused on clicks rather than covering what news is deemed most important to report on.[22] Hyperpersonalization of news and ads can undermine journalism and its public service mission and can fail to provide citizens with common points of reference to enhance public debate.[23] If news publishers bowed out of surveillance advertising, this would not do much to reduce the amount of misinformation, but it would likely help increase trust in the media, which is a related challenge.

What about Using Blacklisting, Whitelisting, or Ad Blockers?

Even if the four players referenced above decided they wanted to take action to stop subsidizing misinformation, a bigger hurdle involves figuring out what information should be defunded. Blacklists are created to ban specific harmful sites, and whitelists are created to approve specific trustworthy sites; both have serious shortcomings in terms of severing the ties between money and misinformation.

Blacklisting entails identifying and banning specific websites that contain false or offensive content. These sites can then be prevented from displaying and receiving payment for ad placements. Most ad servers already have blacklists of sites with which they will not do business, but blacklists can only contain sites that have already been identified. Large platforms such as Google AdSense manage to blacklist millions of sites a year, but they have thousands of new sites needing to be reviewed every day.[24]

In addition, many misinformation sites avoid detection by "cloaking"—serving up reliable versions of a web page for review and then performing a bait and switch to later serve up fake content to the user. Other sites impersonate reputable publishers by using fake metadata to fool algorithms. Publishers of false content are often skilled at deception and can quickly morph into a new web page template one step ahead of the ad server review. Despite the challenges, blacklisting can be effective to the degree that ad servers are willing to devote significant resources to both automated and human detection systems.[25]

Whitelisting involves placing ads with sites that have been screened ahead of time and identified as having reliable content. The challenge is that whitelisting is nearly impossible to carry out at the scale at which large ad servers conduct business.[26] Ideally, a central service used by all ad server companies—such as Trust Metrics or Brandguard—could provide a whitelist to companies for a fee, though a side effect would be to drive up the price of ads. This would create challenges for smaller publishers. Another issue is that once a site has been whitelisted, the site can change its content, so ongoing tracking would be needed.

Algorithms are not sophisticated enough to catch low-credibility sites, especially when they mimic the look, content, and metadata of reputable publishers.[27] Sorting out content about whether Justin Bieber really did announce he is studying to become a minister (he is not) is likely to remain beyond the scope of advanced machine learning for some time. Pairing AI systems with humans can be effective, though costly.[28]

Ad blockers that prevent false content from making money from ads also prevent credible content from making money. Content on the internet is "free" because of advertising. Legitimate news sites now tell readers to turn off their ad-blocking software or pay for the content if they want to continue to have access. Some ad blockers also whitelist ads for certain companies by arranging to take a cut of the profits from these ads.[29]

The programmatic advertising bubble may burst in the coming years, as younger and more valuable users are less likely to click on ads, and calls for more transparency may show that ads do not work as well as ad servers are claiming.[30] Click farming—a form of click fraud where a large group of low-paid workers are hired to click on paid advertising links—can create fake clicks on ads, which puts money in content producers' pocketbooks but does not result in actual views and purchases by real consumers. While media could still be funded by advertising, it does not have to involve surveillance advertising, a funding mechanism that commodifies user attention.[31] Instead, ads could be based on the content itself and the likelihood that consumers would be interested in that content.

REGULATION: INFORMATION AS A HUMAN RIGHT

There is widespread agreement that some type of regulation is needed to rein in the power that social media platforms have over much of the information we consume.[32] Like clean water, access to reliable information should be a human right. New technologies have disrupted the albeit imperfect structures that were in place to ensure access to a free press and trustworthy information that are essential for democracy. In 2021, the UN stated that "the production of local information, such as local news, is under great stress. At the same time, humanity faces a confusing abundance of content that drowns out even those facts that are produced and circulated at both global and local levels."[33]

Social media platforms need to be designed in a way that protects the public and helps foster a healthy media environment and thriving digital public square. New policies can ensure that these structures are built to support a diversity of opinions and prioritize access to reliable information.

What about Free Speech?

Any suggestion of regulating information raises a red flag about the protection of our First Amendment right to free speech. Regulation should be approached cautiously so that minority or unpopular opinions remain protected. At the same time, we need to recognize that speech in the United States has always been regulated: there are restrictions on obscenity, fraud, child sexual abuse material, speech integral to illegal conduct, speech that incites imminent lawless action, speech that violates intellectual property law, true threats, false advertising, and defamation that causes harm to reputation.[34]

Traditional publishers are held liable for publishing illegal or legally actionable content, but platforms have been exempted from responsibility for the information they provide. Section 230 of the Communications Decency Act of 1996 designates platform companies as *services* rather than *publishers*. The original intent of the exemption was to foster innovation, but these supports are no longer needed, as platforms have become dominant media providers.[35] The line between what is a "publisher" and what is a "platform" is no longer clear, and yet information by legacy media is heavily regulated and platforms are not held liable for what appears on their sites.[36]

The Aspen Institute has proposed two amendments to Section 230 that could help reduce misinformation without jeopardizing free speech. The first states that platforms should have the same liability for ad content as TV networks or newspapers do, which would require them to ensure they meet the standards imposed on these other industries. The second amendment to Section 230 would remove platform immunity with respect to the ways in which they design their algorithms and recommender engines. This would minimize harmful content and misinformation: it would prevent design features that promote extreme content, and it would also avoid threatening free speech rights.[37]

Access to a Free Press

Having a few private tech companies in charge of most of the information to which we have access creates a direct threat to our democratic system of government. The opaque algorithms used by platforms shape the information we view.[38] Legacy media sites and local news are often downranked in platform news feeds, and less credible, more entertaining sources are promoted. These search and news-feed rankings impact everything we view.

As constitutional scholar Martha Minow points out, "Freedom of the press defended by the First Amendment . . . assumes the existence and durability of a private industry. [The argument of this book is that] initiatives by the government and by private sector actors are not only permitted but required as transformations in technology, economics, and communications jeopardize the production and distribution of and trust in news that are essential in a democratic society."[39]

Minow goes on to argue that not only does the First Amendment *not* forbid government involvement in strengthening news creation and distribution but, for more than two hundred years, "the First Amendment has coexisted with the aid and activity of government, shaping enterprises for generating and sharing news. An even more ambitious interpretation would treat the First Amendment as mandating such efforts."[40]

Philip Napoli, a foremost expert on media policy, also calls for a stronger role to be played by the state to ensure that the speech conditions required for democratic self-governance are being supported. This includes ensuring that citizens have access to a diversity of credible sources and restoring gatekeeping functions to protect citizens from excessive exposure to misinformation.[41]

For centuries, the "counterspeech doctrine," a central component of the First Amendment, was sufficient to avoid having the government overly involved in the regulation of speech. The doctrine stated that the best response to negative speech was to counter it with positive speech, the assumption being that audiences can weigh for themselves the values of competing ideas and will likely follow the best of these ideas.[42] This doctrine rested on the healthy functioning of a "marketplace of ideas," but our marketplace of ideas is now drowned out, as misinformation is prioritized and trustworthy media curation has been gutted or is behind paywalls.[43]

Hyperpersonalization adds to the mix by targeting the most vulnerable. The rapid spread and sheer quantity of poor-quality information triggers quick thinking, encourages likes and shares, and leaves little time for analysis or rebuttal.[44] The idea that the solution to negative speech is to counter it with positive speech seems quaint in a time where we all have way too much speech, with much of it of questionable veracity.

Platforms as Public Utilities for Democracy

When Facebook chose to provide Trump with a megaphone to incite violence during the George Floyd protests—"when the looting starts, the shooting starts"—it exerted enormous control over what "news" the public would view that day. At the same time, Twitter also exerted powerful control by "hiding" the post and later shutting down Trump's account.[45] Regardless of how you feel about the former president of the United States being silenced in this particular case, who should be making these decisions?

Platforms create some filters to demote what is deemed misinformation or hate speech, but these filters can sometimes reflect baked-in social inequities and biases that stem from the data they are built on and the biases of the designers.[46] Content is also treated differently based on political or "star" power and the desire to quell potential public relations nightmares.[47] In other words, powerful people get access to larger megaphones online.

There is a strong argument to be made for platforms being regulated as public utilities that are required to serve the public good, due to the powerful influence they have over people's lives. Facebook and Google control roughly 70 percent of all internet traffic.[48] About a third of US adults get news regularly on Facebook, 22 percent from YouTube, 13 percent from Twitter, and 11 percent from Instagram.[49] Overall, Facebook has 2.7 billion users; YouTube, owned by Google, has 2 billion; and Instagram has 1 billion.[50]

Algorithms are designed to shape how content is prioritized and presented, based on personalization and driven by financial gain. This is far different from national and local newspapers, where editors meet every day to determine the most important stories to report. Algorithm design is at the heart of the misinformation problem. By shaping the information people see, it is, by its nature, political, and its design prioritizes revenue over reliability.

The argument for regulating platforms goes beyond just information delivery. Facebook and Google are becoming indispensable and now serve as the primary mode of communication as well as security and data management for many corporations, schools, and cities. Similar to the railroads and electric power grids that provide infrastructure for essential goods and services, platforms have a similar control over services to the public.

If the United States fails to regulate large social media platforms, we continue to place the onus on platforms to self-regulate. So far this has been ineffective.[51] Some platforms are now blatantly abusing their power, such as when Facebook rolled out "Project Amplify," which buried negative articles and promoted positive articles about the company in users' news feeds.[52] In the case of COVID, platforms finally swung into action to remove misinformation about vaccines and mask wearing, but it was late in the game and the damage was done. They demonstrated that they can rise to the occasion of effective content moderation when they choose to do so. But should they be exclusively in charge of choosing what is important to moderate and when it is important to do so?

What Is a Public Utility?

Public utilities are corporations that have tremendous power and influence over fundamental areas of our everyday lives. Our associations with public utilities often call to mind railroads or telephone companies that have enormous control over the pipelines through which goods and services are delivered.

Railroads and phone companies needed to be regulated as utilities because they had monopolistic control over a public good. Facebook and Google may not be precisely defined as monopolies,[53] but using a wider lens, they fit well under the goals of regulating excessive corporate power that has an undue influence on citizens' day-to-day lives.[54]

Legal scholars view Facebook, Google, Twitter, Instagram, TikTok, and a few other large platforms as controlling the infrastructure of the digital public square. This infrastructure is vital to the flow of information and ideas in our society.[55] Platforms should be regulated as a new kind of public utility—a "utility for democracy"—because they have control over so much of our daily activities. Unlike railroads and telephone companies that needed to be regulated for economic reasons, these new "utilities for democracy" need to be regulated because they threaten the existence and functioning of a free press and the sharing of ideas necessary for democracy.

This new concept of a utility for democracy conceives of social media platforms as social actors designed to promote the public good. Scholars from different disciplines have arrived at similar conclusions about platforms serving the public interest—for example, framing platforms as information fiduciaries,[56] or as public trustees,[57] or calling for a completely public media system owned and controlled by those it serves.[58]

Structural Regulation: Going after Root Causes

The most important piece of instituting a public utility model is that the focus should be on creating regulatory tools that address the underlying structural issues of platform design. Platforms need to be designed to promote reliable content and demote or remove misinformation. Only a comprehensive structural redesign can succeed, and it will only be accomplished through regulation. Designating platforms as public utilities introduces a new model for providing access to reliable information and acknowledges that information is an essential human right.

The focus of many scholars has been on ways to identify and delete or demote harmful content through human reviewers and AI, but so far these measures have been ineffective or piecemeal. These efforts need to continue, but by changing platform architecture and reward structures, there will be greater strides toward reducing the quantity of misinformation being created and promoted. Pulling the plug on funding will zap a significant percentage of poor-quality information, as there will be less incentive for it to exist.[59]

Structural regulation also has the advantage of not wandering down the road of speech regulation. Focusing on systemic reforms can avoid placing government, private companies, or civic institutions in the role of censor or arbiter of information.[60] Models can be designed that foster and promote constructive and reliable content over harmful content and can be built to foster equity. They will be imperfect and will need to be continually modified and improved under human oversight.

More than a dozen governments around the world have started to provide some regulatory oversight, though most policies continue to take a top-down approach by focusing on identifying and removing content or using the legal process to hold platforms liable.[61] Legal liability, combined with revising Section 230, is another good tool in the arsenal, but regulation needs to focus on the root causes of the problem—specifically, the design features that are causing harm.[62]

By regulating the architecture of platforms, "the goal is prophylactic: to limit the very structure and business models of these firms and to alter the dynamics of the markets in which they operate, thereby reducing at the source the incentives and conflicts of interest that magnify risks of exploitation, extraction, and fraud."[63]

These structural regulations should address the current advertising system, the collection of personal data for microtargeting, and should reduce the incentivizing of misinformation and poor-quality information generally.

Legal scholar K. Sabeel Rahman argues that four kinds of "obligations" should be rolled out through legislation to call attention to the special duties large platforms have as public entities. The focus is not to serve as a censor and determine whether a piece of content should be removed; rather, the focus is on how algorithms can be designed to best serve the public interest.

First, platform infrastructures can be designed to provide public safety, privacy, and equal access. Fairness and transparency can be prioritized over hyperpersonalization and the sale of private data. Algorithms can be designed to counter the systemic bias, racism, and inequity that are built into our data and our machine learning systems.[64]

Second, platforms can be required to provide transparency in the design of algorithms so that independent groups and regulators can confirm that the designs promote trustworthy information and adhere to goals set forward to protect information as a public good.[65] Recommender engines, run by algorithms, are one of the most powerful spreaders of misinformation. They are currently not subject to external review.[66]

Tech companies are resistant to providing access because it would force them to disclose proprietary source code.[67] Researchers argue that ethical responsibility needs to be prioritized over market forces.[68] Developing carefully constructed agreements with independent researchers would enable investigations into what strategies are most effective in combating misinformation and help verify that platform companies are carrying out the strategies to which they have agreed.[69]

Transparency should also be instituted for the use of user data. People should be able to easily manage and restrict the use of their data and be provided with information about how their data might be used to control recommended content. Independent auditors will be needed to identify algorithmic recommendations that cause harm or bias.[70]

Transparency is also needed to understand potential biases in algorithms. Algorithms are designed using machine learning that calls for large amounts of data to train on and make predictions and judgments, but often the data used for training is biased and can produce harmful effects.

Third, firewalls can be designed over time to meet evolving concerns and potential threats. Firewalls can be set up to separate out commercial interests that influence how and what information is created and provided to users. These firewalls and contextual information could be similar to requirements that journalists adhere to by providing clear lines between editorial articles, ads, and objective news reporting.[71]

Fourth, governing the design of algorithms will be the most challenging aspect of these "utilities for democracy." Democracy is a messy process, and decisions made about what is in the public interest and what content should be promoted in the public square will involve participatory decision-making. These collaborative bodies consisting of government players, platform companies, and independent outside institutions could evolve to provide the public with fairness and accountability in algorithm design.[72] Citizen juries and public involvement in decisions on the design and functioning of algorithms can give the public input on decisions that impact the public square and their access to quality information.[73]

While Rahman argues for transparency and an easier opt-out system for data collection, Shoshana Zuboff goes one step further while keeping the focus on structural change over regulating content and tricky First Amendment issues. Zuboff advocates for regulation that prevents the extraction and use of personal data.[74] Platform design can then shift away from promoting content that favors profit-maximizing personalized engagement to designs focused on trustworthy content that is in the public interest. This prevents tech companies from having an oversized influence over our news feeds and shaping our behavior and beliefs and also provides for easier monitoring. Perhaps Google could go back to its original mission of organizing all the world's information, and Facebook could be more about connecting people rather than targeting them. As of this writing, new laws are being proposed by Congress to ban surveillance advertising in the United States, but it is unclear whether they will have enough teeth for effective enforcement.

The European Union (EU) is light years ahead of the United States in passing two laws that regulate social media platforms so that they can better serve the public interest. The Digital Services Act compels large platforms to set up new policies for removing hate speech, propaganda, and content deemed illegal by the EU. It also requires these companies to disclose how their services amplify divisive content with transparency measures, and it bans targeting online ads based on a person's ethnicity, religion, or sexual orientation. In addition, the Digital Markets Act was passed to counter anticompetitive behavior by the largest tech firms. There are concerns about how these two laws will be enforced, but they are a good first step toward adjusting communication policies so that the public can be better protected and our digital spaces can be improved.

Frances Haugen points out that transparency is the key to making any new laws effective, by allowing regulators and civil society to verify that companies are following the rules. She has written that these rules are like the systems set up in the United States to require pharmaceutical companies to ensure drugs are safe and to enable the Food and Drug Administration (FDA) to verify that the rules are being followed.[75] The road to regulation in the United States will be much tougher than in the EU. Meta, the parent company of Facebook, and Alphabet, the parent company of Google, have strong lobbying arms with powerful influence.

The Facebook documents Haugen leaked demonstrate that the company knows that it is prioritizing divisive and extreme content and it knows how to reverse those choices. By addressing structural issues, the United States can avoid infringing on rights to free expression while at the same time enhancing universal access to reliable information and reducing the promotion of misinformation. Platforms can be encouraged to experiment and use flexible design practices, but with transparency and oversight. New platforms serving the public interest will need to be created if current platforms are unwilling to shift their practices and do not agree to serve the public.

6

Repair Journalism and Roll
Out New Curators

*E*very con game involves a grifter and a mark. Online or off, grifters follow the same path: target marks with a personalized approach and then seduce and pull them in. Successful grifters are clever. They tell us what we want to hear, and they appeal to our emotions, desires, and beliefs. They have us at hello.

Dr. Joseph Mercola, an osteopathic doctor, is one of the best of the best. He has been designated as one of the "Disinformation Dozen," because he and eleven other people are responsible for sharing 65 percent of all anti-vaccine messaging on social media. Dr. Mercola has capitalized on the COVID pandemic by subtly spreading anti-vaccine misinformation.[1] Agile and deft, he plays social media like a fiddle and optimizes his content to come up first on Google searches and Facebook feeds.

Posting a video titled "Kitten and Chick Nap So Sweetly Together," he lures in his marks and then tells them about research studies that question the efficacy of vaccines for COVID and about his own research that finds natural cures more effective. Links to purchase Dr. Mercola's vitamin supplements have earned him millions of dollars a year. He nimbly sidesteps clunky algorithmic filters by providing nuanced content that does not trigger their alarm system on rule violations. At the same time, his posts are so appealing to a public desperate for an easy cure for COVID that in the English language alone, he has 1.7 million Facebook followers and hundreds of thousands of Twitter and YouTube followers.[2]

While reliable news outlets do not spread Dr. Mercola's gospel, many people no longer get their information from trustworthy news sites. Platforms prioritize engagement and promote Dr. Mercola over reliable news articles that warn about Dr. Mercola and other scam artists. Platforms have replaced news editors as our online information gatekeepers. They have swallowed up advertisers who used to fund our news organizations. Local news media in particular are now scrambling to keep their heads above water.

Essential to maintaining a healthy democracy is an independent press and an educated public to ensure that elected leaders will represent the public's best interests. The news media provides citizens with a way of understanding the societal challenges we face and gives us accurate information about ways to address these challenges. To have healthy debates, we need to all have access to truth that is based on evidence and facts. Maintaining an independent press has always been a struggle, but today, access to neutral, reliable reporting is facing extreme and novel threats.

As funding models for the news collapse and information gatekeeping is in the hands of a few large tech platforms, our right to accurate information suffers. Misinformation amplified by platforms buries trustworthy content. At the same time, content from reliable sources that *is* promoted is stripped of its context and mixed together with unverified content. This mixing together of news, opinion pieces, advertising, and misinformation has resulted in confusion and a decline of trust in reliable news outlets.

The transition from print to digital news accelerated the gutting of the traditional media industry. Over forty billion dollars in annual ad revenues have now shifted from news outlets to social media platforms.[3] We relied on the news industry to uphold strong journalistic standards and ethical practices when curating our information and deciding what was deemed important and newsworthy.

The loss of access to independent local news is especially concerning.[4] Local news outlets used to provide important coverage of community issues and events, and their decline has corresponded to a decline in local government accountability and civic engagement.[5] With the disappearance of local news sources, people have turned to more partisan TV, national news, and large social media sites. Google search and social media news feeds make decisions that impact what content is available to us. This consolidation of power in a few hands has created a distribution model for news that emphasizes revenue growth over truth.

New funding models that recognize the news as an essential public service, new tools and practices for journalists that can help them effectively compete in the current information disorder and restore public trust, along with the return of human curators working in collaboration with ethically designed algorithms are all necessary to fix our current digital ecosystem.

CREATING NEW FUNDING MODELS FOR THE NEWS

On January 6, 2022, I pop onto Google and search the word "Biden." Google tells me that the top story for my search term is "Biden to mark anniversary of Capitol attack with speech" and gives me a selected list of articles. The *Washington Post* headline is "Biden to clearly blame Trump for Capitol assault [in his speech]." Similar stories are offered from a few other news outlets. Biden has given few speeches so far in his presidency, and this is a major news event.

A few items down in my Google selected list is Fox News: "Hannity: Democrats should hold Biden 'accountable for his failures'" and a *Wall Street Journal* article about Biden and COVID. There's no mention of President Biden's upcoming speech on this day. I click on the *Post* story about the speech, and it tells me I have to buy a monthly ninety-nine-cent subscription to view the article. I then click on Fox, and I get the story in full about Biden's failures. Fox then suggests I might also like to read "Giant crab splits golf club in half with pincers in viral video."

Hmmm. Tempting . . .

Paywalls for high-quality reputable news outlets have become increasingly common as newspapers struggle to stay afloat. This can create ethical dilemmas: On the one hand, subscription fees allow journalists to cover important news rather than writing puff pieces on Ariana Grande to garner clicks. On the other hand, while ninety-nine cents a month doesn't seem like much, most people will not pay it when they can get other news online for free. The people who will pay for the news tend to be wealthier and more educated. And so it goes. The gap widens between those who read vetted, fact-checked news and those who are targeted with personalized content that may lead them down some dark paths or at the very least, to giant crabs crushing golf clubs.[6]

More than a year after the 2020 election, two-thirds of Republicans continue to believe that voter fraud helped Joe Biden win the US presidency, even though this has been verified as false.[7] More than half of Republicans describe the January 6 assault on the Capitol as a "riot that got out of control," whereas more than half of Democrats call it an "attempted coup or insurrection." And for those cordoned off into an even more detached information space, one-third of Trump voters say the January 6 event was actually carried out by enemies of Trump that included Antifa and government agents, a conspiracy theory that has been disproven.[8]

In 2022, two-thirds of Americans reported that they feel democracy is in crisis and at risk of failing.[9] These fears may, in part, be tied to a broken news system where people get their news from vastly different—and sometimes unreliable—sources. We are seeing a breaking point in our democracy that is closely tied to the lack of access to trustworthy news.[10] With many of the more reliable news outlets behind paywalls, the situation becomes further exacerbated.

What we define as "news" needs to shift to recognize that while many news outlets lean left or right, others serve as blatant propaganda machines. Fox News should be categorized as a political organization rather than a news network because of the misinformation included in its reporting. Six renowned reporters have recently left Fox to protest the misinformation the network spreads. The CEO of Fox, Lachlan Murdoch, stated outright that Fox News would act as "the loyal opposition" to President Biden when he was elected.[11] This doesn't exactly scream independence. Fox News should no longer be eligible for the $1.8 billion in carriage fees they receive annually from cable subscribers.[12]

The crisis in journalism is a public policy problem that is more pronounced in the United States than in many other industrialized countries. We can look to these other countries for healthier funding models to emulate. The only way the press can be free of interference from government or special interests is to develop funding mechanisms that are clearly separated from, and independent of, powerful interests. A free and independent press should not be kept behind paywalls for only the elite to consume. While foundations can work to provide seed money to pilot new models, what we need is a more robust, publicly funded, independent system that enacts safeguards against government and corporate intrusion.

Foundations: Seeding New Models

Foundation support can provide some help for independent news outlets. Philanthropists have ponied up funds in an attempt to reduce the powerful influence big business currently has over the press. But foundation support, while important, continues to be a drop in the bucket—offering tens of millions—against the billions provided through corporate "sponsorships."

Foundations can be most effective by targeting new funding-model pilot programs and finding ways to promote access to a diversity of voices. For example, the American Journalism Project has provided $79 million to fund dozens of independent nonprofit news organizations to beef up local investigative reporting. Philanthropic funds can be especially useful in providing seed money to create stronger community-based reporting models and promote coverage of, and participation by, underrepresented communities.

Successful nonprofit models such as those of universities and hospitals can be followed, but there remain challenges ahead for creating sustainable nonprofit entities. Foundation money can also sometimes come with strings attached. This is less common than corporate or government media capture, but donor capture of the news can create similar challenges. Drawing sharp lines between funding and potential special interests of the funders is imperative.

Funding the News as an Essential Public Service

We need to view consumption of the media as less like buying a cup of coffee and more like an essential public service. The US media system differs greatly from systems in other industrialized countries, such as the robustly funded BBC in the UK. The funding of public media in the United States has been miniscule: $1.40 per person annually as compared to other countries that devote $50 to $160 per person.[13]

The news media in the United States has been heavily dependent on ad revenue, with success closely connected to the selling of consumer products. A flawed funding model at best, this model is in sharp decline. While ownership of the news was at one time attractive as a way to make money, ownership is now driven almost solely by the desire for power and influence.[14] A handful of large corporations dominate the US media landscape for news and entertainment today.[15] The consolidation of news ownership is a threat to an independent press no matter how carefully powerful owners maintain their independence. While it may seem that there are many news media sources online, only a handful of mostly legacy outlets dominate online users' attention.[16]

With the consolidation of private ownership of the press and the unwillingness of many readers to pay subscriptions, the time is ripe for publicly funded news media that is protected from outside influence. Funding can be provided through a public trust that has a firewall so that funders will not know exactly what content they are funding and journalists will be protected from knowing the funders in order to maintain objectivity.

There are many public funding models to experiment with, including models used by other countries; public vouchers for people to select their own media from a list of reliable, independently vetted sources; government subsidized journalism job programs; local worker-run cooperatives; and the public media licensing expansion to nonprofits, community groups, colleges, and universities. A number of researchers have suggested taxing the hyperpersonalized advertising done by platforms to support public service media.[17] This could be done in a similar fashion to the way carbon taxes are used to offset a company's carbon dioxide emissions.

JOURNALISTS ARE UPPING THEIR GAME

Journalists have had to up their game with the transition from print to digital news. Their role has shifted from being the first to report a news story to serving in a more reactive mode as other players push information out into the digital space. Taking on misinformation has presented journalists with the need to create a new approach that includes deciding if, when, and how to report on misinformation.

A journalist's job description now includes strategic reporting on misinformation that exposes details about the sources and motives behind the content, learning new tools such as data tracking, infiltrating private messaging apps, and learning forensic strategies to uncover deepfakes. Practices such as community journalism and engaged journalism are helping reporters better compete for eyeballs, provide stories that are more relevant to their communities, and earn the trust of the citizens they serve.

Strategic Amplification

Strategic amplification—selecting what news to promote and what news to bury—has historically been the role of news editors and ideally is done to promote the public good. Not all decisions made are good ones, but with transparency and public accountability, course corrections can be made. In the 1960s, for example, there was recognition that the press was providing little coverage of White violence against Black civil rights groups. This recognition led to greater coverage of the civil rights movement, resulting in better public understanding of these events.[18]

Decisions about what *not* to report on are ethically tricky. Many journalists now deemphasize or do not name the shooter in a mass killing to avoid giving fame to the perpetrator and encouraging future shooters. Most news outlets do not put the shooter's name in a headline and will make only one mention of the name within the article. Some journalists have also made the decision to not link to a shooter's manifesto or quote directly from it, as this can attract some vulnerable people to the shooter's "cause."

With platform companies in the gatekeeping driver's seat, attempts by journalists at strategic amplification are now thrown to the wind. In 2022, seven years after mass murderer Dylann Roof published his racist manifesto online, Google's top link when searching for it provides a "knowledge panel" that links to Google Books for a digital copy of Roof's manifesto. In 2015, many news articles about Roof also linked to the manifesto, but today, journalism practices have evolved. The point is not to censor and completely remove access to the manifesto, but at the same time, make careful decisions not to amplify content promoting hate speech and racism.

Journalists follow an ethical code to serve the public, making complex decisions about what to promote and demote. Now that tech companies wield so much power over viewers' news feeds, can we start encouraging them to make ethical choices and develop standards that better serve society? Media scholars argue that strategic amplification needs to be deployed by journalists *and* platform companies to carefully decide when to pick up a story that involves misinformation and how to promote reliable over false content. This includes the adjustment of platform algorithms but at the same time will require human involvement and difficult judgment calls.[19]

We now see platforms and Google search rolling out strategic amplification in special situations such as the global COVID pandemic. If we Google "COVID," we are now fed information from credible sources such as the Centers for Disease Control and Prevention. In the first six months of the pandemic, this was not the case. But these extreme situations—such as public health emergencies—are still the exception, not the rule. In most cases, platform companies promote divisive content that will engage the largest number of viewers over content that is the most reliable.

Best Practices for Covering Misinformation

Journalists regularly make decisions about when and how to cover misinformation. Reporters need to tread carefully so that they avoid unintentionally spreading misinformation. Journalists competing for eyeballs are under pressure to attract viewers, and this sometimes results in propagating false content.[20] During the Trump presidency, many people learned of false information tweeted by Trump via the news media rather than directly from Trump's Twitter feed. In two-thirds of the media re-tweets of Trump's false claims, journalists spread false information but failed to note that the information was false.[21]

Best practices are emerging to help journalists determine when they should report on a story that involves misinformation and when they should not give the story more oxygen. If the story is already spreading virally or will likely spread soon, then it often makes sense to cover it. Identifying the tipping point is challenging: What exactly determines virality or potential virality? And at what point does the importance of holding someone accountable for the false content outweigh the importance of not spreading a story further?

Once a journalist makes the decision to cover a story, how can the misinformation be reported on without amplifying it? Simply reporting on and saying that something is not true—that wind turbines do not cause cancer—can sometimes have the effect of planting an idea into people's heads.[22] If you are old enough, think back to when President Nixon said, "I am not a crook!" This had the immediate effect of people thinking that perhaps he was a crook.[23]

In some situations, it is appropriate to use what journalists call the "truth sandwich" method. Write the truth first, then the falsehood, and then repeat the truth.[24] Misinformation researcher Joan Donovan suggests the following example: "Vaccines don't cause autism. While the myth persists that vaccines cause this condition, doctors across the globe have proven that vaccines do not cause autism and are a benefit [to] the whole of society."[25]

Truth sandwiches can be effective in some situations, but in other cases, putting the truth first is awkward because the story is really about the lie. A headline that says "Barack Obama Was Born in Hawaii" isn't going to draw people in the way a headline would that says "Trump Falsely Claims Obama Was Born in Kenya."

There is disagreement about the direct role the news media should play in fact-checking. A journalist who reports on a story must verify the facts of the story, but having independent fact-checking organizations such as FactCheck.org or PolitiFact may be preferable to having in-house news media fact-checking. There has been an increase in the number of global fact-checking organizations that focus on debunking political misinformation. These groups provide a resource for journalists and communities to have access to legitimate, unbiased fact-checking, and they work to establish standards and practices to help build trust. Over time and with proven track records, these groups can be a powerful aid to journalists and the public.[26]

Focusing on Sources and Motives

When Mark Grenon and his Genesis II Church of Health and Healing began promoting the Miracle Mineral Solution (a form of toxic bleach) as a cure for COVID, reporting that bleach was not a cure had little impact. At the time, the bleach cure for COVID was making the rounds on conspiracy sites and was even briefly advocated for by President Trump. To poke holes in the story, it was important to focus on the source. Who was Mark Grenon, and what did he get out of the deal? Apparently, he raked in more than a million dollars in the early months of the pandemic, was indicted for fraud, and at the time of this writing is awaiting trial.[27]

Understanding the source and the motivations behind a piece of misinformation can help the public better understand *why* a piece of information is false. Articles that include political and financial motives help people better understand why something that they may be inclined to believe—"miracle cure!"—is false. Journalists need to point out the origins of a lie and why the lie is being posted, which can be an effective strategy in debunking misinformation.

Journalists also need to help the public better understand scientific findings and the motivations of those who are throwing doubt on proven factual information. The fossil fuel industry has been questioning proven climate science because it is a threat to the industry's bottom line. These motives need to be clearly spelled out. It's like believing big tobacco companies when they said smoking was not dangerous to our health. Oh, wait. . . .

Scientific reporting can be especially tricky to understand, because scientific "truths" can shift over time, and that can undermine confidence in our understanding of scientific facts. Over the centuries, there have been many bad actors who have thrown doubt on scientific findings for political or financial gain. Calling out these people and their motives, explaining how science works, and being clear about the facts can help address these challenges.

In 2022, the *Boston Globe* announced that it would no longer engage in debate about the reality of climate change because the science is clear. In the past, there had been some pressure to "report on the other side." When science stories are undergoing a lot of debate about findings, reporting on all sides of the story is essential. But when 99 percent of scientists agree about, for example, climate change, reporting on the "other side" is falling into the trap of presenting a false equivalence: suggesting that there are two sides to this story and spreading misinformation by suggesting that the other side has some credence.

Learning New Tools

Journalists are getting up to speed on new tools in order to be more effective at going after misinformation. Resources such as the Media Manipulation Casebook provide journalists with sophisticated ways to detect and debunk misinformation.[28]

Journalists now use data science and machine learning tools to track the origin and spread of misinformation, including the role platforms play in spreading false content.[29] CrowdTangle, a Facebook-owned data analytics tool, is used by thousands of journalists to analyze Facebook trends and track the performance of posts.

In 2021, a "Facebook's Top 10" list was posted regularly to Twitter by reporter Kevin Roose using CrowdTangle to demonstrate right-wing bias in Facebook feeds. Much to the dismay of Facebook, Roose's Top 10 reports racked up tens of thousands of likes and shares daily on Twitter. Other than "Go Awesome Animals," the Top 10 posts regularly demonstrated that the sites with the most traffic on Facebook were right-wing commentators:

Facebook's Top 10
@FacebooksTop10
The top performing posts by U.S. Facebook pages in the last 24 hours are from:

1. Ben Shapiro
2. Ben Shapiro
3. Sean Hannity
4. Don Bongino
5. Ben Shapiro
6. Go Awesome Animals
7. Ben Shapiro
8. The Daily Caller
9. Dan Bongino
10. Sean Hannity[30]

A struggle ensued at Facebook between staff who wanted to allow reporters more transparent access to data to understand the degree to which Facebook was amplifying harmful content and staff that were worried about the impact this would have on the company's reputation. As top executives prioritized their reputation over transparency, several staff left the company in protest. Facebook's Vice President of Global Affairs sent an email to top executives at the company writing: "our own tools are helping journos [journalists] to consolidate the wrong narrative."[31]

Journalists are also learning to dig deeper into private messaging apps and alternative social media sites where misinformation bubbles up on platforms such as Reddit, 4chan, WhatsApp, Telegram, and Discord. Journalists are creating best practices for tracking misinformation at the earliest stages of its development in order to prevent viral spread. Perhaps things could have played out differently if the first QAnon post that emerged on 4chan had been nipped in the bud. An anonymous user named "Q" claimed to have top-level US security clearance and left a series of "Q drops" that included the Pizzagate conspiracy theory that there was a pedophile ring run by Hillary Clinton's campaign out of the basement of a pizza parlor. As late as mid-2021, 15 percent of Americans agreed with the QAnon statement that the US government, media, and financial worlds "are controlled by a group of Satan-worshipping pedophiles who run a global child sex trafficking operation."[32]

Journalists are starting to "prebunk" stories to quickly rebut misinformation before it takes hold and becomes viral.[33] Monitoring private and semi-private spaces can be tricky both technically and ethically: Should journalists use pseudonyms when accessing closed platforms? Is it ethical for them to be digitally undercover for the purpose of investigative journalism?[34]

Deepfakes present an especially challenging area for journalists. Deepfakes are digitally manipulated audio and video that are almost indistinguishable from real content and can be used to spread misinformation.[35] While there are many lighthearted uses of deepfakes—such as a video of Rasputin singing a Beyoncé song, other uses are more concerning. Deepfake videos can be used to make a world leader appear to say something that the person did not say, and nonconsensual pornography is being created that shows what appears to be Natalie Portman, Billie Eilish, and Taylor Swift engaging in sexual acts, though it is actually their heads imposed on others' bodies.

Journalists working for the *Wall Street Journal*, the *Washington Post*, and Reuters are being trained to detect deepfakes, and AI experts and platforms are working to develop new forensic tools.[36] The Content Authenticity Initiative created by Adobe, the *New York Times*, and Twitter is developing ways to track the provenance, source, and manipulation of videos and images to assist journalists in calling out deepfakes.[37]

There is also an increasing demand for reporters trained in "open source" news investigations that use publicly available resources such as satellite images, mobile phone or security camera recordings, and geolocation. Intercepted radio transmissions from Russian soldiers during the Ukraine war helped tell the story of Russian soldiers talking about the invasion being in disarray. Assembled footage filmed by the perpetrators of the January 6, 2021, attack on the Capitol has been pieced together to provide a play-by-play of how the attack unfolded. Journalism schools are now teaching these new strategies. The websites Storyful and Bellingcat pioneered this work that first started during the Arab Spring, when protests were being coordinated online and journalists could track what was happening in real time.[38]

Engaged Journalism

It is challenging to report the news while competing with sensationalized and entertaining misinformation. Clickbait such as "Cannabis Gummies Leave Doctors Speechless!" often has an advantage over less enticing content. The truth can sometimes be boring. Journalists can compete for attention by becoming more relevant to the communities they serve. Several new initiatives are reinvigorating journalism and strengthening people's trust and engagement with the news.

Reconnecting at the local level and writing stories that the community is passionate about can develop greater engagement and trust.[39] Engagement journalism uses participatory practices such as crowdsourced reporting, moderated comments connected to articles, and coproduction of news. Building networks with local communities and providing space for discussions to promote community engagement can lead to the creation of more relevant stories.[40] Using participatory design and building new platforms for news and civic engagement will be a part of this process. One exciting and innovative example is Nabur.org, which is a platform created to help local citizens interact with the news, ask questions, suggest story ideas, discuss issues, and share information about local events.

Engagement journalism, also called community journalism, involves journalists working collaboratively with community members. The journalist's role is viewed as helping unpack local issues in a way that makes them easy to understand and that focuses on potential solutions while remaining unbiased. Focusing on solutions has sometimes been confused with engaging in advocacy journalism, but the focus should be on providing a critical exploration of potential solutions to a problem and not advocating for any one solution. This focus can also provide hope that constructive solutions to social problems can be found to counter the hopelessness many people feel when reading the news. Bringing in experts and specialists with knowledge of specific issues can also provide deeper explorations of potential solutions.

News organizations have never served all citizens equally, and the current crisis in local news has increased long-running inequities. Creating engaged local journalism can involve communities of color and low-income or other marginalized communities in news reporting. A 2022 study shows a positive trend: analysis of Black media coverage during the pandemic and protests against racial injustice showed that community news outlets provided six times more coverage than mainstream media on issues of importance to Black communities such as racism, health disparities, and voting access.[41]

Community-based Asian media outlets have stepped up with more in-language reporting covering a linguistically diverse population. Asian media is now providing stronger connections to the communities they serve and reporting on stories of interest, including the pandemic, hate crimes, political polarization, and news from citizens' countries of origin. Local online media is better serving immigrant communities with boots on the ground and the development of strong, engaged journalism practices. National and other local media outlets need to partner and collaborate with community journalists.[42]

BRINGING BACK HUMAN CURATION

In 1987, every afternoon at 5:30, fewer than a dozen older White male editors sat in the executive editor's office at the *New York Times* and decided what news should be placed on the front page of the paper. Editors pitched their stories, and a select few were deemed the most important news of the day:

government announcements, meetings between world leaders, and images of business leaders announcing new initiatives were commonly chosen. The news was curated according to the cultural traditions and biases of the day.

Today, twice a day, about fifty *Times* editors around the world, representing a greater diversity of voices, gather to curate the news. Being placed "above the fold" in print, or as one of the top stories on the web page, provides an important service for subscribers. The *Times*'s mission is to "seek the truth and help people understand the world."[43] Online, where we are buried in information, carefully curated content is a valuable service. But curation comes at a cost: the paywall at the *Times* makes their articles inaccessible for many.

Like the *Times*, but with an even broader mission, public media editors—NPR, PBS, and their more than one thousand local affiliates—strategize on how best to inform, educate, and culturally enrich citizens to promote truth and support democracy. Public media across the United States provide citizens with local and nationally relevant news and strive to promote accurate content. They curate our world, but only when they can get viewers to see their content.

In 2022, at a school board meeting in Michigan, a parent angrily rants that she has heard that litter boxes have been added to the unisex bathrooms for students who identify as cats. This information is then promoted by Meshawn Maddock, cochair of the Michigan Republican Party, who posts it to her official public Facebook page: "Kids who identify as 'furries' get a litter box in the school bathroom. Parent heroes will TAKE BACK our schools."

Our new media gatekeepers—Facebook, Google, Twitter, Apple News—then promote and amplify the story. As it goes viral, national news outlets pick it up. It has been deemed newsworthy because it went viral and is an emotionally charged story. Our new gatekeepers curate information for vitriol over truth, and the downstream impact is the promotion of political propaganda and false information. The platforms are being played, but they are laughing all the way to the bank. Kitty litter in school bathrooms is clickbait. Even trusted news outlets are playing the game. If they don't report on sensationalized stories, they lose viewers.

There is no such thing as neutral curation. Platform companies claim to be neutral, but by prioritizing revenue, they often bury reliable and useful information. They sweep up the ethically curated content produced by public media and trustworthy news outlets and throw it into their algorithmic centrifuge, removing contextual clues and then popping it out to viewers based on engagement data. Stripped of its context, cat videos, opinion pieces, and accurate news stories sit side by side, making it challenging to decipher reliability.

Public media outlets, in particular, are struggling for survival. They are making hard choices about whether they should give away content to platforms or create their own platforms. By using the big platforms, they can gain access to large audiences. The downside is that they are disconnected from the relationship with their viewers. Their trustworthy brand is detached from their content and placed side by side next to similarly formatted content that is quite different: news, opinions, ads, and misinformation. By relinquishing their relationship with their audience, public media loses the ability to understand who is viewing its content. It also loses a vital connection to its local donors.[44]

In an ideal world, high-quality content would be expertly curated and promoted by a combination of ethical algorithmic filtering, human curation, and content moderation. Joan Donovan and her colleagues make the case for new media platforms in the public interest curated by editors and librarians and focusing on content that is accurate, timely, local, and relevant.[45] Over time, human curation could help create a digital world that favors quality over quantity and slower engagement instead of addictive doom scrolling. Misinformation and clickbait would no longer be promoted and incentivized, and with fewer viewers, this low-credibility information would gradually decline.

How exactly would this work? Who should have the power to curate the information and news we view? And can algorithms be designed to provide unbiased filters for the millions of pieces of content being loaded onto the web every day? Can we create public service algorithms to work in conjunction with new public service platforms to promote accurate content?

What Is Human Curation?

People are becoming increasingly disaffected with algorithms that control much of what we see and do online. The value of human curation is regaining popularity. As AI-powered platforms blasted misinformation about COVID at the beginning of the pandemic, many realized too late that misinformation about vaccines, masking, and treatment was being promoted and going viral. In the case of the pandemic, platforms started to recalibrate when they realized that they needed to rely more on human curation to help mitigate the harm. By upping the use of human curation to address COVID misinformation, platforms tacitly acknowledged that they had the means to promote reliable information.[46]

Curation involves people gathering, selecting, organizing, and adding qualitative judgment to content. Curators work to select the most accurate, useful, and timely content to provide people with information most relevant to their needs. A good curator knows that when you search "how can I repair my lawn mower?" you do not want to *buy* a new lawn mower; you *actually want* information that will help you fix the lawn mower you already own.

At its best, curation links information together to create meaning and knowledge. Think of it like one of the better articles on Wikipedia: a combination of current, accurate, and cited research and data that is brought together to explain a concept or entity. Curators make evaluative judgments about validity and truth and use various methodologies for verification. Curators tell a story by carefully selecting pieces of content to convey meaning. To create trusted content, curation needs to be done ethically and adhere to explicit standards.

Netflix and other streaming platforms have turned to human reviewers to better curate videos so that there is less "Oh, you like Meryl Streep? Then you might also like *Mamma Mia!* and *The Deer Hunter.*" Not necessarily! Unlike humans, algorithms do not watch movies, have opinions, or provide critical reviews. More platforms are recognizing the shortcomings of algorithms and are turning to humans to create greater value for their subscribers. Curators can have expertise in particular areas—news editors, film or book critics, librarians with subject matter expertise, and so on—or they can be passionate fans that provide a service to other fans. Combining algorithms with human curation can be effective. Sites like Rotten Tomatoes use algorithms to crunch data from reviews by expert and amateur critics and then provide curated lists of recommended films.

Adding In Ethical Algorithms

Algorithms are relied on because they can sort massive amounts of information efficiently and inexpensively. But they can only interpret and make recommendations based on data and patterns. Acting alone, algorithms can have serious shortcomings. They are extremely effective for filtering unambiguous data, such as solving a Rubik's Cube or following a recipe for baking a cake. But even following a recipe can quickly go awry if the recipe says, "Bake until done," because algorithms have no way of determining what "done" means. Algorithms are unable to understand context, recognize humor, pick up on nuance, have empathy, or process emotions. They are also subject to biases that can then be reinforced and magnified over time.

The new field of critical algorithmic studies investigates how to develop more useful algorithms to promote reliable information and how to work in conjunction with human curators. Determining who benefits when some content is ranked more highly than other content can help inform this work. Care needs to be taken when algorithms pre-curate content for human review, and transparency is essential so that valuable content is not screened out before it gets to a human reviewer. At the same time, developing algorithms that are better at screening traumatic content such as beheadings or child sexual abuse material can provide great value in lessening the burden on human reviewers who currently work to flag this content.

Work on designing new public-service algorithms is in its early days. There is agreement that fairness, accountability, and transparency are key ingredients. Prominent algorithm failures are often understood—after the fact—and can then inform algorithmic solutions. The algorithms that Google, Facebook, and TikTok use are succeeding in what they were designed to do—prioritize engagement that then results in increasing revenue. They are not ethical, fair, accountable, or transparent. We have the means to create better algorithms, but regulations are needed to require their development. Silicon Valley will not voluntarily give up the billions it makes from the current setup.[47]

New ethical algorithms can prefilter content that is then reviewed by curators—librarians, editors, news reporters, and others with expertise—following carefully created and transparent standards developed by professional bodies, such as medical organizations. The curators will need to be nonpartisan, to be accountable to public oversight, and to have a code of ethics.

In the current digital information space, this combination of ethical algorithms and expert curators is not scalable, but by starting with disincentivizing misinformation and incorporating new tools that create friction to decrease the amount of information pollution online, we may start to get our footing.

Curators can also be involved in establishing signals of quality to improve trust in vetted content. When someone searches online "Do home COVID tests work?," the search engine can prioritize trustworthy news articles and provide context and transparency in the content it selects. Information about the reputation of a news outlet or website—how it fact-checks and verifies its content and whether there is independent verification and a policy for corrections—could be embedded in search results. Information about industry awards, when the outlet was founded, and the background of its writers can provide signals of reliability.[48]

Establishing trust with disenfranchised communities will take time. Providing a track record of accurate reporting, transparency, and inclusion can help build trust. The Trust Project has created eight "trust indicators" for hundreds of news sites around the world. They provide a global transparency standard so that people can know who is behind a news story, including details about who funds or owns a news site, journalistic expertise, commitment to fairness and accuracy, local connections, access to diverse voices, and actionable feedback.[49]

Content moderators combined with community input can bring up the rear by catching inevitable mistakes that will come through the system. Unlike proactive curation, content moderation is after the fact and much less effective because it often comes after many viewers have latched on to a false story.

With ethical algorithms, someone like Meshawn Maddock would still have the right to post inflammatory content misrepresenting a school board meeting to try to generate anger among her constituents, but in an online world where accuracy and truth are valued and promoted, far fewer people would see these inaccurate posts. Maddock has the right to free speech, but she doesn't have the right to dominate news feeds by gaming a system that prioritizes anger and false content over truth. No one disputes Maddock's right to free speech. She can stand up in the digital public square and rant, but she does not have the right to a megaphone and automatic virality.

7

Build New Digital Public Squares

$\mathcal{I}$ have these two conflicting images that I can't get out of my head.

One image is a video of Mark Zuckerberg surfing on a hydrofoil surf-board holding an enormous American flag accompanied by a John Denver soundtrack. I cannot unsee this. A headline from *The Wrap* sums it up with "What the Zuck? Mark Zuckerberg Goes Full Cringe with Flag-Waving Surfing Video."[1]

In the other image, I see a large, runaway mozzarella cheese ball rolling down a city street as someone chases and then rescues it before it rolls into traffic.

I can explain.

Facebook is moving away from its "apologize and promise to do better" strategy in dealing with accusations that it is sowing misinformation and imperiling democracy. Leaked Meta documents show a new tactic being rolled out called "Project Amplify," which involves using the Facebook News Feed to promote pro-Facebook news articles, some of which are written by the company. I guess it finally dawned on Meta that not only do they control much of the news people consume but they can also start writing this "news" themselves. Several executives expressed shock at this proposal, but that did not alter the course of Project Amplify. And so, we get Zuck, surfboard, giant flag, *Go Facebook!* You get the idea.

As for the large cheese ball rolling down the street. . . . The following is a post from Front Porch Forum, a popular, neighborhood-based community platform in Vermont that is pretty much everything that Facebook is not:

> Did you drop a cheese ball on Berlin St. Friday afternoon? I saw it rolling
> down the sidewalk too late to get your attention. We have it safe in the
> fridge, hopefully it wasn't for tonight's dinner!" —Ken in Montpelier

99

If it weren't for Front Porch Forum would we even know about the run-away mozzarella ball rolling down Berlin Street, rescued by kind strangers? Good to know [of] these oddball random acts of kindness. —Kristin in Montpelier

Where Facebook is a company designed to make money, Front Porch is designed to provide value. The purpose of Front Porch is to build community and solve community problems. Front Porch is funded by donations and set up as a benefit corporation (B Corp). It allows local ads based on where someone lives, but it does not track user behavior, and advertising does not drive platform design.

Where Facebook is a national company that works on the global stage, Front Porch is locally owned and operated, with eighteen employees. Where Facebook is designed to keep users online and engaged as long as possible to drive profits, Front Porch is designed for slow engagement. Most people spend five or ten minutes a day online to get news that their immediate neighbors have posted: lost dogs, bake sales, and announcements of upcoming school board meetings.

Facebook users are not always real people. Bots can set up fake profile accounts, or people can use fake names when posting. On Front Porch, everyone must sign up using a real Vermont address, and when you are on the site, you are interacting with real neighbors. More than a quarter of all people in Vermont now use their neighborhood's Front Porch.

Facebook is opaque about how it addresses complaints, how harmful content is handled, and how its algorithms are designed to promote or demote content. Content is posted immediately, and sometimes harmful posts are pulled down but often after the content has been widely viewed. In countries outside the United States—that is, for 90 percent of Facebook's users—harmful content is much less likely to be pulled. In countries such as India, which has twenty-two officially recognized languages, there are no content moderators reviewing posts in some of these languages.[2] On Front Porch, all posts are first reviewed by paid human moderators and then posted within twenty-four hours. If someone behaves badly, such as writing insults about a neighbor, that person is contacted, and the guidelines are explained: neighbors can disagree with something someone has posted and voice their opinion, but personal attacks are not allowed.

Facebook has been able to scale globally; Front Porch is not designed to be scalable. Local staff deal with a few thousand posts a week on Front Porch, with 98 percent of posts approved through these human filters. Local businesses are limited to a few labeled promotional posts and are then asked to pay for a placed ad. Illegal activities, such as selling drugs, cannot be posted on Front Porch. On Facebook, there are 4.75 billion posts shared daily. Selling drugs, child sexual abuse material, human trafficking, and other illicit activities can all be found on Facebook.

We are influenced by where we live. This is true in digital worlds as well as physical ones. The most important difference between these two platforms is that Facebook is optimized for increasing revenue. Facebook makes more money by keeping us engaged with highly emotional and charged content, and this influences how we behave with each other online. Front Porch is optimized for building social cohesion. The intentional design of Front Porch is to strengthen in-person interactions in the physical community. In his work on social connection, Nicholas Christakis, director of the Human Nature Lab at Yale University, has found that the fundamental principle of human social networks is that they "magnify whatever they are seeded with." They don't give rise to things on their own, but once something is put into the network, the network will amplify it. As Christakis says, "If you put Nazism into the network you get more Nazis; if you put love into the network you get more love."[3]

Facebook is not devoid of building social cohesion. Lots of wonderful positive social interactions occur on Facebook, but Facebook is not optimized for this purpose. Facebook has caused tremendous damage by choosing our news feeds and not verifying information that is promoted on these feeds. Outside of the United States, Facebook has been directly responsible for inciting offline violence in India, Ethiopia, and Myanmar. In Myanmar, as cell phones were being widely adopted, the Facebook app came preloaded and without data charges. Overnight, Facebook became the primary news source for more than half of the country. A few years later, the platform was weaponized to spread political misinformation. UN human rights investigators have since concluded that Facebook played a key role in inciting violence and was complicit in the Rohingya genocide in Myanmar.[4]

Independent research on Front Porch shows that it improves social cohesion and is improving the resilience of local Vermont communities.[5] Building stronger community cohesion produces many intangible benefits such as high civic engagement, more instances of neighbors helping neighbors, and lower crime rates. Connecting trusted local news outlets to Front Porch may be the next step toward enhancing social capital throughout Vermont.

Front Porch Forum provides many design features that foster healthier online interactions, but not everyone will want what Vermont wants. It can still serve as a useful model of what can happen when platforms are value-based rather than profit-seeking. New value-based online communities can come in many flavors: Neighborhoods in Las Vegas may want something different from neighborhoods in rural Kansas. Other online communities may be built around common interests and can transcend geographical boundaries and also be designed to foster healthy interactions.

Ethan Zuckerman, head of the new Institute for Digital Public Infrastructure, points out that in addressing the issue of misinformation, we may be too focused on trying to fix our old social media platforms. Instead, we should focus on creating new spaces that have explicit civic goals and are designed for equity, inclusion, and social cohesion. Real-world communities need to be involved in carefully designing their own local digital public spaces rather than leaving this work to tech companies looking to create the next enormous global platform.[6]

DIGITAL THIRD PLACES?

"Where everybody knows your name, and they're always glad you came."[7]

Third places are places outside of our homes and workplaces that provide essential neutral places where we can relax, interact with friends and strangers, and enjoy ourselves. Ray Oldenburg first described third places decades ago, at a time when people were moving to the suburbs, and third places were disappearing. These informal community gathering places provide a sense of belonging and connection that can strengthen community ties. Coffee shops, barbershops, churches, libraries, and parks can be accessible to everyone; conversation and community building, rather than solely pursuing commerce, are a top priority.

More recently, sociologist Eric Klinenberg's book *Palaces for the People*, traces the importance of public squares throughout history. These "palaces" can offer transparent, neutral spaces where everyone is welcome. Klinenberg argues that the future of democratic society rests on developing shared values *and* shared spaces. Libraries, gyms, cafes, and childcare centers provide connections where people can linger and make friends across group lines. These places for hanging out strengthen entire communities and are often intentionally designed to promote socialization and connection.

Rates of loneliness, anxiety, and depression are rising in our hyper-connected world. Robert Putnam, the author of *Bowling Alone*, called attention to our declining social capital even prior to the rise of social media. Social capital consists of the networks of relationships among people who live and work together and are essential for the effective functioning of society. These networks provide us with a shared understanding and shared values. They foster trust, cooperation, and reciprocity and help feed our strong need for connection and belonging.

When online platforms were first developed decades ago, bulletin board systems focused on connecting people, sharing information, and being social. But platforms that promised to connect us soon evolved into capitalizing on our desire for connection. TikTok, YouTube, and other platforms are not set up to be third places. They foster consumerism, asynchronous communication, passive doomscrolling, hyperpersonalization, high engagement, and misinformation. A small number of Silicon Valley companies have driven our attention toward consumerism rather than community building.

The design choices made by tech executives result in behavior that can sometimes be aggressive, illegal, or predatory. Leaked documents from Facebook in 2021 indicated that the platform knew it was underenforcing checks against abusive activity including the selling of Filipina maids. Only when Apple threatened to remove Facebook and Instagram from its app store over this issue did these platforms relent and remove these accounts, though later images of maids with their ages and prices could still be seen on the platform.[8]

Meta has experimented with tweaking its algorithms to make its platform "friendlier." Meta altered its news feed algorithm to downrank unreliable news before the 2021 election and shortly after the January 6 insurrection, but we have no access to what decisions were made, whether they were successful, and whether some of these tweaked algorithms are still in place. Platforms have the capacity to design healthier spaces that could prioritize truth and encourage more civil interactions online, but doing so would harm their bottom line.[9]

Digital worlds will never replace physical third places, but they can serve to augment and enhance our physical world and do a better job of focusing on our best interests rather than our wallets. Creating platforms to serve the public interest will not happen organically. These types of platforms are possible, but they need to be intentionally and collaboratively built and maintained.

HUMANE PLATFORM DESIGN

Ethan Zuckerman is at the forefront of a growing movement dedicated to creating more humane technologies that can foster healthy civic engagement. Zuckerman points out that the internet is currently made up of public infrastructures, such as Facebook, that are designed to display ads to users, not to enable citizenship. These platforms bear little resemblance to other public institutions such as libraries, museums, arboretums, and community centers. Zuckerman suggests that future healthy platforms may not involve Facebook or Twitter at all.[10]

New_ Public, an organization that seeks to connect designers and technologists to build healthier digital public spaces, conducted a large study to determine what qualities are essential for creating better online communities. It identified fourteen signals that support healthy spaces: invite everyone to participate, encourage the humanization of others, ensure people's safety, keep people's information secure, cultivate belonging, build bridges between groups, strengthen local ties, make power accessible, elevate shared concerns, show reliable information, build civic competence, promote thoughtful conversation, boost community resilience, and support civic action.[11] How are we doing so far? It concluded that few platforms scored well on any of the signals and that all the platforms studied were greatly lacking in encouraging the humanization of others and ensuring people's safety.

When designing better online communities, we need to think about what makes our physical spaces function smoothly. When we enter a public library or park, there are social norms and structures that encourage being respectful toward others. We don't, for the most part, walk down the street shrieking at people, and if we do, there are consequences. Sahar Massachi, from the Integrity Institute and formerly on the Civic Team at Facebook, views his work as an integrity designer as similar to that of an urban planner. Online neighborhoods need to be designed from the ground up to help people and democracies thrive.[12]

Massachi advocates for using the physical city as a model for digital spaces but at the same time recognizing that there are differences between the two. A city has clear physical limits; online worlds are limitless. In the physical world, the ability to disguise yourself and communicate with large groups of people is constrained: you can only be in one place at a time. Online, people can more easily disguise themselves and post unlimited amounts of content across platforms for little cost in time or money.

Digital spaces can use nudges and develop infrastructure that encourages people to behave. These can include curb cuts that make some things easier to do and speed bumps that can slow some things down. Creating these new spaces will not necessarily be commercially successful, in the same way that building a public park or a school is not a commercial endeavor. These new spaces will also need effective content moderators and established guidelines. Until recently, integrity work has been a small department inside tech companies, and the work can be at odds with company goals. When push comes to shove, the ethics team loses. Ethicists are now leaving large tech companies and engaging in ethics work from the outside, realizing that change from the inside has had a limited impact.

Some of the best and brightest minds in tech are breaking ranks to speak out against harmful technology practices and are working to create better digital spaces. In addition to Sahar Massachi, former Facebook staffers Frances Haugen and Tim Kendall, who have testified about harmful practices to Congress, former Google staffer Tristan Harris, who founded the Center for Humane Technology, and Timnit Gebru, a computer scientist who led an ethical AI team at Google and has founded the Distributed Artificial Intelligence Research Institute (DAIR), have tried to push ethical design from within companies that were unwilling to prioritize humane design practices.

People are experimenting with ways to build more humane platforms. The following sections dig more deeply into design choices about platform size, content moderation practices, the role of anonymity, and the dangerous externalities that can occur if we improve some platforms while not addressing larger issues for all platforms.

Large or Small?

Should new public interest platforms be large or small? Centralized or decentralized? Public or private? The answer may be all of the above, but we don't really know yet. We do know that we can do better.

Creating smaller platforms within larger federated systems that are decentralized and distributed across distinct service providers is one idea. Users could use a central social media browser to access these various spaces, helping new platforms compete with existing more addictively designed spaces.[13] People are not going to come running from engaging platforms like TikTok unless the new choices provide them with value and have an easy on-ramp. If people can pop onto a dashboard and see a site like Front Porch alongside their usual feeds, they may go on to view the handful of posts each day that come from actual neighbors. From this same personalized dashboard, designers could promote value-based platforms and make it easy for us to pop onto a virtual yoga class, attend a lecture, read the news, or go to a church service, while at the same time minimizing our exposure to misinformation or hate groups.

The Buy Nothing Project has experimented with the issue of size since its founding. Two women set up a local gift economy on Facebook in 2013 that gives away goods and services within neighborhoods. Their goal is to enrich connections between neighbors with the belief that communities can be more "resilient, sustainable, equitable and joyful" when they have gift economies.[14]

Gifts on the platform—leftover paint, an unused bicycle—are given away with no expectation of any reward. The guidelines are clear: no buying, selling, trading, referrals, or fundraisers. People express interest in selected gifts, and then the Givers are encouraged to take their time in choosing the recipient, often waiting twenty-four hours to gauge interest, need, and the creativity of the Askers. Encouraging Givers to wait promotes slower engagement and avoids rewarding people that constantly monitor the app. It can also discourage resellers. Gratitude is intentionally promoted to establish a norm of goodwill toward others.

Like Front Porch, the Buy Nothing Project provides us with an early model of how to build a value-based platform. Its growing pains and tweaks provide lessons for what to embrace and what to avoid. Today, Buy Nothing has more than six thousand federated groups and millions of users. It has clear policies about online behavior and has established an equity team to monitor and remove harmful discussions.

The biggest challenge for Buy Nothing was realizing that Facebook was not conducive to supporting local gifting. The design of Facebook actively encourages people to stay online and join more groups. Many Facebook private groups are wonderful—groups that support cancer patients, new moms, church youth groups—but the platform's focus on growth and keeping people online, rather than fostering better social cohesion and improving our offline lives, sets the wrong tone.

Buy Nothing has now created its own app to better foster community as it transitions off of Facebook. It has found that size matters and small is better. When a group gets larger than one thousand people, just too many Asks and Gives go unseen or unmet due to sheer numbers.[15] Size also impacted feelings of safety, as real-life local connections were more difficult when the group got too big. The project developed a system of sprouting and capping to keep groups small, but this has not been easy. Some people felt segregated when boundaries often reflected real-life inequities between local neighborhoods. Facebook was inflexible in this area, insisting that clear boundaries be set. The new app provides a flexible approach that can be customized by local communities, though being off Facebook may result in fewer people finding their service.

The small communities we develop online will look different and have different rules. "Local logic" platforms may resemble larger platforms in appearance, but their posts and members would be tied to local areas such as a small town or a city block. These local online communities may require proof of identity and may connect people's posts directly or indirectly to their real identity. It could use centralized technology in the way that Front Porch does, use advertising that is tied to geography rather than personal data capture, and involve the community in creating customized guidelines.[16] Small communities online could also include groups for knitting or spaces to connect with the friends we see in the physical world. These spaces are not without their challenges, and while connecting orchid lovers, they will also likely house hate groups.

Having many different types of platforms with different rules benefits society. No one group—or just three or four—should be making decisions about what content is allowed and promoted online. Different communities can create different norms about acceptable behavior, and people can make choices about where they want to hang out. The US government has set up a limited set of civility and safety norms while carefully balancing free speech rights, but private groups can create their own rules depending on their purpose.[17] A children's YouTube channel can have strict guidelines about what types of content and behavior are allowed, and other spaces will also choose to set limits that are more conservative than what the law allows. On the other hand, an adult erotica fan club will set the bar much lower on allowable content and behavior—you can opt in if you want, but you don't get hit with this content on your news feed.

While a diverse set of smaller spaces online may be preferred, we also need platforms designed for larger groups. danah boyd writes about how we can create healthier spaces even in larger ecosystems through intentional design. She points to Grateful Dead concerts, whose average audience size was eighty thousand. A shared love of the Dead certainly promoted positive interactions at these concerts, but there were design choices made to promote pro-social behavior. One nudge used the concept of "familiar strangers." If you bought a ticket for a concert in Denver, the ticket sellers kept a record of who was seated near you. If you later bought a ticket for a show in Austin, they would seat you with the same people. By the time you went to your third concert—typical among Deadheads—you would start recognizing and interacting with this same collection of familiar strangers, and this could facilitate positive interactions.[18]

Work is in the planning stages to create public service platforms that might serve an entire country. The Public Square Project in Australia is attempting to create a countrywide public service platform. Australia had a frightening wake-up call when it passed legislation requiring Facebook and Google to start paying news outlets for content that they were hosting. Google complied, but Facebook fought back by temporarily blocking access to news organizations as well as blocking access to essential government services, such as Fire and Rescue, that are housed on Facebook.

Australians realized how much power one foreign company had over their online interactions and access to news and services. In addition, the infrastructure of Facebook was fueling misinformation and divisive public discourse and resisting regulations to change their model. The Public Square Project is creating a platform that is not driven by revenue goals but at the same time is not state run, so a healthy exchange of ideas can be protected. The new platform will be centered around principles of public broadcasting by being publicly funded and independent.[19]

Stronger Content Moderation

Content moderation is a vital component in the design of value-based digital spaces. Human content moderators differ from curators in that their purpose is to demote or remove content deemed harmful or inappropriate rather than to select and promote accurate and useful content. Content moderation comes in three flavors: algorithms powered by AI, crowd-generated user reporting, and human review. Each of these strategies comes with challenges.

Algorithms are useful for spotting and removing especially obvious content that violates a rule, such as child sexual abuse material, but AI has difficulty with understanding more nuanced content. Crowdsourced up- and down-voting, or reporting of bad behavior on a platform, is the most common type of content moderation. It is inexpensive and can scale if users are invested in the platform. Unfortunately, content is often already viewed by thousands of people before it is down-voted or reported. Trained human content moderators are much better than algorithms at spotting harmful or false content. Unfortunately, humans are labor intensive and expensive. Working in combination with carefully designed AI, and with the right system of checks and balances to minimize individual biases, they can be effective. With billions of dollars in revenue, platforms could be required to use more humans to improve moderation. In addition, if platforms were regulated more like publishers, they would be highly motivated to use friction to limit the vast amounts of content coming over their transom.

In extreme situations, such as the recent pandemic or the Russian invasion of Ukraine, platforms have used more robust content moderation, but this is the exception and not the rule. Most point to their community guidelines and ask users not to violate these. On Reddit, these consist of a few sentences that state that its purpose is to create community and that posters are not allowed to attack, threaten, or bully anyone—and if they do, they will be banned. On Twitter there are extensive guidelines with reassuring statements about keeping the community safe, while at the same time Twitter states that it will not act as a publisher or censor. Banning content can create bad publicity for a platform.[20] Most platforms are not transparent in how content moderation is done: we don't know what content is permitted; how it is promoted, demoted, or removed; or what recourse a person has whose content is banned. With more rigorous, fair, and transparent content moderation, digital spaces could be far less toxic.

In the case of Spotify, it didn't have to worry much about the issue of content moderation until it added podcasts. The platform did try to remove R. Kelly's music when he was accused of sexual misconduct, but protests led to a quick reversal. Now Spotify has entered the market of podcasts, and it is struggling with pushback about the misinformation and hateful content on its platform.

Neil Young, Joni Mitchell, India.Arie, and others pulled their music from Spotify in protest of its star podcaster, the controversial Joe Rogan, who brought on guests who were peddling coronavirus misinformation. Spotify barely blinked at the protest: Rogan's contract with the platform was for $200 million. Podcasting has become more lucrative than music because it attracts more listeners and there is no percentage cut sent to music industry executives.

Spotify is doing what most large platforms do after being busted for spreading misinformation: beefing up its guidelines that bar dangerous, deceptive, and illegal content. But what are its plans for enforcing these guidelines? It is adding content advisory flags to podcasts that cover the pandemic. And for his part, Rogan has promised to provide more "balance" on his show. This is unlikely to do much to reduce the impact and amount of harmful content.

In addition to the desire to dodge accusations of censorship, there are also the issues of scale and technical challenges with policing content, especially audio content. There are almost four million podcasts on Spotify, and transcribing and analyzing audio is time-consuming and expensive. Spotify claims it has removed twenty thousand podcasts that had false information about the coronavirus, but it refuses to reveal how much money it spends on content moderation, how many employees are dedicated to reviewing content, or what technologies are used to police content.[21] We do know that new podcasts are approved in a matter of minutes.[22]

Beyond COVID misinformation, Spotify also hosts racist, anti-Semitic, and other offensive hate speech. We can't know for certain, but it appears that their main strategy for content moderation is crowdsourced: users can report material that is then reviewed and, in some cases, taken down. Taking down content happens after Spotify has served as a megaphone that promotes sensationalized content for its 460 million listeners.

We now have much more information about what makes content moderation effective and what types of design changes can decrease the amount of toxicity online.[23] We also know that existing platform companies are not likely to adopt many of these design changes on their own. At Meta, a team of integrity workers tests new ideas for improving interactions on their platform, but often if there is even a tiny impact on growth, these new ideas are tossed.[24]

Twitter's live audio platform "Spaces" provides a megaphone for White nationalists, Taliban supporters, and hate speech. This audio is not policed or moderated by Twitter. It reports that it does not have the technology to police live audio. Internal reports indicate that employees who expressed concern were ignored.[25] Radio DJs are regularly held accountable and, in some cases, fired over hateful speech.[26] Why do digital platforms get a free ride?

Stronger content moderation practices need to be required to reduce the scale and speed at which platforms approve and host content. We need elected officials, regulators, and the public to decide on rules and norms that should govern online spaces. What if platforms were required to function more like publishers and put the brakes on the excessive amount of poor content blasting through their pipes? What if they actually had reviewers, editors, and curators who signed off on the content that they were willing to host? More selectivity in what content is published would add great value to the user and reduce toxic content.

One downside of providing stronger content moderation and establishing norms and consequences for people who are misbehaving is that without overall regulations, this can drive problematic behavior into the darker corners of the internet. When large platforms crack down on harmful behavior, groups flee to lesser-known platforms that are willing to host this behavior. Reddit, and other platforms, can sometimes unintentionally provide a megaphone for recruiting members for White supremacist or terrorist groups because they fail to act swiftly on groups that violate their guidelines. Their process involves warnings, quarantine, and eventually removal, but as this process plays out, the groups are able to attract new members more easily on a platform of 430 million members.[27]

Google search also plays a role in recruitment by promoting these harmful groups. An ethical search engine designed for public service could demote hate groups and false content. Alphabet, Google's parent company, eventually chose to demote online misinformation about COVID, but in many other areas it continues with an allegedly hands-off policy. Minimizing the publicity these groups and their messages get through platforms and search can reduce the amount of attention these groups receive.[28]

Proactive Community Stewards

One of the key differences between Front Porch Forum and Nextdoor—two platforms designed to foster local connections—is that on Front Porch, harmful posts are rare due to proactive content moderation by paid professionals who serve as community stewards. Content that violates community guidelines is flagged before it is posted and before it can spread and undermine community goodwill. If you have a problem with content that is banned, you can appeal to professionals and plead your case.

On Nextdoor, moderation policies are at the whim of whichever volunteer in your neighborhood stepped up first, and members are relied on to report content. Nextdoor has prioritized growth over community cohesion, and as a result, there have been a lot of negative interactions on the platform. This is in part because Nextdoor communities have become large—a design decision built into the platform—but also because harmful content is often left up or viewed by many people before it is removed, normalizing negative behavior.

The lack of content moderation and an overreliance on crowdsourced reporting has been a problem for many years. In 2013, the number of teenagers joining Yik Yak grew rapidly to almost two million before its extreme toxicity, bomb threats, racist posts, and threats to rape or kill specific individuals finally shut it down.[29] Its design was focused on being local—user groups were confined to a five-mile radius—but its lack of moderators and its anonymity resulted in harmful posts. Librex, one of a handful of anonymous platforms created for college students, jumped in to fill the void. Designed initially for Yale students, it got big quickly, and was known for its abusive and hateful content but also for providing an anonymous place for students to speak freely, ask dumb questions, gossip, and say what they were thinking without fear of reprisals. Content on the platform was a mixed bag at best.

Hiring trained moderators is expensive, especially for Librex's creator, who was a sophomore in college. But it's possible that an anonymous platform like Librex could provide great value to its community if it invested in stronger moderation in the form of community stewards.[30] A platform such as Librex could be broken up and designed for different purposes with different rules and moderation practices: one place to discuss mental health concerns, another to post events, another for discussing concerns about campus life, and another to share humor and memes. People could choose what communities they would want to participate in, and norms could be established with community input.

Professional community stewards are essential for managing and caring for people in digital public spaces. The public servants hired might be the digital counterpart to police and security officers, social workers, journalists, educators, and librarians, to provide the appropriate care work similar to the work done in physical spaces. For community stewards to succeed, these spaces would need to be small enough to manage. Public buildings and parks in the physical world have limits on the numbers of people that can enter, and online communities could also set limits.

Wikipedia is one site that—after some struggles—has managed to grow a healthy and productive space despite being a large community. How is it that Wikipedia has managed to be so successful? The community has a clear vision and an ethical goal to create "a world in which every single human being can freely share in the sum of all knowledge."[31] Anyone can join Wikipedia and contribute, but there are clear, community-created guidelines and some friction involved in joining and contributing content—you can't just jump in and start editing. Known as a commons-based, peer-production platform, the focus is on social value rather than revenue, making it easier to prioritize ethical practices. Wikipedia's success is not accidental. The community has embedded what Elinor Ostrom has determined are the eight principles for managing a commons, which include user-made procedures and monitoring, conflict resolution policies, and other practices to ensure community health.[32]

Ethan Zuckerman has said, "If the contemporary internet is a city, Wikipedia is the lone public park; all the rest of our public places are shopping malls—open to the general public, but subject to the rules and logic of commerce."[33] Wikipedia is not without its challenges. Like many large tech spaces, it tends to be White male dominant, and encyclopedia entries skew in that direction, but this can be changed.[34]

The Place for Anonymity

Whether a platform should provide anonymity to its users is a complex issue. LinkedIn does not provide anonymity and has far fewer problems with harmful content. Its vibe of being a professional, work-related platform also helps convey a sense of responsibility and establishes norms that are like rules found in the workplace. This helps limit controversial posts.

Ahwaa, on the other hand, is a platform that would not exist if there was not anonymity. Ahwaa is a special-purpose social network for Arab LGBTQ teenagers. Avatars are used, and profile pictures are not allowed. People cannot post comments or start new conversations until they have logged on multiple times, and their first comments need to have received supportive responses from others for them to stay. These policies protect youth from political or religious persecution and also prevent drive-by trolls from harassing users. Anonymity can protect marginalized communities and enable people to discuss issues such as sexuality in a safe space. In addition to guidelines and speed bumps, clear norms spell out acceptable community behavior and cue users to support each other.

Anonymous platforms have clear value but can also generate a set of problems that can be hard to combat unless there are strong, proactive content moderators. People online—whether anonymous or identifiable—behave differently than in real life and frequently not in a good way. There is an online disinhibition effect that is sometimes strengthened by being able to hide one's identity. This can result in positive behavior, such as the useful conversations that would sometimes take place on Yale's Librex, but anonymity also provided free rein for extreme hate speech on that platform.

Anonymity may not be the causal factor in toxic behavior online.[35] The online disinhibition effect does not just occur when the poster is anonymous. People post harmful content and misinformation under their real names on social media. Passing laws to ban anonymity online may not address the root causes of toxic online behavior. What seems to be more crucial to fostering better behavior are designs that nudge appropriate behavior, agreed-upon norms, and strong moderation. In particular, platforms provide cues that indicate to people what types of behaviors will be tolerated or are even encouraged. This is similar to the physical world, where you walk into a library or a frat house party and you have pretty clear social cues about what behavior will be tolerated in those spaces.

Anonymous spaces Yik Yak and Librex failed to push back on toxic behavior and quickly spun out of control. Calling on existing platforms to take greater responsibility for the types of behaviors that are tolerated will, in part, go after the source of the problem. On some platforms, anonymity can provide a safe place for people to share thoughts that they are too afraid or too shy to share under their own name. Twitter has long defended its use of pseudonymity as a way to enable self-expression and free speech, especially in countries where censorship and repression are common.

CAN WE DESIGN ETHICAL PLATFORMS?

Black Twitter—a subset of Twitter—has managed to take a platform that has serious design flaws and provide an online gathering space for Black people to engage in discussions about Black culture, strengthen social ties, share jokes, and live tweet news events to raise awareness about issues that impact the community. Black Twitter is not a separate space but rather an "open secret waiting in plain sight for those who know how to find it," with hashtags that provide a shared Black experience that users find through shared connections on Twitter.[36]

While Twitter has many identity-based communities, Black Twitter remains one of the most successful and popular. Black people were early adopters of Twitter, and Black Twitter has been a force in community building and social justice work. It is responsible for promoting effective national campaigns for racial justice, including being the first to promote #BlackLivesMatter as well as #OscarsSoWhite, which called attention to issues of race and representation in Hollywood.

Black Twitter has successfully claimed a piece of internet real estate that "decenters whiteness as the default internet identity."[37] The premiere of the first *Black Panther* film became one of many shared cultural moments for Black Twitter users. The release of the film created a slew of fans posting movie-inspired outfits, masks, and dashikis under #WakandaForever.

Many people have found ways to thrive on Black Twitter, but being on Twitter is not without its challenges. Platformed racism is the result of a design ethos in Silicon Valley that applauds a hands-off philosophy in support innovation and growth.[38] Outsiders sometimes jump on Black Twitter hashtags and post racist comments, and there are reports of police gathering information from Black Twitter. Trolls, cancel culture, and online harassment can make Twitter a traumatizing place for many people, especially those from communities of color. Algorithms designed to drive engagement end up calling attention to offensive content. Community guidelines addressing negative behavior are underenforced or are arbitrarily enforced for different communities.[39]

Twitter's design encourages simplicity, impulsivity, and incivility.[40] It cues our fast thinking rather than encouraging us to slow down and analyze content or reconsider making a post. The platform promotes negative behavior in part by allowing people to post under a cloak of anonymity. More than anything, the sheer size of Twitter—with two hundred million people posting daily—has made it extremely difficult to effectively police.

Despite its design flaws, small private groups on Twitter that provide users with the ability to hold group chats have been able to thrive. People are learning how to build smaller communities, block racist posters, and curate their own feeds to minimize the toxicity that is built into the platform. Black Twitter users have been on the forefront of using private groups to communicate with and support each other. Student networks that started among friends who attended historically Black colleges and universities (HBCU) continue after graduation to provide community and networking across these institutions.

Victoria Ogoegbunam Okoye writes about her experience as one of the only Black graduate students at Sheffield University in the UK. She started a private space on Twitter to build connections to other Black colleagues locally and globally. Okoye discusses the dearth of Black British scholars due to structural racism. The structures built into the academy perpetuate whiteness as the norm, and she realized she needed to create her own support community. She calls these private groups "constellations of relation and care" and "outer spaces." In her new private digital community on Twitter, she experienced nurturing conversations and friendships. She was able to connect with other Black scholars, some of whom were local and others who were global and whom she might not ever meet in person.

Both the larger Black Twitter public space and the small private groups provide members with valuable support and shared experiences, despite the design of Twitter, not because of it. Can we find ways to create a broader culture of ethics that can inform the design of our online spaces as we do in our physical world?

CREATING A BROADER CULTURE OF
ETHICS-INFUSED TECHNOLOGIES

Internet pioneer Brad Templeton advocates for the adoption of a new, society-wide moral theory that states that it is wrong to exploit human weaknesses and that our online spaces need to be designed in a way that does not take advantage of people. Media studies professor Mark Davis concurs, saying that we need to start making active choices in designing an internet where accountability matters and that we develop a commonly agreed-upon ethics of public culture.[41]

Many companies attempt to correct harmful AI design by approaching the issue as if it were a broken part—data or code—that just needs to be repaired. Social media platforms approach problems regarding misinformation as if there were some tweaks or tools that could correct the problem, when the entire system is structurally flawed. Putting warning labels on some antivaxxer misinformation, demoting content that incites violence, and creating a quasi-independent oversight board to rule on challenging content decisions need to be done, but they are Band-Aid solutions that address only the tip of the iceberg.[42] Companies need to establish a culture of ethical behavior at the organizational level that goes beyond simply writing a policy manual.

A new course created by the Center for Humane Technology teaches people working in the tech industry how to design ethics-infused technologies. Course participants learn to think about supporting human vulnerabilities by treating attention as sacred rather than something to be exploited, developing a mindset that minimizes harm and that holds creators accountable to those using the technology.

If we walk away from the commercial constraints that have created harmful platform designs, we can start looking at design from an entirely different vantage point. It is exciting to think about what may be possible if we design digital spaces with ethical imperatives that promote pro-social behaviors and create digital town squares that augment our physical spaces, encourage productive discussions, and deprioritize misinformation.[43]

Ending the practice of behavioral data harvesting will reduce the hyperpersonalization that assists platforms in becoming so addictive. Rather than having users opt out by clicking on a complex series of screens to stop the tracking, systems could be required to have an opt-in feature that clearly explains the ramifications of opting into a data tracking system. Features such as the "Like" button and "Retweet" button are addictive and could be eliminated or minimized. Twitter has experimented with a new design change that would require users to click on a link before sharing it. It sounds minor, but this small tweak could decrease the number of shares substantially.[44]

Safety features such as speed bumps could flag and slow down a user who is suddenly posting hundreds of videos, or we could institute constraints such as a cost—maybe in small amounts of time or money—to slow down someone after their nth post or comment.[45] Instituting a fee of twenty-five cents for posting and sharing after you have gone over your daily limit would reduce the amount of junk content. Integrity teams can help design ways to slow down postings, and these limits can also reduce the workload of moderators.[46]

Platforms also need to be designed to be interoperable so that one service can easily interact with another. This can help people transition over to better-designed public service platforms and put pressure on existing platforms to improve. Existing platforms have an enormous advantage as a result of network effects. For example, if all your friends are on Facebook, you will not want to use another platform, because your friends are still on Facebook.[47] Interoperability will let you take your friends with you. Interoperability isn't a simple twist-of-a-wrench fix, but we do have the means to create these plug-and-play systems.[48]

Replacing Google search with more ethical public service search engines, or even search engines that specialize in specific areas such as education or health, could have a huge impact on our information crisis. Google search dominates the internet, accounting for 85 percent of all searches.[49] Similar to social media feeds, Google controls much of the information we view daily, and it influences the type of content that is created. Google devotes roughly half of its first-page search results to companies that Alphabet, Google's parent company, owns.[50]

We have the technical knowledge to create search engines that are designed to promote reliable information. Germany and France have experimented with public interest search engines, and Australia is pursuing this as well.[51] Imagine what it would be like if we incentivized useful and reliable content. We do this with book publishers and scholarly content and high-quality journalism. The biggest obstacles are not in technical development but in the social and political challenges we will have to solve because large platform companies have so much power.[52]

CHALLENGES ON THE ROAD AHEAD

If you take a person and put them into a new culture, they change their behavior. If you move a person to the Netherlands, they are likely to be happier.[53] The Netherlands ranks as one of the top countries in the UN World Happiness Report and is famous for its strong social welfare policies, its promotion of mutual trust and freedom, and its strong support for equality and equity in the workplace. We like to think of ourselves as autonomous in the ways we behave and interact with others, but the structures that surround us greatly influence how we feel and how we behave toward others.[54]

The great migration to digital spaces—accelerated during the pandemic—is impacting how we treat each other. We spend too much time living in digital spaces that are designed like shopping malls and roller derbies. The challenge of figuring out how to gather groups of strangers together and facilitate social cohesion are not new. We have been wrestling with these challenges for centuries in the physical world. We've created zoning laws, public education, and third places to improve social capital and support our democracy. The school picnic and the Zumba class at the community center are informal places that can help people bond and get to know each other without focusing on political differences.

There are too few online spaces that promote the public good. We do not have to continue to be held captive by the "nine people" in Silicon Valley.[55] We can design features that benefit the public, and we can pass regulations to ensure that our interests are better served. Technology can provide us with amazing affordances—opportunities that technology facilitates—so that we can continue to build more Wikipedias and Front Porch Forums and fewer massive toxic platforms.

The biggest challenge ahead will be to dismantle the stranglehold a few tech companies have over much of our lives. These companies have promised to do better—to reduce the amount of private data they take from us and to crack down on misinformation—but we see little evidence of progress on these fronts. Leaked documents from platform companies and congressional testimony from former staffers indicate that platform companies are ramping up their efforts to maintain their market dominance by engaging in practices that exacerbate our information disorder.

Legal scholar Cass Sunstein argues that people have a right to not be manipulated. He suggests that a recent Supreme Court ruling might have implications for how platforms are designed in the future. The case had to do with a group of school employees being offered an enormous and confusing array of retirement savings plans, including some that were not well suited for them. The school said it offered freedom of choice and should not be held responsible if employees made poor choices. The court disagreed and stated that the school had some obligation to provide a more simple and practical choice architecture to help employees better understand their options and make informed choices.[56]

Platform designs that use addiction, manipulation, and surveillance take away the user's autonomy. Legal scholar Preston Torbert puts it succinctly: it is against the law "because it is wrong." [57] Torbert argues that the user's consent to allow the company to gather and monetize personal data is illegal because it goes against good morals, is unconscionable, and is contrary to public policy.[58] We need to shift from measuring new tools by how efficient they are to also evaluating them based on their ability to enhance our humanity. Platforms have significant influence over a user's experience, and that influence is carried out in opaque and complex ways that are difficult for the public to fully understand.

Misinformation researcher Joan Donovan and others argue that the right to freedom of expression is a human right that includes the right to have access to truth.[59] By creating systems that hold the world's information and using opaque algorithms that are prone to abuse, we are being deprived of our right to trustworthy content.[60] Social media platforms started out with so much promise and hope, but along the way they went down the wrong path. It is time to shift our mindset about the purpose of our digital public squares. We need to change their core designs so that they can better serve the public interest. We need to think about our online worlds as more similar to public parks and libraries and less like shopping malls and roller derbies. The problem of misinformation is not insurmountable. We can fix this.

Notes

INTRODUCTION

1. Nadja Popovich, Josh Williams, and Denise Lu, "Can Removing Highways Fix America's Cities?" *New York Times*, May 27, 2021, https://www.nytimes.com/interactive/2021/05/27/climate/us-cities-highway-removal.html; Christina Pazzanese, "Their Assignment? Design a More Equitable Future," *Harvard Gazette*, February 17, 2022, https://edib.harvard.edu/news/their-assignment-design-more-equitable-future.

2. Pazzanese, "Design a More Equitable Future."

3. Pazzanese, "Design a More Equitable Future."

4. Michael Schulman, "Bo Burnham's Age of Anxiety," *New Yorker*, June 25, 2018, https://www.newyorker.com/magazine/2018/07/02/bo-burnhams-age-of-anxiety.

5. Marc Rotenberg, "Regulating Privacy," *New York Times*, May 6, 2018, https://www.nytimes.com/2018/05/06/opinion/letters/regulating-privacy.html.

6. Dipayan Ghosh, "It's All in the Business Model: The Internet's Economic Logic and the Instigation of Disinformation, Hate, and Discrimination," *Georgetown Journal of International Affairs* 21 (Fall 2020): 129–35, https://doi.org/10.1353/gia.2020.0012.

7. Gillian Reagan, "The Evolution of Facebook's Mission Statement," *Observer*, July 13, 2009, https://observer.com/2009/07/the-evolution-of-facebooks-mission-statement.

8. Shoshana Zuboff, *The Age of Surveillance Capitalism* (New York: Public Affairs, 2019).

9. Jason A. Gallo and Clare Y. Cho, *Social Media: Misinformation and Content Moderation Issues for Congress* (Washington, DC: Congressional Research Service, 2021), https://crsreports.congress.gov/product/pdf/R/R46662.

10. Rotenberg, "Regulating Privacy."

11. Adrianne Jeffries and Leon Yin, "Google's Top Search Result? Surprise, It's Google," The Markup, July 28, 2020, https://themarkup.org/google-the-giant/2020/07/28/google-search-results-prioritize-google-products-over-competitors.

12. Heidi Legg and Joe Kerwin, "The Fight against Disinformation in the U.S.: A Landscape Analysis," Shorenstein Center on Media, Politics and Public Policy, November 2018, https://shorensteincenter.org/the-fight-against-disinformation-in -the-u-s-a-landscape-analysis; quoted with permission under a Creative Commons Attribution-NoDerivs 3.0 Unported License.

13. Julia Angwin, "The Challenge of Regulating Algorithms," Revue, October 23, 2021, https://www.getrevue.co/profile/themarkup/issues/the-challenge-of -regulating-algorithms-813783.

14. Amy O'Hara and Jodi Nelson, "Combatting Digital Disinformation: An Evaluation of the William and Flora Hewlett Foundation's Disinformation Strategy," Hewlett Foundation, October 2020, https://hewlett.org/wp-content/uploads/2020/ 10/Final-Hewlett-evaluation-report-on-disinformation-.pdf.

15. Aspen Digital, "Experts Weigh In on Scope of Commission on Information Disorder," *Commission on Information Disorder* (blog), April 20, 2021, https:// www.aspeninstitute.org/blog-posts/experts-weigh-in-on-scope-of-commission-on -information-disorder.

16. Tom Miles, "U.N. Investigators Cite Facebook Role in Myanmar Crisis," Reuters, March 12, 2018, https://www.reuters.com/article/us-myanmar-rohingya -facebook-idUKKCN1GO2PN.

17. Nik Popli, "The 5 Most Important Revelations From the 'Facebook Papers,'" *Time*, October 26, 2021, https://time.com/6110234/facebook-papers-testimony -explained.

18. Cailin O'Connor and James Owen Weatherall, *The Misinformation Age: How False Beliefs Spread* (New Haven, CT: Yale University Press, 2019).

19. R. Kelly Garrett, "The 'Echo Chamber' Distraction: Disinformation Campaigns Are the Problem, Not Audience Fragmentation," *Journal of Applied Research in Memory and Cognition* 6, no. 4 (2017): 370–76, https://doi.org/10.1016/j.jarmac.2017 .09.011.

20. K. Sabeel Rahman, "The New Utilities: Private Power, Social Infrastructure, and the Revival of the Public Utility Concept," *Cardoza Law Review* 39, no. 5 (2018): 1621–89; Alexis Wichowski, "The U.S. Can't Regulate Big Tech Companies When They Act Like Nations," *Washington Post*, October 20, 2020, https://www.washington post.com/outlook/2020/10/29/antitrust-big-tech-net-states.

21. Jameson M. Wetmore, "Implementing Restraint: Automobile Safety and the US Debate over Technological and Social Fixes," in *Car Troubles: Critical Studies of Automobility and Auto-Mobility*, ed. Jim Conley and Arlene Tigar McLaren (London: Ashgate, 2009), 111–26.

22. Wetmore, "Implementing Restraint," 111–26.

23. Wetmore, "Implementing Restraint," 111–26.

24. National Highway Traffic Safety Administration, "Seat Belt Use in 2016: Use Rates in the States and Territories," US Department of Transportation, May 2017, https://crashstats.nhtsa.dot.gov/Api/Public/ViewPublication/812417; Wetmore, "Implementing Restraint," 111–26.

25. National Highway Traffic Safety Administration, "Seat Belts," US Department of Transportation, n.d., https://www.nhtsa.gov/risky-driving/seat-belts.

26. Tom Slee, *What's Yours Is Mine: Against the Sharing Economy* (New York: OR Books, 2017), 167.

CHAPTER 1

1. Amanda Seitz and Hannah Fingerhut, "Americans Agree That Misinformation Is a Problem, Poll Shows." Associated Press, October 8, 2021, https://apnorc.org/americans-agree-misinformation-is-a-problem-poll-shows.

2. Julia Angwin, "The Challenge of Regulating Algorithms," Revue, October 23, 2021, https://www.getrevue.co/profile/themarkup/issues/the-challenge-of-regulating-algorithms-813783.

3. Kate Cox, "Facebook's Latest 'Groups' Disaster Will Only Make It More Toxic," arsTechnica, October 6, 2020, https://arstechnica.com/tech-policy/2020/10/facebooks-endless-quest-for-engagement-is-dangerous-for-us-all.

4. Tim Kendall, "Testimony of Tim Kendall," House Committee on Energy and Commerce, September 24, 2020, https://energycommerce.house.gov/sites/demo crats.energycommerce.house.gov/files/documents/09.24.20%20CPC%20Witness%20 Testimony_Kendall.pdf.

5. Safiya Umoja Noble, *Algorithms of Oppression: How Search Engines Reinforce Racism* (New York: New York University Press, 2018).

6. Dipayan Ghosh, "It's All in the Business Model: The Internet's Economic Logic and the Instigation of Disinformation, Hate, and Discrimination." *Georgetown Journal of International Affairs* 21 (Fall 2020): 129–35, https://doi.org/10.1353/gia.2020.0012.

7. Gillian Reagan, "The Evolution of Facebook's Mission Statement," *Observer*, July 13, 2009, https://observer.com/2009/07/the-evolution-of-facebooks-mission -statement.

8. Shoshana Zuboff, *The Age of Surveillance Capitalism* (New York: Public Affairs, 2019).

9. Zuboff, *Age of Surveillance Capitalism*.

10. Jason A. Gallo and Clare Y. Cho, *Social Media: Misinformation and Content Moderation Issues for Congress* (Washington, DC: Congressional Research Service, 2021), https://crsreports.congress.gov/product/pdf/R/R46662.

11. Zuboff, *Age of Surveillance Capitalism*.

12. Sean O'Kane, "New Study Will Show Misinformation on Facebook Gets Way More Engagement Than News," The Verge, September 3, 2021, https://www .theverge.com/2021/9/3/22656036/nyu-researchers-study-facebook-misinformation -engagement-election.

13. Steven Lee Myers and Cecilia Kang, "Barack Obama Takes on a New Role: Fighting Disinformation," *New York Times*, April 20, 2022, https://www.nytimes .com/2022/04/20/technology/barack-obama-disinformation.html.

14. David Dayen, "What's Up with Twitter's Content Moderation Policies?" *American Prospect* (blog), March 5, 2021, https://prospect.org/power/whats-up-with -twitters-content-moderation-policies.

15. Ethan Zuckerman, "Building a More Honest Internet," *Columbia Journalism Review*, Fall 2019, https://www.cjr.org/special_report/building-honest-internet-public-interest.php.

16. Rebecca Heilweil, "Why Algorithms Can Be Racist and Sexist," Vox, February 18, 2020, https://www.vox.com/recode/2020/2/18/21121286/algorithms-bias-discrimination-facial-recognition-transparency.

17. Heilweil, "Why Algorithms Can Be Racist and Sexist."

18. Robert Epstein and Ronald E. Robertson, "The Search Engine Manipulation Effect (SEME) and Its Possible Impact on the Outcomes of Elections," *PNAS* 112, no. 33 (August 2015): E4512–21, https://doi.org/10.1073/pnas.1419828112.

19. Matteo Cinelli et al., "The Echo Chamber Effect on Social Media," *Computer Sciences* 118, no. 9 (2021): 1–8, https://www.pnas.org/doi/10.1073/pnas.2023301118.

20. Disinformation Research Group, "Disinformation Reports," Federation of American Scientists, last modified 2022, https://fas.org/ncov/disinformation-reports.

21. Amy Ross Arguedas et al., "Echo Chambers, Filter Bubbles, and Polarisation: A Literature Review," Reuters, January 19, 2022, https://reutersinstitute.politics.ox.ac.uk/echo-chambers-filter-bubbles-and-polarisation-literature-review.

22. Alice Marwick, Benjamin Clancy, and Katherine Furl, "Far-Right Online Radicalization: A Review of the Literature," *Bulletin of Technology & Public Life*, 2022, https://citap.pubpub.org/pub/jq7l6jny; Cory Collins, "The Miseducation of Dylann Roof: How Does a Kid Become a Killer?" *Learning for Justice Magazine* 57, Fall 2017, https://www.learningforjustice.org/magazine/fall-2017/the-miseducation-of-dylann-roof.

23. World Health Organization (WHO). "Let's Flatten the Infodemic Curve," n.d., https://www.who.int/news-room/spotlight/let-s-flatten-the-infodemic-curve.

24. CBS, "Mark Zuckerberg Says Facebook Has Removed 18 Million Posts with COVID Misinformation, but Won't Say How Many People Viewed Them," CBS News, August 18, 2021, https://www.cbsnews.com/news/mark-zuckerberg-facebook-covid-misinformation-post; Daniel Zuidijk, "Misinformation Is Bigger Than Facebook, but Let's Start There," *Bloomberg Business Week*, August 30, 2021, https://www.bloomberg.com/news/articles/2021-08-30/how-to-fix-covid-vaccine-misinformation-on-facebook-fb-social-media.

25. Reuters Fact Check, "Fact Check: Indiana Doctor Makes False Claims in Viral Video," Reuters, August 12, 2021, https://www.reuters.com/article/fact-check-indiana-doctor/fact-check-indiana-doctor-makes-false-claims-in-viral-video-idUSL1N2PJ1KR.

26. "Biden Rows Back on Facebook 'Killing People' Comment," BBC, July 20, 2021, https://www.bbc.com/news/technology-57901710.

27. Sheera Frenkel and Katie Benner, "To Stir Discord in 2016, Russians Turned Most Often to Facebook," *New York Times*, February 17, 2018, https://www.nytimes.com/2018/02/17/technology/indictment-russian-tech-facebook.html.

28. Greg Miller, "As U.S. Election Nears, Researchers Are Following the Trail of Fake News," Science, October 26, 2020, https://www.science.org/content/article/us-election-nears-researchers-are-following-trail-fake-news.

29. Chuck Todd, Mark Murray, and Carrie Dann, "Study Finds Nearly One-in-Five Americans Believe QAnon Conspiracy Theories," NBC News, May 27, 2021, https://www.nbcnews.com/politics/meet-the-press/study-finds-nearly-one-five-americans-believe-qanon-conspiracy-theories-n1268722.

30. Nicholas Confessore, "How Tucker Carlson Stoked White Fear to Conquer Cable," *New York Times*, April 30, 2022, https://www.nytimes.com/2022/04/30/us/tucker-carlson-gop-republican-party.html.

31. Kayla Gogarty, "Trump Used Facebook to Amplify Fox News and Its Personalities. Of Course the Network Wants Him Reinstated," Media Matters for America, May 11, 2021, https://www.mediamatters.org/fox-news/trump-used-facebook-amplify-fox-news-and-its-personalities-course-network-wants-him.

32. John Cook, "Understanding and Countering Misinformation about Climate Change," in *Research Anthology on Environmental and Societal Impacts of Climate Change*, ed. Management Association, Information Resources (Hershey, PA: IGI Global, 2022), 1633–58, https://doi.org/10.4018/978-1-6684-3686-8.ch081.

33. Kathie M. d'I. Treen, Hywel T. P. Williams, and Saffron J. O'Neill, "Online Misinformation about Climate Change," *WIREs Climate Change* 11 (May 2020): 1–20, https://wires.onlinelibrary.wiley.com/doi/pdf/10.1002/wcc.665.

34. Treen, Williams, and O'Neill, "Online Misinformation about Climate Change."

35. Katarina Kertysova, "Artificial Intelligence and Disinformation," *Security and Human Rights* 29 (2018): 55–81, https://doi.org/10.1163/18750230-02901005.

36. Kashmir Hill and Jeremy White, "Designed to Deceive: Do These People Look Real to You?" *New York Times*, November 21, 2020, https://www.nytimes.com/interactive/2020/11/21/science/artificial-intelligence-fake-people-faces.html.

37. Stephan Lewandowsky et al., "Science by Social Media: Attitudes towards Climate Change Are Mediated by Perceived Social Consensus," *Memory & Cognition* 47, no. 18 (June 2019): 1445–56, https://doi.org/10.3758/s13421-019-00948-y.

38. Colin M. Gray et al., "The Dark (Patterns) Side of UX Design," *Proceedings of the 2018 CHI Conference on Human Factors in Computing Systems—CHI '18* (New York: ACM Press, 2018), 1–14. https://doi.org/10.1145/3173574.3174108.

39. Harry Brignull, "Types of Deceptive Design," Deceptive Design, accessed May 2022, https://www.deceptive.design/types.

40. Israr Khan, "How Can States Effectively Regulate Social Media Platforms?" *Oxford Business Law Blog*, January 13, 2021, https://www.law.ox.ac.uk/business-law-blog/blog/2021/01/how-can-states-effectively-regulate-social-media-platforms.

41. "The Philippines Social Network Has Been Weaponized by Bots to Spread Fake News," *Networks* (blog), November 12, 2020, https://blogs.cornell.edu/info2040/2020/11/12/the-philippines-social-network-has-been-weaponized-by-bots-to-spread-fake-news.

42. Knight Foundation, "Disinformation, 'Fake News' and Influence Campaigns on Twitter," Knight Foundation, October 4, 2018, https://knightfoundation.org/reports/disinformation-fake-news-and-influence-campaigns-on-twitter.

43. Knight Foundation, "Disinformation, 'Fake News' and Influence Campaigns on Twitter."

44. Knight Foundation, "Disinformation, 'Fake News' and Influence Campaigns on Twitter."

45. CMU Ambassadors, "Many Twitter Accounts Spreading COVID-19 Falsehoods May Be Bots," Carnegie Mellon University, July 2020, https://www.cmu.edu/ambassadors/july-2020/covid-falsehoods.html.

46. Aspen Institute, "Experts Weigh In on Scope of Commission on Information Disorder," *Commission on Information Disorder* (blog), April 20, 2021, https://www.aspeninstitute.org/blog-posts/experts-weigh-in-on-scope-of-commission-on-information-disorder.

47. Aspen Institute, "Experts Weigh In on Scope."; Jennifer Kavanagh and Michael D. Rich, *Truth Decay: An Initial Exploration of the Diminishing Role of Facts and Analysis in American Public Life* (Santa Monica, CA: RAND Corporation, 2018), https://www.rand.org/pubs/research_reports/RR2314.html.

48. Megan Brenan, "Americans Remain Distrustful of Mass Media," Gallup, September 30, 2020, https://news.gallup.com/poll/321116/americans-remain-distrustful-mass-media.aspx.

49. Kavanagh and Rich, "Truth Decay."

50. Alexa Wehsener, Vera Zakem, and M. Nina Miller, "Future Digital Threats to Democracy: Trends and Drivers," IST Institute for Security and Technology, 2021, https://securityandtechnology.org/wp-content/uploads/2021/05/IST-RWT_2.0-FDTD-Trends-Drivers_FA_Final.pdf; Sarah Kreps and Miles McCain, "Not Your Father's Bots: AI Is Making Fake News Look Real," *Foreign Affairs*, August 2, 2019, https://www.foreignaffairs.com/articles/2019-08-02/not-your-fathers-bots; Tristan Harris, "Our Brains Are No Match for Technology," *New York Times*, December 5, 2019, https://www.nytimes.com/2019/12/05/opinion/digital-technology-brain.html.

51. Wehsener, Zakem, and Miller, "Future Digital Threats to Democracy."

52. Paul Mihailidis, "Civic Media Literacies: Re-Imagining Engagement for Civic Intentionality," *Learning, Media and Technology* 43, no. 2 (2018): 152–64, https://doi.org/10.1080/17439884.2018.1428623.

53. Newton Minow, "Preface," in *Saving the News*, by Martha Minow (New York: Oxford University Press, 2021).

54. Marc Rotenberg, "Regulating Privacy," *New York Times*, May 6, 2018, https://www.nytimes.com/2018/05/06/opinion/letters/regulating-privacy.html.

55. Katy Cook, *The Psychology of Silicon Valley: Ethical Threats and Emotional Unintelligence in the Tech Industry* (London: Palgrave Macmillan, 2020), https://doi.org/10.1007/978-3-030-27364-4; Nicholas Carlson, "Googlers Say Larry Page Is a 'Rude' 'Egomaniacal' 'Jerk,' Who Is an 'Intellectually Honest Visionary,'" Insider, January 24, 2011, https://www.businessinsider.com/googlers-say-larry-page-is-a-rude-egomanical-jerk-who-is-an-intellectually-honest-visionary-2011-1; Ryan Mac, Cade Metz, and Kate Conger, "'I Don't Really Have a Business Plan': How Elon Musk Wings It," *New York Times*, May 3, 2022, https://www.nytimes.com/2022/05/03/technology/elon-musk-twitter-plan.html.

56. Cat Zakrzewski et al., "Facebook Whistleblower Frances Haugen Tells Lawmakers That Meaningful Reform Is Necessary 'For Our Common Good,'" *Washington*

Post, October 5, 2021, https://www.washingtonpost.com/technology/2021/10/05/facebook-senate-hearing-frances-haugen.

57. Anya Schiffrin, ed., *Media Capture: How Money, Digital Platforms, and Governments Control the News* (New York: Columbia University Press, 2021).

58. Craig I. Forman, "Solutions to America's Local Journalism Crisis: Consolidated Literature Review," Harvard Kennedy School: Shorenstein Center on Media, Politics and Public Policy, October 12, 2021, https://shorensteincenter.org/solutions-americas-local-journalism-crisis-consolidated-literature-review/#_ftn2; Keach Hagey, Lukas I. Alpert, and Yaryna Serkez, "In News Industry, a Stark Divide between Haves and Have-Nots," *Wall Street Journal*, May 4, 2019, https://www.wsj.com/graphics/local-newspapers-stark-divide.

59. Mary Fitzgerald, James Cusick, and Peter Geoghegan, "The Capture of Britain's Feral Beast," in *Media Capture: How Money, Digital Platforms, and Governments Control the News*, ed. Anya Schiffrin (New York: Columbia University Press, 2021), 188–213.

60. Nikki Usher, "How Facebook and Google Buy Off the Press," *Washington Monthly*, October 25, 2020, https://washingtonmonthly.com/magazine/november-december-2020/how-facebook-and-google-buy-off-the-press.

61. Mason Walker, "U.S. Newsroom Employment Has Fallen 26% Since 2008," Pew Research Center, July 13, 2021, https://www.pewresearch.org/fact-tank/2021/07/13/u-s-newsroom-employment-has-fallen-26-since-2008; Penelope Muse Abernathy, "Preface," in "News Deserts and Ghost Newspapers: Will Local News Survive?," UNC: Hussman School of Journalism and Media, 2020, https://www.usnewsdeserts.com/reports/news-deserts-and-ghost-newspapers-will-local-news-survive.

62. Muse Abernathy, "Preface."

63. Penelope Muse Abernathy, "The Rise of the Ghost Newspaper," in "The Expanding News Desert," UNC: Hussman School of Journalism and Media, 2018, https://www.usnewsdeserts.com/reports/expanding-news-desert/loss-of-local-news/the-rise-of-the-ghost-newspaper/#easy-footnote-bottom-9-2820.

64. Paul Glastris, "Introduction: Can Journalism Be Saved?" *Washington Monthly*, October 25, 2020, https://washingtonmonthly.com/magazine/november-december-2020/can-journalism-be-saved-2.

65. Usher, "How Facebook and Google Buy Off the Press."

66. David Ardia et al., "Addressing the Decline of Local News, Rise of Platforms, and Spread of Mis- and Disinformation Online," UNC: Center for Information, Technology, and Public Life, December 2020, https://citap.unc.edu/local-news-platforms-mis-disinformation.

67. Julie Gerstein, "Fox News Pundit Steve Hilton Pushed a Ridiculous Conspiracy Theory That Dr. Fauci Is behind the Coronavirus," Insider, January 26, 2021, https://www.businessinsider.com/fox-news-pushing-conspiracy-that-fauci-created-coronavirus-2021-1.

68. Michiko Kakutani. *The Death of Truth* (New York: Duggan Books, 2018).

69. Cailin O'Connor and James Owen Weatherall, *The Misinformation Age: How False Beliefs Spread* (New Haven, CT: Yale University Press, 2019).

70. R. Kelly Garrett, "The 'Echo Chamber' Distraction: Disinformation Campaigns Are the Problem, Not Audience Fragmentation," *Journal of Applied Research in Memory and Cognition* 6, no. 4 (2017): 370–76. https://doi.org/10.1016/j.jarmac.2017.09.011.

71. K. Sabeel Rahman, "The New Utilities: Private Power, Social Infrastructure, and the Revival of the Public Utility Concept," *Cardoza Law Review* 39, no. 5 (2018): 1621–89; Alexis Wichowski, "The U.S. Can't Regulate Big Tech Companies When They Act Like Nations," *Washington Post*, October 20, 2020, https://www.washingtonpost.com/outlook/2020/10/29/antitrust-big-tech-net-states.

72. Adrianne Jeffries and Leon Yin, "Google's Top Search Result? Surprise, It's Google," The Markup, July 28, 2020, https://themarkup.org/google-the-giant/2020/07/28/google-search-results-prioritize-google-products-over-competitors.

73. Steven Overly and Alexandra S. Levine, "Facebook Announces First 20 Picks for Global Oversight Board," *Politico*, May 6, 2020, https://www.politico.com/news/2020/05/06/facebook-global-oversight-board-picks-240150; Philip M. Napoli, *Social Media and the Public Interest: Media Regulation in the Disinformation Age* (New York: Columbia University Press, 2019).

CHAPTER 2

1. Soroush Vosoughi, Deb Roy, and Sinan Aral, "The Spread of True and False News Online," *Science* 359, no. 6380 (March 2018): 1146–51, https://doi.org/10.1126/science.aap9559.

2. S. C. Matz et al., "Psychological Targeting in Digital Mass Persuasion," *PNAS* 114, no. 48 (November 2017): 12714–19, https://doi.org/10.1073/pnas.1710966114.

3. Daniel Kahneman, *Thinking, Fast and Slow* (New York: Farrar, Straus and Giroux, 2011).

4. Judith E. Rosenbaum and Jennifer Bonnet, "Looking Inward in an Era of 'Fake News': Addressing Cognitive Bias," Young Leaders of the Americas Initiative, June 10, 2019, https://ylai.state.gov/looking-inward-in-an-era-of-fake-news-addressing-cognitive-bias.

5. Norbert Schwarz and Madeline Jalbert, "When (Fake) News Feels True: Intuitions of Truth and the Acceptance and Correction of Misinformation," in *The Psychology of Fake News: Accepting, Sharing, and Correcting Misinformation*, ed. Rainer Greifeneder, Mariela Jaffé, Eryn J. Newman, and Norbert Schwarz (New York: Routledge, 2021), 73–89; P. N. Johnson-Laird, "Mental Models and Consistency," in *Cognitive Consistency: A Unifying Concept in Social Psychology,* ed. Bertram Gawronski and Fritz Strack (New York: Guilford Press, 2012), 225–44; Rolf Reber and Norbert Schwarz, "Effects of Perceptual Fluency on Judgments of Truth," *Consciousness and Cognition* 8, no. 3 (September 1999): 338–42, https://doi.org/10.1006/ccog.1999.0386; Daniel M. Oppenheimer, "Consequences of Erudite Vernacular Utilized Irrespective of Necessity: Problems with Using Long Words Needlessly," *Applied Cognitive Psychology* 20 (October 2005): 139–56, https://doi.org/10.1002/acp.1178; Norbert Schwarz, "Metacognitive Experiences in Consumer Judgment and Decision Making,"

Journal of Consumer Psychology 14, no. 4 (2004): 332–48, https://doi.org/10.1207/s15327663jcp1404_2.

6. Nathan Novemsky et al., "Preference Fluency in Choice," *Journal of Marketing Research* 44 (August 2007): 347–56, https://doi.org/10.1509/jmkr.44.3.347.

7. Adam L. Alter and Daniel M. Oppenheimer, "Predicting Short-Term Stock Fluctuations by Using Processing Fluency," *PNAS* 103, no. 24 (2006): 9369–72, https://doi.org/10.1073/pnas.0601071103.

8. Gerd Gigerenzer, "Towards a Rational Theory of Heuristics," in *Minds, Models and Milieux: Archival Insights into the Evolution of Economics*, ed. Roger Frantz and Leslie Marsh (London: Palgrave Macmillan, 2016), 34–59, https://doi.org/10.1057/9781137442505_3; Amos Tversky and Daniel Kahneman, "Judgment under Uncertainty: Heuristics and Biases," in *Judgment under Uncertainty: Heuristics and Biases*, ed. Daniel Kahneman, Paul Slovic, and Amos Tversky (Cambridge: Cambridge University Press, 1982), 3–20, https://doi.org/10.1017/CBO9780511809477.

9. Corine Reichert, "5G Coronavirus Conspiracy Theory Leads to 77 Mobile Towers Burned in UK, Report Says," *CNET*, May 7, 2020, https://www.cnet.com/health/5g-coronavirus-conspiracy-theory-sees-77-mobile-towers-burned-report-says.

10. Gordon Pennycook, Tyrone D. Cannon, and David G. Rand, "Prior Exposure Increases Perceived Accuracy of Fake News," *Journal of Experimental Psychology-General* 147, no. 12 (December 2018): 1865–80, https://doi.org/10.1037/xge0000465.

11. Mallika Mitra, "Nike Won Its First 'Outstanding Commercial' Emmy in 17 Years for an Ad Featuring Colin Kaepernick," CNBC, September 16, 2019, https://www.cnbc.com/2019/09/16/nike-wins-emmy-for-ad-featuring-colin-kaepernick.html.

12. Michael D. Robinson and Gerald Clore, "Belief and Feeling: Evidence for an Accessibility Model of Emotional Self-Report," *Psychological Bulletin* 128, no. 6 (December 2002): 934–60, https://doi.org/10.1037//0033-2909.128.6.934; Norbert Schwarz, Eryn Newman, and William D. Leach, "Making the Truth Stick and the Myths Fade: Lessons from Cognitive Psychology," *Behavioral Science & Policy* 2, no. 1 (2016): 85–95.

13. Paul Slovic et al., "The Affect Heuristic," *European Journal of Operational Research* 177, no. 3 (March 2007): 1333–52, https://doi.org/10.1016/j.ejor.2005.04.006.

14. Carola Salvi et al., "Going Viral: How Fear, Socio-Cognitive Polarization and Problem-Solving Influence Fake News Detection and Proliferation during COVID-19 Pandemic," *Frontiers in Communication* 5 (January 2021), https://doi.org/10.3389/fcomm.2020.562588.

15. Lee Ross, David Greene, and Pamela House, "The False Consensus Effect: An Egocentric Bias in Social Perception and Attribution Processes," *Journal of Experimental Social Psychology* 13, no. 3 (2004): 279–301, https://doi.org/10.1016/0022-1031(77)90049-X.

16. Tommy Shane, "The Psychology of Misinformation: Why We're Vulnerable," First Draft, June 30, 2020, https://firstdraftnews.org/latest/the-psychology-of-misinformation-why-were-vulnerable.

17. Craig R. Fox and Martin Weber, "Ambiguity Aversion, Comparative Ignorance, and Decision Context," *Organizational Behavior and Human Decision Processes* 88, no. 1 (May 2022): 476–98, https://doi.org/10.1006/obhd.2001.2990.

18. William Hart et al., "Feeling Validated versus Being Correct: A Meta-Analysis of Selective Exposure to Information," *Psychological Bulletin* 135, no. 4 (2009): 555–88, https://doi.org/10.1037/a0015701.

19. Amy Ross Arguedas et al., "Echo Chambers, Filter Bubbles, and Polarisation: A Literature Review," Reuters, January 19, 2022, https://reutersinstitute.politics.ox
.ac.uk/echo-chambers-filter-bubbles-and-polarisation-literature-review.

20. Cailin O'Connor and James Owen Weatherall, *The Misinformation Age: How False Beliefs Spread* (New Haven, CT: Yale University Press, 2019).

21. James T. Spartz et al., "YouTube, Social Norms and Perceived Salience of Climate Change in the American Mind," *Environmental Communication* 11, no. 1 (2017): 1–16, https://doi.org/10.1080/17524032.2015.1047887; Singularex, "The Black Market for Social Media Manipulation," NATO Strategic Communications Centre of Excellence, 2019. https://www.stratcomcoe.org/black-market-social-media
-manipulation.

22. Rachel L. Kendal et al., "Social Learning Strategies: Bridge-Building between Fields," *Trends in Cognitive Sciences* 22, no. 7 (July 2018): 651–65, https://doi.org/
10.1016/j.tics.2018.04.003.

23. Kathleen H. Corriveau, Maria Fusaro, and Paul L. Harris, "Going with the Flow: Preschoolers Prefer Non-Dissenters as Informants," *Psychological Science* 20, no. 3 (March 2009): 372–77, https://doi.org/10.1111/j.1467-9280.2009.02291.x

24. Penny Visser and Robert R. Mirabile, "Attitudes in the Social Context: The Impact of Social Network Composition on Individual-Level Attitude Strength," *Journal of Personality and Social Psychology* 87, no. 6 (January 2005): 779–95, https://
doi.org/10.1037/0022-3514.87.6.779; Adam J. L. Harris and Ulrike Hahn, "Bayesian Rationality in Evaluating Multiple Testimonies: Incorporating the Role of Coherence," *Journal of Experimental Psychology: Learning, Memory, and Cognition* 35, no. 5 (September 2009): 1366–73, https://doi.org/10.1037/a0016567; Robert B. Cialdini, *Influence: Science and Practice* (Boston: Pearson Education, 1984).

25. Michael Muthukrishna, Thomas J. H. Morgan, and Joseph Henrich, "The When and Who of Social Learning and Conformist Transmission," *Evolution and Human Behavior* 37, no. 1 (January 2016): 10–20, https://doi.org/10.1016/j.evolhumbe-
hav.2015.05.004.

26. Solomon E. Asch, "Studies of Independence and Conformity: A Minority of One against a Unanimous Majority," *Psychological Monographs: General and Applied* 70, no. 9 (1956): 1–70, https://doi.org/10.1037/h0093718.

27. Stephan Lewandowsky et al., "Misinformation and Its Correction: Continued Influence and Successful Debiasing," *Psychological Science in the Public Interest* 13 (September 2012): 106–13, https://doi.org/10.1177/1529100612451018.

28. Rainer Greifeneder et al., eds. *The Psychology of Fake News: Accepting, Sharing, and Correcting Misinformation* (New York: Routledge, 2021).

29. CMU Ambassadors, "Many Twitter Accounts Spreading COVID-19 False-hoods May Be Bots," Carnegie Mellon University, July 2020, https://www.cmu.edu/ambassadors/july-2020/covid-falsehoods.html.

30. O'Connor and Weatherall, *Misinformation Age.*

31. Pennycook, Cannon, and Rand, "Prior Exposure."

32. Gordon Pennycook and David Rand, "Lazy, Not Biased: Susceptibility to Partisan Fake News Is Better Explained by Lack of Reasoning Than by Motivated Reasoning," *Cognition* 188 (July 2019): 39–50, https://doi.org/10.1016/j.cognition.2018.06.011; Robert M. Ross, David G. Rand, and Gordon Pennycook, "Beyond 'Fake News': Analytic Thinking in the Detection of Inaccuracy and Partisan Bias in News Headlines," *Judgment and Decision Making* 16, no. 2 (March 2021): 484–504, https://doi.org/10.31234/osf.io/cgsx6.

33. Bence Bago, David G. Rand, and Gordon Pennycook, "Fake News, Fast and Slow: Deliberation Reduces Belief in False (but Not True) News Headlines," *Journal of Experimental Psychology: General* 149, no. 8 (2020): 1608–13, https://doi.org/10.1037/xge0000729.

34. Pennycook and Rand, "Lazy, Not Biased."

35. Michael V. Bronstein et al., "Belief in Fake News Is Associated with Delusionality, Dogmatism, Religious Fundamentalism, and Reduced Analytic Thinking," *Journal of Applied Research in Memory and Cognition* 8, no. 1 (March 2019): 108–17, https://doi.org/10.1016/j.jarmac.2018.09.005.

36. Bronstein et al., "Belief in Fake News."

37. Bronstein et al., "Belief in Fake News."

38. Case Western Reserve University, "Why Some People Are So Sure They're Right, Even When They Are Not: Insight Suggests Ways to Communicate with People Who Ignore Evidence That Contradicts Cherished Beliefs," ScienceDaily, July 26, 2017, www.sciencedaily.com/releases/2017/07/170726103017.htm.

39. Gordon Pennycook et al., "Correction: Atheists and Agnostics Are More Reflective Than Religious Believers: Four Empirical Studies and a Meta-Analysis," *PLoS ONE* 12, no. 4 (2017), https://doi.org/10.1371/journal.pone.0176586; Bob Altemeyer, "Dogmatic Behavior among Students: Testing a New Measure of Dogmatism," *Journal of Social Psychology* 142, no. 6 (April 2010): 713–21, https://doi.org/10.1080/00224540209603931.

40. Monika Grzesiak-Feldman, "The Effect of High-Anxiety Situations on Conspiracy Thinking," *Current Psychology* 32, no. 1 (January 2013): 100–118, https://doi.org/10.1007/s12144-013-9165-6.

41. Joseph E. Uscinski, Casey Klofstad, and Matthew Atkinson, "What Drives Conspiratorial Beliefs? The Role of Informational Cues and Predispositions," *Political Research Quarterly* 69 (January 2016), https://doi.org/10.1177/1065912915621621.

42. Joshua Hart and Molly Graether, "Something's Going On Here: Psychological Predictors of Belief in Conspiracy Theories," *Journal of Individual Differences* 39, no. 4 (2018): 229–37, https://doi.org/10.1027/1614-0001/a000268.

43. Joanne M. Miller, Kyle L. Saunders, and Christine E. Farhart, "Conspiracy Endorsement as Motivated Reasoning: The Moderating Roles of Political Knowledge

and Trust," *American Journal of Political Science* 60, no. 4 (November 2015): 824–44, https//doi.org/10.1111/ajps.12234.

44. Uscinski, Klofstad, and Atkinson, "What Drives Conspiratorial Beliefs?"

45. Uscinski, Klofstad, and Atkinson, "What Drives Conspiratorial Beliefs?"

46. danah boyd, "You Think You Want Media Literacy . . . Do You?" *Points* (blog), March 8, 2018, https://points.datasociety.net/you-think-you-want-media literacy-do-you-7cad6af18ec2.

47. Daniel Goleman, *Emotional Intelligence: Why It Can Matter More Than IQ* (New York: Bantam Dell, 1994).

48. Stephanie Preston et al., "Detecting Fake News on Facebook: The Role of Emotional Intelligence," *PLoS ONE* 16, no. 3 (March 2021), https://doi.org/10.1371/journal.pone.0246757.

49. Gordon Pennycook and David G. Rand, "Who Falls for Fake News? The Roles of Bullshit Receptivity, Overclaiming, Familiarity, and Analytic Thinking," *Journal of Personality* 88, no. 2 (March 2019): 1–16, https://doi.org/10.1111/jopy.12476.

50. Richard Boyatzis, Melvin L. Smith, and Ellen Van Oosten, *Helping People Change: Coaching with Compassion for Lifelong Learning and Growth* (Boston: Harvard Business Review Press, 2019).

51. Julia Galef, *The Scout Mindset: Why Some People See Things Clearly and Others Don't* (New York: Penguin, 2021).

52. Morgan Marietta and David C. Barker, *One Nation, Two Realities: Dueling Facts in American Democracy* (New York: Oxford University Press, 2019).

53. Aviv J. Sharon and Ayelet Baram-Tsabari, "Can Science Literacy Help Individuals Identify Misinformation in Everyday Life?" *Science Education* 104, no. 5 (May 2020): 873–94, https://doi.org/10.1002/sce.21581; Sarit Barzilai and Clark A. Chinn, "On the Goals of Epistemic Education: Promoting Epistemic Performance," *Journal of the Learning Sciences* 27, no. 3 (2018): 353–89, https://doi.org/10.1080/10508406.2017.1392968.

CHAPTER 3

1. "The Top 5 Celebrities Who Love a Vape in 2021," *Chief of Vapes* (blog), March 11, 2021, https://www.chiefofvapes.com/the-top-5-celebrities-who-love-a-vape-in -2021.

2. Karen Cullen et al., "E-Cigarette Use among Youth in the United States," *JAMA* 21, (2019): 2095–103. https://doi.org/doi:10.1001/jama.2019.18387.

3. Sheila Kaplan, "Juul to Pay $40 Million to Settle N.C. Vaping Case," *New York Times*, June 28, 2021, https://www.nytimes.com/2021/06/28/health/juul-vaping -settlement-north-carolina.html.

4. Tanya Schevitz and Sandra Gharib, "New Survey Reveals Teens Get Their News from Social Media and YouTube," Common Sense Media, August 12, 2019, https://www.commonsensemedia.org/press-releases/new-survey-reveals-teens-get -their-news-from-social-media-and-youtube; Mason Walker and Katerina Eva Matsa,

"News Consumption Across Social Media in 2021," Pew Research Center, September 2021, https://www.pewresearch.org/journalism/2021/09/20/news-consumption -across-social-media-in-2021.

5. Alessio Giussani, "Competing over Truth: A Critical Analysis of EU Initiatives to Counter Disinformation (2015–2019)" (master's diss., Aristotle University of Thessaloniki, 2020); Ryan M. Milner and Whitney Phillips, "Cultivating Ecological Literacy," in *You Are Here: A Field Guide for Navigating Polarized Speech, Conspiracy Theories, and Our Polluted Media Landscape*, by Whitney Phillips and Ryan M. Milner, April 2020 (excerpt), https://you-are-here.pubpub.org/pub/fc80dnhc (Cambridge, MA: MIT Press, 2021).

6. Nathaniel Kublin, "The [BLEEP] You Can't Say on TV: A History of Swearing in Television," *Brown Political Review*, August 13, 2018, https://brownpoliticalreview .org/2018/08/the-bleep-you-cant-say-on-tv-a-history-of-swearing-in-television.

7. Peggy Orenstein, "If You Ignore Porn, You Aren't Teaching Sex Ed," *New York Times*, June 14, 2021, https://www.nytimes.com/2021/06/14/opinion/sex-ed -curriculum-pornography.html.

8. Yonty Friesem, Diane Quaglia, and Ed Crane, "Media Now: A Historical Review of a Media Literacy Curriculum," *Journal of Media Literacy Education* 6, no. 2, (2014): 35–55, https://digitalcommons.uri.edu/cgi/viewcontent .cgi?article=1162&context=jmle; R. Curtis, Project Film Now—Title III Review of Materials (Office of Education, dissemination review panel, Elizabeth Thoman Archive, University of Rhode Island, Kingston, RI, 1970).

9. Friesem, Quaglia, and Crane, "Media Now."

10. David Kamerer, "Media Literacy," *Communication Research Trends* 32, no. 1 (2013).

11. Alice Marwick et al., *Critical Disinformation Studies: A Syllabus* (Chapel Hill: Center for Information, Technology, and Public Life [CITAP], University of North Carolina, 2021), https://citap.unc.edu/critical-disinfo.

12. Lena V. Nordheim et al., "Effects of School-Based Educational Interventions for Enhancing Adolescents Abilities in Critical Appraisal of Health Claims: A Systematic Review," *PLoS ONE* 11, no. 8 (2016), https://doi.org/10.1371/journal .pone.0161485.

13. Joel Breakstone et al., "Students' Civic Online Reasoning: A National Portrait," Stanford History Education Group and Gibson Consulting, 2019, https://purl .stanford.edu/gf151tb4868.

14. Päivi Rasi, Hanna Vuojärvi, and Susanna Rivinen, "Promoting Media Literacy among Older People: A Systematic Review," *Adult Education Quarterly* 71, no. 1 (2021): 37–54, https://doi.org/10.1177/0741713620923755.

15. Renee Hobbs, "Propaganda in an Age of Algorithmic Personalization: Expanding Literacy Research and Practice," *Reading Research Quarterly* 55, no. 3 (February 2020): 521–33, https://doi.org/10.1002/rrq.301.

16. Megan Brenan, "Americans Remain Distrustful of Mass Media," Gallup, September 30, 2020, https://news.gallup.com/poll/321116/americans-remain-distrustful -mass-media.aspx.

17. danah boyd, "Did Media Literacy Backfire?" *Points* (blog), January 5, 2017, https://points.datasociety.net/did-media-literacy-backfire-7418c084d88d.

18. Alison J. Head, Barbara Fister, and Margy MacMillan, *Information Literacy in the Age of Algorithms: Student Experiences with News and Information, and the Need for Change,* Project Information Research Institute, January 2020, https://projectinfolit.org/publications/algorithm-study.

19. Shari Tishman and Edward Clapp, "Agency by Design: Exploring Documentation and Assessment Strategies for Maker-Centered Learning," Project Zero, 2020, https://pz.harvard.edu/projects/agency-by-design.

20. Tishman and Clapp, "Agency by Design."

21. "Design a Program or App to Prevent Bullying," Smithsonian Teacher, Teacher Resources, n.d., accessed May 24, 2022, https://www.tweentribune.com/teacher/lessonplans/design-program-or-app-prevent-bullying.

22. Megan Schmit, "Providence Students Develop a New Social Media Platform Catered to College Kids," *Providence Monthly,* May 27, 2021, https://providenceonline.com/stories/providence-students-develop-a-new-social-media-platform-catered-to-college-kids,37127.

23. Pete Davis, "Open Book: The Case for Commitment: Pete Davis Expands on his Commencement Address," *Harvard Magazine,* July–August 2021, https://www.harvardmagazine.com/2021/06/montage-pete-davis; Pete Davis, *Commitment in an Age of Infinite Browsing* (New York: Avid Reader/Simon & Schuster, 2021).

24. Tristian Stobie, "Reflections on the 100th Year Anniversary of John Dewey's 'Democracy and Education,'" *Cambridge Assessment International Education* (blog), September 8, 2016, https://blog.cambridgeinternational.org/reflections-on-the-100th-year-anniversary-of-john-deweys-democracy-and-education.

25. Eric Gordon and Paul Mihailidis, eds., *Civic Media: Technology, Design, Practice* (Cambridge, MA: MIT Press, 2016).

26. Gordon and Mihailidis, *Civic Media.*

27. David Buckingham, "Media Theory 101: Agency," *Journal of Media Literacy* 64, nos. 1 and 2 (2017): 12–15, https://aml.ca/wp-content/uploads/2019/09/jml-agency.pdf.

28. Gordon and Mihailidis, *Civic Media.*

29. Stephania Milan, "Liberated Technology: Inside Emancipatory Communication Activism," in *Civic Media: Technology, Design, and Practice,* ed. Eric Gordon and Paul Mihailidis (Cambridge, MA: MIT Press, 2016), 107–24.

30. Paul Mihailidis, "Civic Media Literacies: Re-Imagining Engagement for Civic Intentionality," *Learning, Media and Technology* 43, no. 2 (2018): 152–64, https://doi.org/10.1080/17439884.2018.1428623.

31. Barbara Fister, "Lizard People in the Library," Project Information Literacy: Provocation Series, February 3, 2021, https://projectinfolit.org/pubs/provocation-series/essays/lizard-people-in-the-library.html.

32. Whitney Phillips and Ryan Milner, *You Are Here: A Field Guide for Navigating Polarized Speech, Conspiracy Theories, and Our Polluted Media Landscape* (Cambridge, MA: MIT Press, 2021).

33. Rodrigo Ferreira and Moshe Y. Vardi, "Deep Tech Ethics: An Approach to Teaching Social Justice in Computer Science," *Proceedings of the 52nd ACM Technical Symposium on Computer Science Education* (March 2021): 1041–47, https://doi.org/10.1145/3408877.3432449.

34. Head, Fister, and MacMillan, *Information Literacy in the Age of Algorithms.*

35. Monica Bulger and Patrick Davison, "The Promises, Challenges and Futures of Media Literacy," *Journal of Media Literacy Education* 10, no. 1 (2018): 1–21, https://digitalcommons.uri.edu/cgi/viewcontent.cgi?article=1365&context=jmle.

CHAPTER 4

1. Richard Thaler and Cass R. Sunstein, *Nudge: Improving Decisions about Health, Wealth, and Happiness* (New York: Penguin, 2009).

2. Christopher Ingraham, "What's a Urinal Fly and What Does It Have to Do with Winning a Nobel Prize?," *Washington Post*, October 9, 2017, https://www.washingtonpost.com/news/wonk/wp/2017/10/09/whats-a-urinal-fly-and-what-does-it-have-to-with-winning-a-nobel-prize.

3. Cass R. Sunstein, "Nudges.gov: Behavioral Economics and Regulation," in *Oxford Handbook of Behavioral Economics and the Law*, ed. Eyal Zamir and Doron Teichman (February 16, 2013), https://papers.ssrn.com/sol3/papers.cfm?abstract_id=2220022.

4. Mark Petticrew et al., "Dark Nudges and Sludge in Big Alcohol: Behavioral Economics, Cognitive Biases, and Alcohol Industry Corporate Social Responsibility," *Millbank Quarterly* 98, no. 4 (September 15, 2020), https://doi.org/10.1111/1468-0009.12475.

5. Mark Nitzberg and Camille Carlton, "Technology Solutions for Disinformation," BRIE Working Paper 2021-7, Berkeley Roundtable on the International Economy (August 2021), https://brie.berkeley.edu/sites/default/files/brie_wp_2021_7_tech_solutions_for_disinformation.pdf; Xichen Zhang and Ali A. Ghorbani, "An Overview of Online Fake News: Characterization, Detection, and Discussion," *Information Processing & Management* 57, no. 2 (March 2020), https://doi.org/10.1016/j.ipm.2019.03.004; Marianela García Lozano et al., "Veracity Assessment of Online Data," *Decision Support Systems* 129 (2020), https://doi.org/10.1016/j.dss.2019.113132.

6. Christopher Mims, "Without Humans, Artificial Intelligence Is Still Pretty Stupid," *Wall Street Journal*, November 12, 2017, https://www.wsj.com/articles/without-humans-artificial-intelligence-is-still-pretty-stupid-1510488000.

7. Lia Bozarth and Ceren Budak, "Market Forces: Quantifying the Role of Top Credible Ad Servers in the Fake News Ecosystem," in *Proceedings of the Fifteenth International AAAI Conference on Web and Social Media*, ed. Ceren Budak, Meeyoung Cha, Daniele Quercia, and Lexing Xie (2021), https://ojs.aaai.org/index.php/ICWSM/article/view/18043/17846.

8. Deanna Pan, "Boston Officials Reach Out to Chinatown to Quell Coronavirus Fears, Misinformation," *Boston Globe*, February 13, 2020, https://www.bostonglobe

.com/2020/02/13/metro/boston-officials-reaching-out-elderly-chinatown-quell
-coronavirus-fears-misinformation.

9. Nitzberg and Carlton, "Technology Solutions for Disinformation"; Zhang and Ghorbani, "Overview of Online Fake News"; Lozano et al., "Veracity Assessment of Online Data."

10. Nitzberg and Carlton, "Technology Solutions for Disinformation"; Katarina Kertysova, "Artificial Intelligence and Disinformation: How AI Changes the Way Disinformation Is Produced, Disseminated, and Can Be Countered," *Security and Human Rights* 29 (2018): 55–81, https://doi.org/10.1163/18750230-02901005.

11. Kertysova, "Artificial Intelligence and Disinformation."

12. Malaka Gharib, "WHO Is Fighting False COVID Info on Social Media. How's That Going?" NPR, February 9, 2021, https://www.npr.org/sections/goatsandsoda/2021/02/09/963973675/who-is-fighting-false-covid-info-on-social-media-hows-that-going.

13. Kai Shu et al., "Combating Disinformation in a Social Media Age," *WIREs Data Mining and Knowledge Discovery* 10, no. 6 (August 2020), https://doi.org/10.1002/widm.1385; Jooyeon Kim et al., "Leveraging the Crowd to Detect and Reduce the Spread of Fake News and Misinformation," in *WSDM 2018: The Eleventh ACM International Conference on Web Search and Data Mining: Marina Del Rey, CA, USA, February 05–09, 2018* (New York: Association for Computing Machinery, 2018), 324–32, https://doi.org/10.1145/3159652.3159734.

14. Eric Szeto, Katie Pedersen, and Asha Tomlinson, "Marketplace Flagged over 800 Social Media Posts with COVID-19 Misinformation. Only a Fraction Were Removed," CBC News, March 30, 2021, https://www.cbc.ca/news/marketplace/marketplace-social-media-posts-1.5968539.

15. James Vincent, "YouTube Brings Back More Human Moderators after AI Systems Over-Censor," The Verge, September 21, 2020, https://www.theverge.com/2020/9/21/21448916/youtube-automated-moderation-ai-machine-learning-increased-errors-takedowns.

16. Shu et al., "Combating Disinformation in a Social Media Age."

17. Kate Cox et al., *COVID-19, Disinformation and Hateful Extremism: Literature Review Report* (Cambridge, UK: RAND Europe for the Commission for Countering Extremism, March 2021), https://assets.publishing.service.gov.uk/government/uploads/system/uploads/attachment_data/file/993841/RAND_Europe_Final_Report_Hateful_Extremism_During_COVID-19_Final_accessible.pdf.

18. Cox et al., *COVID-19, Disinformation and Hateful Extremism.*

19. Israr Khan, "How Can States Effectively Regulate Social Media Platforms?" *Oxford Business Law Blog*, January 13, 2021, https://www.law.ox.ac.uk/business-law-blog/blog/2021/01/how-can-states-effectively-regulate-social-media-platforms.

20. Kelly Born, "The Future of Truth: Can Philanthropy Help Mitigate Misinformation?" Hewlett Foundation, June 8, 2017, https://hewlett.org/future-truth-can-philanthropy-help-mitigate-misinformation.

21. Knight Foundation, "Disinformation, 'Fake News' and Influence Campaigns on Twitter," Knight Foundation, October 4, 2018, https://knightfoundation.org/reports/disinformation-fake-news-and-influence-campaigns-on-twitter.

22. Knight Foundation, "Disinformation, 'Fake News' and Influence Campaigns on Twitter."

23. Knight Foundation, "Disinformation, 'Fake News' and Influence Campaigns on Twitter."

24. CMU Ambassadors, "Many Twitter Accounts Spreading COVID-19 Falsehoods May Be Bots," Carnegie Mellon University, July 2020, https://www.cmu.edu/ambassadors/july-2020/covid-falsehoods.html.

25. Nellie Bowles, "The Complex Debate over Silicon Valley's Embrace of Content Moderation," *New York Times*, June 5, 2020, https://www.nytimes.com/2020/06/05/technology/twitter-trump-facebook-moderation.html.

26. Philip Lorenz-Spreen et al., "How Behavioural Sciences Can Promote Truth, Autonomy and Democratic Discourse Online," *Nature Human Behaviour* 4 (June 2020): 1102–109, https://doi.org/10.1038/s41562-020-0889-7.

27. M. Harbach et al., "Using Personal Examples to Improve Risk Communication for Security and Privacy Decisions," in *Proceedings of the SIGCHI Conference on Human Factors in Computing Systems* (New York: ACM, 2014), 2647–56, https://doi.org/10.1145/2556288.2556978.

28. Lorenz-Spreen et al., "How Behavioural Sciences Can Promote Truth"; Richard H. Thaler and Cass R. Sunstein, *Nudge: Improving Decisions about Health, Wealth, and Happiness* (New York: Penguin Press, 2009); George Pennycook et al., "Fighting COVID-19 Misinformation on Social Media: Experimental Evidence for a Scalable Accuracy Nudge Intervention," *Association for Psychological Science* 31, no. 7 (2020): 770–80, https://doi.org/10.1177/0956797620939054.

29. Gharib, "WHO Is Fighting False COVID Info."

30. Claire Wardle and Hossein Derakhshan, *Information Disorder: Toward an Interdisciplinary Framework for Research and Policymaking* (Strasbourg, France: Council of Europe, September 27, 2017); Briony Swire and Ullrich Ecker, "Misinformation and Its Correction: Cognitive Mechanisms and Recommendations for Mass Communication," in *Misinformation and Mass Audiences*, ed. B. Southwell, E. Thorson, and L. Sheble (Austin: University of Texas Press, 2018), https://brionyswire.files.wordpress.com/2019/03/swireecker2018.pdf; David Scales et al., "Effective Ways to Combat Online Medical and Scientific Misinformation: A Hermeneutic Narrative Review and Analysis," *MediArXiv*, February 2021, https://doi.org/10.33767/osf.io/rcugs; Gordon Pennycook et al., "The Implied Truth Effect: Attaching Warnings to a Subset of Fake News Stories Increases Perceived Accuracy of Stories without Warnings," *Management Science* 66, no. 11 (February 2020), https://doi.org/10.1287/mnsc.2019.3478; Katherine Clayton et al., "Real Solutions for Fake News? Measuring the Effectiveness of General Warnings and Fact-Check Tags in Reducing Belief in False Stories on Social Media," *Political Behavior* 42 (February 2019): 1073–95, https://doi.org/10.1007/s11109-019-09533-0.

31. Born, "Future of Truth"; Briony Swire-Thompson, Joseph DeGutis, and David Lazer, "Searching for the Backfire Effect: Measurement and Design Considerations," *Journal of Applied Research in Memory and Cognition* 9, no. 3 (September 2020): 286–99, https://doi.org/10.1016/j.jarmac.2020.06.006; Amy Sippit, "The Backfire Effect: Does it Exist? And Does It Matter for Factcheckers?" Full Fact, March 2019,

https://fullfact.org/media/uploads/backfire_report_fullfact.pdf; Thomas Wood and Ethan Porter, "The Elusive Backfire Effect: Mass Attitudes' Steadfast Factual Adherence," *Political Behavior* 41, no. 1 (March 2019): 135–63, https://doi.org/10.1007/s11109-018-9443-y.

32. Wood and Porter, "Elusive Backfire Effect."

33. Born, "Future of Truth."

34. Wardle and Derakhshan, "Information Disorder."

35. Donie O'Sullivan, "Doctored Videos Shared to Make Pelosi Sound Drunk Viewed Millions of Times on Social Media," CNN, May 24, 2019, https://www.cnn.com/2019/05/23/politics/doctored-video-pelosi/index.html.

36. Kertysova, "Artificial Intelligence and Disinformation."

37. Ralph Hertwig and Till Grüne-Yanoff, "Nudging and Boosting: Steering or Empowering Good Decisions," *Perspectives on Psychological Science* 12, no. 6 (2017): 973–86, https://doi.org/10.1177/1745691617702496.

38. Anastasia Kozyreva, Stephan Lewandowsky, and Ralph Hertswig, "Citizens versus the Internet: Confronting Digital Challenges with Cognitive Tools," *Psychological Science in the Public Interest* 21, no. 3 (December 2020): 103–56, https://doi.org/10.1177/1529100620946707.

39. Katherine Miller, "Radical Proposal: Middleware Could Give Consumers Choices over What They See Online," HAI Stanford University, October 20, 2021, https://hai.stanford.edu/news/radical-proposal-middleware-could-give-consumers-choices-over-what-they-see-online.

40. See NewsGuard, https://www.newsguardtech.com.

41. Wardle and Derakhshan, "Information Disorder."

42. Ciara Nugent, "WhatsApp's Fake News Problem Has Turned Deadly in India. Here's How to Stop It," *Time*, August 1, 2018, https://time.com/5352516/india-whatsapp-fake-news.

43. Filippo Menczer and Thomas Hills, "Information Overload Helps Fake News Spread, and Social Media Knows It: Understanding How Algorithm Manipulators Exploit Our Cognitive Vulnerabilities Empowers Us to Fight Back," *Scientific American*, December 1, 2020, https://www.scientificamerican.com/article/information-overload-helps-fake-news-spread-and-social-media-knows-it.

44. Shu et al., "Combating Disinformation in a Social Media Age."

45. Born, "Future of Truth."

46. Sakari Nieminen and Lauri Rapeli, "Fighting Misperceptions and Doubting Journalists' Objectivity: A Review of Fact-Checking Literature," *Political Studies Review* 17, no. 3 (July 2018): 296–309, https://doi.org/10.1177/1478929918786852; Chloe Lim, "Checking How Fact-Checkers Check," *Research and Politics* 5, no. 3 (July 2018), https://doi.org/10.1177/2053168018786848.

47. Man-pui Sally Chan et al., "Debunking: A Meta-Analysis of the Psychological Efficacy of Messages Countering Misinformation," *Psychological Science* 28, no. 11 (September 2017): 1531–46, https://doi.org/10.1177/0956797617714579; Swire and Ecker, "Misinformation and Its Correction"; Ullrich K. H. Ecker et al., "Correcting False Information in Memory: Manipulating the Strength of Misinformation Encod-

ing and Its Retraction," *Psychonomic Bulletin & Review* 18 (February 2011): 570–78, https://doi.org/10.3758/s13423-011-0065-1.

48. Leticia Bode, Emily K. Vraga, and Melissa Tully, "Do the Right Thing: Tone May Not Affect Correction of Misinformation on Social Media," *Harvard Kennedy School Misinformation Review,* June 11, 2020, https://misinforeview.hks.harvard.edu/article/do-the-right-thing-tone-may-not-affect-correction-of-misinformation-on-social-media.

49. Swire and Ecker, "Misinformation and Its Correction."

50. Swire and Ecker, "Misinformation and Its Correction."

51. Swire and Ecker, "Misinformation and Its Correction."

52. Swire and Ecker, "Misinformation and Its Correction."

53. Chris Wells et al., "Information Distortion and Voting Choices: The Origins and Effects of Factual Beliefs in Initiative Elections," *Political Psychology* 30, no. 6 (December 2009): 953–69, https://doi.org/10.1111/j.1467-9221.2009.00735.x.

54. Swire and Ecker, "Misinformation and Its Correction"; Stephan Lewandowsky et al., "Memory for Fact, Fiction, and Misinformation: The Iraq War 2003," *Psychological Science* 16, no. 3 (March 2005): 190–95, https://doi.org/10.1111/j.0956-7976.2005.00802.x.

55. Stephan Lewandowsky et al., "Misinformation and Its Correction: Continued Influence and Successful Debiasing," *Psychological Science in the Public Interest* 13, no. 3 (September 2012): 106–31, https://doi.org/10.1177/1529100612451018.

56. Joseph E. Uscinski, Casey Klofstad, and Matthew D. Atkinson, "What Drives Conspiratorial Beliefs? The Role of Informational Cues and Predispositions," *Political Research Quarterly* 69, no. 1 (January 2016): 57–71, https://doi.org/10.1177/1065912915621621; Joseph E. Uscinski and Joseph M. Parent, *American Conspiracy Theories* (New York: Oxford University Press, 2014); Roland Imhoff and Martin Bruder, "Speaking (Un-)Truth to Power: Conspiracy Mentality as a Generalised Political Attitude," *European Journal of Personality* 28, no. 1 (January 2014): 25–43, https://doi.org/10.1002/per.1930; Jovan Byford, "I've Been Talking to Conspiracy Theorists for 20 Years: Here Are My Six Rules of Engagement," The Conversation, July 22, 2020, https://theconversation.com/ive-been-talking-to-conspiracy-theorists-for-20-years-here-are-my-six-rules-of-engagement-143132.

57. Nathan Walter and Riva Tukachinsky, "A Meta-Analytic Examination of the Continued Influence of Misinformation in the Face of Correction: How Powerful Is It, Why Does It Happen, and How to Stop It?," *Communication Research* 47, no. 2 (June 2019): 155–77.

58. Walter and Tukachinsky, "A Meta-Analytic Examination of the Continued Influence of Misinformation"; Swire and Ecker, "Misinformation and Its Correction"; Bode, Vraga, and Tully, "Do the Right Thing."

59. Chan et al., "Debunking"; Swire and Ecker, "Misinformation and Its Correction"; Rose McDermott, "Psychological Underpinnings of Post-Truth in Political Beliefs," *PS: Political Science & Politics* 52, no. 2 (January 2019): 218–22, https://doi.org/10.1017/S104909651800207X; Lewandowsky et al., "Misinformation and Its Correction."

60. Walter and Tukachinsky, "A Meta-Analytic Examination of the Continued Influence of Misinformation."

61. Chan et al., "Debunking"; Jonas Colliander, "This Is Fake News: Investigating the Role of Conformity to Other Users' Views When Commenting on and Spreading Disinformation in Social Media," *Computers in Human Behavior* 97 (August 2019): 202–15, https://doi.org/10.1016/j.chb.2019.03.032.

62. Swire and Ecker, "Misinformation and Its Correction"; Ullrich K. H. Ecker and Luke M. Antonio, "Can You Believe It? An Investigation into the Impact of Retraction Source Credibility on the Continued Influence Effect," *Memory and Cognition* 49 (January 2021): 631–44, https://doi.org/10.3758/s13421-020-01129-y; Nathaniel Geiger, "Do People Actually 'Listen to the Experts'? A Cautionary Note on Assuming Expert Credibility and Persuasiveness on Public Health Policy Advocacy," *Health Communication* 37, no. 6 (December 2020): 677–84, https://doi.org/10.1080/10410236.2020.1862449.

63. Walter and Tukachinsky, "A Meta-Analytic Examination of the Continued Influence of Misinformation."

64. John Cook, Stephan Lewandowsky, and Ullrich K. H. Ecker, "Neutralizing Misinformation through Inoculation: Exposing Misleading Argumentation Techniques Reduces Their Influence," *PLoS ONE* 12, no. 5 (2017), https://doi.org/10.1371/journal.pone.0175799.

65. Swire and Ecker, "Misinformation and Its Correction."

66. Nicoleta Corbu et al., "They Can't Fool Me, but They Can Fool the Others!: Third Person Effect and Fake News Detection," *European Journal of Communication* 35, no. 2 (February 2020): 165–80, https://doi.org/10.1177/0267323120903686.

67. Swire and Ecker, "Misinformation and Its Correction."

68. Swire and Ecker, "Misinformation and Its Correction"; Chan et al., "Debunking."

69. Michael Hameleers et al., "A Picture Paints a Thousand Lies? The Effects and Mechanisms of Multimodal Disinformation and Rebuttals Disseminated via Social Media," *Political Communication* 37, no. 2 (February 2020): 281–301, https://doi.org/10.1080/10584609.2019.1674979.

70. Nathan Ballantyne, Jared Celniker, and Peter Ditto, "Can Shocking Images Persuade Doubters of COVID's Dangers?" *Scientific American*, January 25, 2021, https://www.scientificamerican.com/article/can-shocking-images-persuade-doubters-of-covids-dangers.

CHAPTER 5

1. Eric Johnson, "Tristan Harris Says Tech Is 'Downgrading' Humanity—But We Can Fix It," Vox, May 6, 2019, https://www.vox.com/recode/2019/5/6/18530860/tristan-harris-human-downgrading-time-well-spent-kara-swisher-recode-decode-podcast-interview.

2. Maelle Gavet, *Trampled by Unicorns: Big Tech's Empathy Problem and How to Fix It* (Hoboken, NJ: Wiley, 2020).

3. Newton Minow, "Preface: From Gutenberg to Zuckerberg," in Martha Minow, *Saving the News* (New York: Oxford University Press, 2021), xv, xvii.

4. Emily Stewart, "Lawmakers Seem Confused about What Facebook Does—and How to Fix It," Vox, April 10, 2018, https://www.vox.com/policy-and-politics/2018/4/10/17222062/mark-zuckerberg-testimony-graham-facebook-regulations.

5. This explanation of the "players" has been simplified. Often there are more than four players involved, as ad firms both internal and external to companies also serve as go-betweens with ad servers.

6. David Ardia et al., *Addressing the Decline of Local News, Rise of Platforms, and Spread of Mis- and Disinformation Online* (Chapel Hill: UNC [University of North Carolina] Center for Media Law and Policy, December 2020), https://citap.unc.edu/local-news-platforms-mis-disinformation/#part-2; Lia Bozarth and Ceren Budak, "Market Forces: Quantifying the Role of Top Credible Ad Servers in the Fake News Ecosystem," in *Proceedings of the Fifteenth International AAAI Conference on Web and Social Media*, ed. Ceren Budak, Meeyoung Cha, Daniele Quercia, and Lexing Xie (2021), https://ojs.aaai.org/index.php/ICWSM/article/view/18043/17846; Jason A. Gallo and Clare Y. Cho, *Social Media: Misinformation and Content Moderation Issues for Congress* (Washington, DC: Congressional Research Service, 2021), https://crsreports.congress.gov/product/pdf/R/R46662.

7. Gallo and Cho, *Social Media.*

8. Gallo and Cho, *Social Media.*

9. Note: ad servers come in different shapes and sizes; some are called ad firms. This information about ad servers has been simplified. For a more comprehensive description, see Bozarth and Budak, "Market Forces"; Megan Graham and Jennifer Elias, "How Google's $150 Billion Advertising Business Works," CNBC, May 18, 2021, https://www.cnbc.com/2021/05/18/how-does-google-make-money-advertising-business-breakdown-.html.

10. Bozarth and Budak, "Market Forces"; Graham and Elias, "How Google's $150 Billion Advertising Business Works."

11. Ruth Reader, "Google Is Placing Ads Next to COVID-19 Misinformation on Conspiracy Sites," *Fast Company*, June 11, 2020, https://www.fastcompany.com/90514329/google-is-placing-ads-next-to-health-misinformation-on-conspiracy-sites.

12. Note: retailers are also called advertisers and refer to any person or company that advertises itself or its products and services.

13. Jeff Pundyk, "Fake News: Awareness, Attitudes, and Actions of Advertisers," Conference Board, February 23, 2018, https://conference-board.org/publications/Advertiser-Fake-News-Awareness.

14. Pundyk, "Fake News."

15. Lia Bozarth and Ceren Budak, "An Analysis of the Partnership between Retailers and Low-Credibility News Publishers," *Journal of Quantitative Description: Digital Media* 1 (April 2021), https://doi.org/10.51685/jqd.2021.010.

16. Joshua A. Braun and Jessica L. Eklund, "Fake News, Real Money: Ad Tech Platforms, Profit-Driven Hoaxes, and the Business of Journalism," *Digital Journalism* 7, no. 1 (January 2019): 1–21, https://doi.org/10.1080/21670811.2018.1556314.

17. Joseph Turow, *The Daily You* (New Haven, CT: Yale University Press, 2011).

18. Braun and Eklund, "Fake News, Real Money."

19. Bozarth and Budak, "Market Forces."

20. Bozarth and Budak, "Market Forces."

21. Tim Marcin and Rachel Kraus, "Here Are the (Many) Companies Pulling Their Ads from Facebook," Mashable, June 27, 2020, https://mashable.com/article/list-facebook-advertisers-pulled-out; Tiffany Hsu and Gillian Friedman, "CVS, Dunkin', Lego: The Brands Pulling Ads from Facebook over Hate Speech," *New York Times*, July 7, 2020, https://www.nytimes.com/2020/06/26/business/media/Facebook-advertising-boycott.html.

22. Braun and Eklund, "Fake News, Real Money."

23. Braun and Eklund, "Fake News, Real Money."

24. Braun and Eklund, "Fake News, Real Money."

25. Bozarth and Budak, "Market Forces."

26. Braun and Eklund, "Fake News, Real Money."

27. Braun and Eklund, "Fake News, Real Money."

28. Braun and Eklund, "Fake News, Real Money."

29. Braun and Eklund, "Fake News, Real Money."

30. Tim Hwang, *Subprime Attention Crisis* (New York: Farrar, Straus and Giroux, 2020).

31. Hwang, *Subprime Attention Crisis*; Tim Hwang, interview by Ethan Zuckerman, *Reimagining the Internet*, Initiative for Digital Public Infrastructure, December 2, 2020, https://publicinfrastructure.org/podcast/07-tim-hwang.

32. Victor Pickard, "Restructuring Democratic Infrastructures: A Policy Approach to the Journalism Crisis," *Digital Journalism* 8, no. 6 (2020): 704–19, https://doi.org/10.1080/21670811.2020.1733433.

33. UNESCO, "Information as a Public Good," 2021, https://en.unesco.org/sites/default/files/wpfd_2021_concept_note_en.pdf.

34. "United States Free Speech Exceptions," Wikipedia, last modified December 13, 2021, https://en.wikipedia.org/wiki/United_States_free_speech_exceptions.

35. Minow, *Saving the News*.

36. Anja Bechmann and Ben O'Loughlin, *Democracy & Disinformation: A Turn in the Debate* (Brussels, Belgium: Koninklijke Vlaamse Academie van België voor Wetenschappen en Kunsten Paleis der Academiën, n.d.), https://www.kvab.be/sites/default/rest/blobs/2557/Final%20Report%20Dem%20&%20Desinfo.pdf.

37. Aspen Digital, "Experts Weigh In on Scope of Commission on Information Disorder," *Commission on Information Disorder* (blog), April 20, 2021, https://www.aspeninstitute.org/blog-posts/experts-weigh-in-on-scope-of-commission-on-information-disorder.

38. Josh Simons and Dipayan Ghosh, "Utilities for Democracy: Why and How the Algorithmic Infrastructure of Facebook and Google Must Be Regulated," Brookings Institution, August 2020, https://www.brookings.edu/research/utilities-for

-democracy-why-and-how-the-algorithmic-infrastructure-of-facebook-and-google
-must-be-regulated.

39. Minow, *Saving the News*.

40. Minow, *Saving the News*.

41. Philip M. Napoli, *Social Media and the Public Interest: Media Regulation in the Disinformation Age* (New York: Columbia University Press, 2019).

42. Simons and Ghosh, "Utilities for Democracy."

43. Minow, *Saving the News*.

44. Philip M. Napoli, "What If More Speech Is No Longer the Solution? First Amendment Theory Meets Fake News and the Filter Bubble," *Federal Communications Law Journal* 70, no. 1 (2018): 55–104, http://www.fclj.org/wp-content/uploads/2018/04/70.1-Napoli.pdf

45. Elizabeth Culliford, "Facebook Suspends Trump until 2023, Shifts Rules for World Leaders," Reuters, June 5, 2021, https://www.reuters.com/world/us/facebook-suspends-former-us-president-trumps-account-two-years-2021-06-04; Sam Shead, "Facebook Staff Angry with Zuckerberg for Leaving Up Trump's 'Looting . . . Shooting' Post," CNBC, June 1, 2020, https://www.cnbc.com/2020/06/01/facebook-staff-angry--zuckerberg.html; Amanda Seitz, "America 'on Fire': Facebook Watched as Trump Ignited Hate," AP News, October 28, 2021, https://apnews.com/article/the-facebook-papers-trump-george-floyd-hate-speech-violence-b0f6f26f3fdf889c090703cc2fa8dce0.

46. Jon Kleinberg et al., "Discrimination in the Age of Algorithms," SSRN, February 5, 2019, http://dx.doi.org/10.2139/ssrn.3329669.

47. Jeff Horwitz, "The Facebook Files," *Wall Street Journal*, September 13, 2021, https://www.wsj.com/articles/the-facebook-files-11631713039.

48. Simons and Ghosh, "Utilities for Democracy."

49. Mason Walker and Katerina Eva Matsa, "News Consumption across Social Media in 2021," Pew Research Center, September 20, 2021, https://www.pewresearch.org/journalism/2021/09/20/news-consumption-across-social-media-in-2021.

50. Israr Khan, "How Can States Effectively Regulate Social Media Platforms?" *Oxford Business Law Blog*, January 13, 2021, https://www.law.ox.ac.uk/business-law-blog/blog/2021/01/how-can-states-effectively-regulate-social-media-platforms.

51. Minow, *Saving the News*; Horwitz, "Facebook Files."

52. Ryan Mac and Sheera Frenkel, "No More Apologies: Inside Facebook's Push to Defend Its Image," *New York Times*, September 9, 2021, https://www.nytimes.com/2021/09/21/technology/zuckerberg-facebook-project-amplify.html.

53. Note: antitrust actions against large platform companies may be needed to address the ways in which these companies have reduced competition through mergers and acquisitions of competitors, but these measures will not address the issue of misinformation head on. It will just mean that a larger number of companies will also be using algorithms designed to incentivize and promote misinformation. For more on this see, for example, Minow, *Saving the News*; Pickard, "Restructuring Democratic Infrastructures."

54. Simons and Ghosh, "Utilities for Democracy," citing (1) Walton H. Hamilton, "Affectation with Public Interest," *Yale Law Journal* 39, no. 8 (June 1930): 1089–1112,

https://digitalcommons.law.yale.edu/fss_papers/4669, and (2) Breck P. McAllister, "Lord Hale and Business Affected with a Public Interest," *Harvard Law Review* 43, no. 5 (March 1930): 759–91.

55. Simons and Ghosh, "Utilities for Democracy."

56. Jack M. Balkin, "Information Fiduciaries and the First Amendment," *UC Davis Law Review* 49, no. 4 (April 2016): 1183–234, https://lawreview.law.ucdavis.edu/issues/49/4/Lecture/49-4_Balkin.pdf.

57. Philip M. Napoli and Fabienne Graf, "Social Media Platforms as Public Trustees: An Approach to the Disinformation Problem," *TPRC48: The 48th Research Conference on Communication, Information and Internet Policy*, SSRN, December 14, 2020, http://dx.doi.org/10.2139/ssrn.3748544.

58. Pickard, "Restructuring Democratic Infrastructures."

59. Not all misinformation is created for financial gain. It is important to acknowledge that different structural changes as well as beefed-up monitoring are needed to control those seeking power and/or political gain through spreading misinformation.

60. Khan, "Effectively Regulate Social Media Platforms."

61. Khan, "Effectively Regulate Social Media Platforms."

62. Khan, "Effectively Regulate Social Media Platforms."

63. K. Sabeel Rahman, "Regulating Informational Infrastructure: Internet Platforms as the New Public Utilities," *Georgetown Law and Technology Review* 2, no. 2 (February 23, 2018): 234–51, https://ssrn.com/abstract=3220737.

64. Rahman, "Regulating Informational Infrastructure."

65. Rahman, "Regulating Informational Infrastructure."

66. Claire Wardle and Hossein Derakhshan, *Information Disorder: Toward an Interdisciplinary Framework for Research and Policymaking* (Strasbourg, France: Council of Europe, September 27, 2017).

67. Katarina Kertysova, "Artificial Intelligence and Disinformation: How AI Changes the Way Disinformation Is Produced, Disseminated, and Can Be Countered," *Security and Human Rights* 29, nos. 1–4 (2018): 55–81, https://doi.org/10.1163/18750230-02901005.

68. Wardle and Derakhshan, *Information Disorder.*

69. Kalina Bontcheva and Julie Posetti, eds., *Balancing Act: Countering Digital Disinformation While Respecting Freedom of Expression* (Geneva, Switzerland, and Paris, France: International Telecommunication Union and UNESCO, for the Broadband Commission for Sustainable Development, September 2020), https://www.broadbandcommission.org//wp-content/uploads/2021/02/WGFoEDisinfo_Report2020.pdf.

70. Spandana Singh, "How Recommendation Algorithms Shape Your Online Experience," *New America* (blog), March 26, 2020, https://www.newamerica.org/oti/blog/how-recommendation-algorithms-shape-your-online-experience.

71. Rahman, "Regulating Informational Infrastructure."

72. Rahman, "Regulating Informational Infrastructure."

73. Jonathan Zittrain, "A Jury of Random People Can Do Wonders for Facebook," *The Atlantic,* November 14, 2019, https://www.theatlantic.com/ideas/archive/2019/11/let-juries-review-facebook-ads/601996.

74. Shoshana Zuboff, "You Are the Object of a Secret Extraction Operation," *New York Times*, November 12, 2021, https://www.nytimes.com/2021/11/12/opinion/facebook-privacy.html.

75. Frances Haugen, "Europe Is Making Social Media Better without Curtailing Free Speech. The U.S. Should, Too," *New York Times*, April 28, 2022, https://www.nytimes.com/2022/04/28/opinion/social-media-facebook-transparency.html.

CHAPTER 6

1. Sheera Frenkel, "The Most Influential Spreader of the Coronavirus Misinformation Online," *New York Times*, July 24, 2021, https://www.nytimes.com/2021/07/24/technology/joseph-mercola-coronavirus-misinformation-online.html.

2. Frenkel, "The Most Influential Spreader."

3. Craig I. Forman, "Solutions to America's Local Journalism Crisis: Consolidated Literature Review," Harvard Kennedy School: Shorenstein Center on Media, Politics and Public Policy, October 12, 2021, https://shorensteincenter.org/solutions-americas-local-journalism-crisis-consolidated-literature-review/#_ftn2; Keach Hagey, Lukas I. Alpert, and Yaryna Serkez, "In News Industry, a Stark Divide between Haves and Have-Nots," *Wall Street Journal*, https://www.wsj.com/graphics/local-newspapers-stark-divide.

4. Mason Walker, "U.S. Newsroom Employment Has Fallen 26% Since 2008," Pew Research Center, July 13, 2021, https://www.pewresearch.org/fact-tank/2021/07/13/u-s-newsroom-employment-has-fallen-26-since-2008; Penelope Muse Abernathy, "Preface," in "News Deserts and Ghost Newspapers: Will Local News Survive?," UNC: Hussman School of Journalism and Media, 2020, https://www.usnewsdeserts.com/reports/news-deserts-and-ghost-newspapers-will-local-news-survive.

5. Paul Glastris, "Introduction: Can Journalism Be Saved?," *Washington Monthly*, October 25, 2020, https://washingtonmonthly.com/magazine/november-december-2020/can-journalism-be-saved-2; David Ardia et al., "Addressing the Decline of Local News, Rise of Platforms, and Spread of Mis- and Disinformation Online," Center for Information, Technology, and Public Life, December 2020, https://citap.unc.edu/local-news-platforms-mis-disinformation.

6. Mike Masnick, "The Paywall Conundrum: Even Those Who Like Paying for News Don't Pay for Much News," *Techdirt* (blog), June 21, 2019, https://www.techdirt.com/articles/20190615/01285842407/paywall-conundrum-even-those-who-like-paying-news-dont-pay-much-news.shtml.

7. Joel Rose and Liz Baker, "6 in 10 Americans Say U.S. Democracy Is in Crisis as the 'Big Lie' Takes Root," NPR, January 3, 2022, https://www.npr.org/2022/01/03/1069764164/american-democracy-poll-jan-6.

8. Rose and Baker, "6 in 10 Americans."

9. Rose and Baker, "6 in 10 Americans."

10. Rose and Baker, "6 in 10 Americans."

11. Matt Walton, "It's Time That Fox News Is Considered a Political Organization, Not a News Network," Insider, March 28, 2021, https://www.businessinsider.com/fox-news-cable-political-organization-subscription-network-tucker-carlson-hannity-2021-3.

12. Walton, "It's Time That Fox News."

13. Victor Pickard, *Democracy without Journalism? Confronting the Misinformation Society* (New York: Oxford, 2020); Yago Zayed and John Woodhouse, *TV Licence Fee Statistics*, House of Commons, January 24, 2022, https://commonslibrary.parliament.uk/research-briefings/cbp-8101.

14. Pickard, *Democracy.*

15. Pickard, *Democracy.*

16. Pickard, *Democracy.*

17. Ethan Zuckerman. "The Case for Digital Public Infrastructure," Knight First Amendment Institute at Columbia University, January 17, 2020, https://knight-columbia.org/content/the-case-for-digital-public-infrastructure; Timothy Karr and Craig Aaron, *Beyond Fixing Facebook,* Free Press, February 2019, https://www.free-press.net/sites/default/files/2019-02/Beyond-Fixing-Facebook-Final_0.pdf; Victor Pickard, *Democracy.*

18. Joan Donovan and danah boyd, "Stop the Presses? Moving from Strategic Silence to Strategic Amplification in a Networked Media Ecosystem," *American Behavioral Scientist* 65, no. 2 (September 2019): 333–50, https://doi.org/10.1177/0002764219878229.

19. Donovan and boyd, "Stop the Presses?"

20. Thomas E. Patterson, "Election Beat 2020: How News Outlets Become Misinformation Spreaders," Journalist's Resource, October 27, 2020, https://journalistsresource.org/politics-and-government/news-misinformation-superspreaders.

21. Patterson, "News Outlets."

22. Susan Benkelman, "The Sound of Silence: Strategic Amplification," American Press Institute, December 11, 2019, https://www.americanpressinstitute.org/publications/reports/strategy-studies/the-sound-of-silence-strategic-amplification.

23. Julia Waldow, "George Lakoff Says This Is How Trump Uses Words to Con the Public," CNN Business, June 15, 2018, https://money.cnn.com/2018/06/15/media/reliable-sources-podcast-george-lakoff/index.html.

24. Waldow, "George Lakoff Says."

25. Joan Donovan, "How Civil Society Can Combat Misinformation and Hate Speech without Making It Worse," Medium, September 28, 2020, https://medium.com/political-pandemonium-2020/how-civil-society-can-combat-misinformation-and-hate-speech-without-making-it-worse-887a16b8b9b6.

26. Lucas Graves, "Boundaries Not Drawn: Mapping the Institutional Roots of the Global Fact-Checking Movement," *Journalism Studies* 19, no. 5 (June 2016): 613–31, https://doi.org/10.1080/1461670X.2016.1196602.

27. Department of Justice, US Attorney's Office, Southern District of Florida, "Florida Family Indicted for Selling Toxic Bleach as Fake 'Miracle' Cure for Covid-19 and Other Serious Diseases, and for Violating Court Orders," press release, April

23, 2021, https://www.justice.gov/usao-sdfl/pr/florida-family-indicted-selling-toxic-bleach-fake-miracle-cure-covid-19-and-other.

28. "Media Manipulation Casebook," Technology and Social Change Project, last modified 2022, https://mediamanipulation.org.

29. Andrew Beers et al., "Examining the Digital Toolsets of Journalists Reporting on Disinformation," in *Proceedings of Computation + Journalism 2020* (New York: ACM, 2020), https://cpb-us-w2.wpmucdn.com/sites.northeastern.edu/dist/0/367/files/2020/02/CJ_2020_paper_50.pdf.

30. Kevin Roose, "Inside Facebook's Data Wars," *New York Times*, July 14, 2021, https://www.nytimes.com/2021/07/14/technology/facebook-data.html.

31. Roose, "Inside Facebook's Data Wars."

32. Chuck Todd, Mark Murray, and Carrie Dann, "Study Finds Nearly One-in-Five Americans Believe QAnon Conspiracy Theories," NBC News, May 27, 2021, https://www.nbcnews.com/politics/meet-the-press/study-finds-nearly-one-five-americans-believe-qanon-conspiracy-theories-n1268722.

33. "Media Manipulation Casebook."

34. Padraic Ryan, "Who's Your 4chan Correspondent? (And Other Questions Storyful Thinks Newsrooms Should Be Asking after the French Election)," NiemanLab, May 22, 2017, https://www.niemanlab.org/2017/05/whos-your-4chan-correspondent-and-other-questions-storyful-thinks-newsrooms-should-be-asking-after-the-french-election.

35. Katarina Kertysova, "Artificial Intelligence and Disinformation: How AI Changes the Way Disinformation Is Produced, Disseminated, and Can Be Countered," *Security and Human Rights* 29, nos. 1–4 (2018): 55–81, https://doi.org/10.1163/18750230-02901005.

36. Ángel Vizoso, Martín Vaz-Álvarez, and Xosé López-García, "Fighting Deepfakes: Media and Internet Giants' Converging and Diverging Strategies against Hi-Tech Misinformation," *Media and Communication* 9, no. 1 (2021): 291–300, https://doi.org/10.17645/mac.v9i1.3494.

37. Sam Gregory, "Deepfakes, Misinformation and Disinformation and Authenticity Infrastructure Responses: Impacts on Frontline Witnessing, Distant Witnessing, and Civic Journalism," *Journalism*, December 11, 2021, https://doi.org/10.1177/14648849211060644.

38. David Bauder, "Detailed 'Open Source' News Investigations Are Catching On," *Boston Globe*, May 8, 2022, https://www.bostonglobe.com/2022/05/08/business/detailed-open-source-news-investigations-are-catching.

39. Paul Mihailidis and Adam Gamwell, "Designing Engagement in Local News: Using FOIA Requests to Create Inclusive Participatory Journalism Practices," *Journalism Practice*, September 16, 2020, 1–20, https://doi.org/10.1080/17512786.2020.1819381.

40. Regina G. Lawrence et al., *Building Engagement: Supporting the Practice of Relational Journalism*, Agora Journalism Center, April 2019, https://agorajournalism.center/wp-content/uploads/2019/04/201904-Agora-Report-Building-Engagement.pdf.

41. Jesenia De Moya Correa, "Community Media Keeps Outpacing Mainstream Media," NiemanLab, 2021, https://www.niemanlab.org/2021/12/community-media-keeps-outpacing-mainstream-media.

42. De Moya Correa, "Community Media."

43. See https://www.nytco.com/company/mission-and-values.

44. Erik Nikolaus Martin, "Can Public Service Broadcasting Survive Silicon Valley? Synthesizing Leadership Perspectives at the BBC, PBS, NPR, CPB and Local U.S. Stations," *Technology in Society* 64 (February 2021): 1–11, https://doi.org/10.1016/j.techsoc.2020.101451.

45. Joan Donovan et al., "Disinformation at Scale Threatens Freedom of Expression Worldwide," Harvard Kennedy School: Shorenstein Center on Media, Politics and Public Policy, 2021, https://www.ohchr.org/Documents/Issues/Expression/disinformation/3-Academics/Harvard-Shorenstein-Center.pdf.

46. Andrea Bras, "How Platforms Curate and Elevate Reliable Information during Emergencies," *NewsQ* (blog), August 14, 2020, https://newsq.net/2020/08/14/how-platforms-curate-and-elevate-reliable-information-during-emergencies.

47. Michael Kearns and Aaron Roth, *The Ethical Algorithm: The Science of Socially Aware Algorithm Design* (New York: Oxford University Press, 2020).

48. Taeyoung Lee et al., "How to Signal Trust in a Google Search," Center for Media Engagement, January 2021, https://mediaengagement.org/research/how-to-signal-trust-in-a-google-search.

49. "#TrustedJournalism," Trust Project, 2022, https://thetrustproject.org/trusted-journalism.

CHAPTER 7

1. Rosemary Rossi, "What the Zuck? Mark Zuckerberg Goes Full Cringe with Flag-Waving Surfing Video," *The Wrap*, July 4, 2021, https://www.thewrap.com/zuckerberg-july-fourth-surfboard-flag-john-denver.

2. Nik Popli, "The 5 Most Important Revelations from the 'Facebook Papers,'" *Time*, October 26, 2021, https://time.com/6110234/facebook-papers-testimony-explained.

3. Elizabeth Gehrman, "The Isolation of Social Media: Social Media Should Promote Conversation and Exchange, yet Increasingly It Doesn't," *Harvard Medicine* (Spring 2022), https://hms.harvard.edu/magazine/viral-world/isolation-social-media.

4. Tom Miles, "U.N. Investigators Cite Facebook Role in Myanmar Crisis," Reuters, March 12, 2018, https://www.reuters.com/article/us-myanmar-rohingya-facebook-idUKKCN1GO2PN.

5. Lynn, "New Survey in Vermont Reveals More Trust among Neighbors," *Front Porch Forum: Ghost of Midnight* (blog), February 14, 2018, https://blog.frontporchforum.com/2018/02/14/new-survey-in-vermont-reveals-more-trust-among-neighbors.

6. Janna Anderson and Lee Rainie, "The Future of Digital Spaces and Their Role in Democracy," Pew Research Center, November 22, 2021, https://www.pewresearch.org/internet/2021/11/22/the-future-of-digital-spaces-and-their-role-in-democracy.

7. "Where Everybody Knows Your Name," Wikipedia, last modified January 27, 2022, https://en.wikipedia.org/wiki/Where_Everybody_Knows_Your_Name.

8. Popli, "Important Revelations."

9. Anne Applebaum and Peter Pomerantsev, "How to Put Out Democracy's Dumpster Fire," *The Atlantic* (April 2021), https://www.theatlantic.com/magazine/archive/2021/04/the-internet-doesnt-have-to-be-awful/618079.

10. Ethan Zuckerman, "What Is Digital Public Infrastructure?," Center for Journalism and Liberty, November 17, 2020, https://www.journalmliberty.org/publications/what-is-digital-public-infrastructure.

11. New_ Public, "The Signals Research," New_ Public, last modified March 7, 2022, https://newpublic.org/signals.

12. Sahar Massachi, "How to Save Our Social Media by Treating It Like a City," *MIT Technology Review*, December 20, 2021, https://www.technologyreview.com/2021/12/20/1042709/how-to-save-social-media-treat-it-like-a-city.

13. Zuckerman, "What Is Digital Public Infrastructure?"

14. "Your Community Commitment," Buy Nothing Project, last modified 2022, https://buynothingproject.org/commitment.

15. "Buy Nothing Project," Buy Nothing Project, last modified 2022, https://buynothingproject.org.

16. Chand Rajendra-Nicolucci and Ethan Zuckerman, "Local Logic: It's Not Always a Beautiful Day in the Neighborhood," *Toward a Better Internet* (blog), November 30, 2020, https://knightcolumbia.org/blog/local-logic-its-not-always-a-beautiful-day-in-the-neighborhood.

17. Jack M. Balkin, "How to Regulate (and Not Regulate) Social Media," Knight First Amendment Institute at Columbia University, Occasional Papers, March 25, 2020, https://knightcolumbia.org/content/how-to-regulate-and-not-regulate-social-media.

18. danah boyd, "Knitting a Healthy Social Fabric," Medium, May 20, 2021, https://zephoria.medium.com/knitting-a-healthy-social-fabric-86105cb92c1c.

19. Jordan Guiao and Peter Lewis, *The Public Square Project*, Australia Institute: Centre for Responsible Technology, n.d., https://australiainstitute.org.au/wp-content/uploads/2021/04/210428-public-square-paper-WEB.pdf.

20. David Dayen, "What's Up with Twitter's Content Moderation Policies?" *American Prospect* (blog), March 5, 2021, https://prospect.org/power/whats-up-with-twitters-content-moderation-policies.

21. Elizabeth Culliford, Dawn Chmielewski, and Supantha Mukherjee, "Spotify's Joe Rogan Saga Spotlights Podcast Moderation Challenges," Reuters, February 22, 2022, https://www.reuters.com/business/media-telecom/spotifys-joe-rogan-saga-spotlights-podcast-moderation-challenges-2022-02-22.

22. Culliford, Chmielewski, and Mukherjee, "Spotify's Joe Rogan Saga."

23. Manoel Horta Ribeiro et al., "Do Platform Migrations Compromise Content Moderation? Evidence from r/The_Donald and r/Incels," CSCW 2021 (2021), https://arxiv.org/pdf/2010.10397.pdf.

24. New_ Public, "The Case for Integrity Workers," New_ Public, last modified February 27, 2022, https://newpublic.substack.com/p/-the-case-for-integrity-workers.

25. Elizabeth Dwoskin et al., "Racists and Taliban Supporters Have Flocked to Twitter's New Audio Service after Executives Ignored Warnings," *Anchorage Daily News*, December 10, 2021, https://www.adn.com/nation-world/2021/12/10/racists -and-taliban-supporters-have-flocked-to-twitters-new-audio-service-after-executives -ignored-warnings.

26. Roberto Scalese, "What Does It Take to Get Fired from Boston Radio?" *Boston*, July 16, 2014, https://www.boston.com/news/local-news/2014/07/16/what -does-it-take-to-get-fired-from-boston-radio.

27. Horta Ribeiro et al., "Do Platform Migrations Compromise Content Moderation?"

28. Horta Ribeiro et al., "Do Platform Migrations Compromise Content Moderation?"

29. Taylor Hatmaker, "Yik Yak Returns from the Dead," TechCrunch, August 16, 2021, https://techcrunch.com/2021/08/16/yik-yak-is-back.

30. Alessia Degraeve and Lucy Hodgman, "Anonymous App Librex Abruptly Shuts Down after Nearly Three Years of Operation," *Yale Daily News*, February 21, 2022, https://yaledailynews.com/blog/2022/02/21/anonymous-app-librex-abruptly-shuts -down-after-nearly-three-years-of-operation.

31. Volker Ralf Grassmuck, "Towards an Infrastructure for a Democratic Digital Public Sphere," in *European Public Spheres, Digitisation and Public Welfare Orientation, iRights*, ed. Alexander Baratsits (October 2021), https://papers.ssrn.com/sol3/papers .cfm?abstract_id=3937500.

32. Elinor Ostrom, *Governing the Commons: The Evolution of Institutions for Collective Action* (Cambridge: Cambridge University Press, 1990).

33. Ethan Zuckerman, "Building a More Honest Internet," *Columbia Journalism Review* (Fall 2019), https://www.cjr.org/special_report/building-honest-internet-public -interest.php.

34. Zachary J. McDowell and Matthew A. Vetter, *Wikipedia and the Representation of Reality* (New York: Taylor and Francis, 2022), https://library.oapen.org/handle/ 20.500.12657/50520.

35. John Suler, "The Online Disinhibition Effect," *CyberPsychology & Behavior* 7, no. 3 (June 2004): 321–26, https://doi.org/10.1089/1094931041291295.

36. Lisa Marshall, "How Black Twitter Has Become the New 'Green Book'—and More," CU Boulder Today, October 27, 2021, https://www.colorado.edu/today/ 2021/10/27/how-black-twitter-has-become-new-green-book-and-more.

37. André Brock Jr., *Distributed Blackness: African American Cybercultures* (New York: New York University Press, 2020).

38. Ariadna Matamoros-Fernández, "Platformed Racism: The Mediation and Circulation of an Australian Race-Based Controversy on Twitter, Facebook and YouTube," *Information, Communication & Society* 20, no. 6 (February 2017): 930–46, https://doi.org/10.1080/1369118X.2017.1293130.

39. Matamoros-Fernández, "Platformed Racism."

40. Matamoros-Fernández, "Platformed Racism."

41. Anderson and Rainie, "Future of Digital Spaces."

42. Dave Lauer, "You Cannot Have AI Ethics without Ethics," *AI and Ethics* 1 (February 2021): 21–25, https://doi.org/10.1007/s43681-020-00013-4.

43. Anderson and Rainie, "Future of Digital Spaces."

44. Carlie Porterfield, "Twitter Begins Asking Users to Actually Read Articles before Sharing Them," *Forbes*, June 10, 2020, https://www.forbes.com/sites/carlieporterfield/2020/06/10/twitter-begins-asking-users-to-actually-read-articles-before-sharing-them.

45. Massachi, "How to Save Our Social Media."

46. Massachi, "How to Save Our Social Media."

47. Cory Doctorow, "alt.interoperability.adversarial," Electronic Frontier Foundation, November 13, 2019, https://www.eff.org/deeplinks/2019/11/altinteroperabilityadversarial.

48. See, for example, Planetary or Solid, the latter developed by Tim Berners-Lee, as possible models.

49. Kyle Chayka, "What Google Search Isn't Showing You," *New Yorker*, March 10, 2022, https://www.newyorker.com/culture/infinite-scroll/what-google-search-isnt-showing-you.

50. Adrianne Jeffries and Leon Yin, "Google's Top Search Result? Surprise, It's Google," The Markup, July 28, 2020, https://themarkup.org/google-the-giant/2020/07/28/google-search-results-prioritize-google-products-over-competitors.

51. Grassmuck, "Towards an Infrastructure for a Democratic Digital Public Sphere."

52. Alexis Wichowski, "The U.S. Can't Regulate Big Tech Companies When They Act Like Nations," *Washington Post*, October 29, 2020, https://www.washingtonpost.com/outlook/2020/10/29/antitrust-big-tech-net-states.

53. David Marchese, "Yale's Happiness Professor Says Anxiety Is Destroying Her Students," *New York Times*, February 18, 2022, https://www.nytimes.com/interactive/2022/02/21/magazine/laurie-santos-interview.html.

54. Marchese, "Anxiety Is Destroying Her Students."

55. Michael Schulman, "Bo Burnham's Age of Anxiety," *New Yorker*, June 25, 2018, https://www.newyorker.com/magazine/2018/07/02/bo-burnhams-age-of-anxiety.

56. Cass R. Sunstein, "Hidden Terms, High Cancellation Fees, Complex Disclaimers Should Be Forbidden," *Boston Globe*, March 3, 2022, https://www.bostonglobe.com/2022/03/17/opinion/hidden-terms-high-cancellation-fees-complex-disclaimers-should-be-forbidden.

57. Preston M. Torbert, "'Because It Is Wrong': An Essay on the Immorality and Illegality of the Online Service Contracts of Google and Facebook," *Case Western Reserve Journal of Law and Technology and the Internet* 12, no. 1 (2021), https://scholarlycommons.law.case.edu/jolti/vol12/iss1/2.

58. Torbert, "'Because It Is Wrong.'"

59. Joan Donovan et al., "Disinformation at Scale Threatens Freedom of Expression Worldwide," Shorenstein Center on Media, Politics and Public Policy, February

15, 2021, https://www.ohchr.org/sites/default/files/Documents/Issues/Expression/disinformation/3-Academics/Harvard-Shorenstein-Center.pdf.
    60. Joan Donovan et al., "Disinformation."

Bibliography

Abernathy, Penelope Muse. "Preface." In "News Deserts and Ghost Newspapers: Will Local News Survive?" UNC: Hussman School of Journalism and Media, 2020. https://www.usnewsdeserts.com/reports/news-deserts-and-ghost-newspapers-will-local-news-survive.

———. "The Rise of the Ghost Newspaper." In "The Expanding News Desert." UNC: Hussman School of Journalism and Media, 2018. https://www.usnewsdeserts.com/reports/expanding-news-desert/loss-of-local-news/the-rise-of-the-ghost-newspaper/#easy-footnote-bottom-9-2820.

Altemeyer, Bob. "Dogmatic Behavior among Students: Testing a New Measure of Dogmatism." *Journal of Social Psychology* 142, no. 6 (April 2010): 713–21. https://doi.org/10.1080/00224540209603931.

Alter, Adam L., and Daniel M. Oppenheimer. "Predicting Short-Term Stock Fluctuations by Using Processing Fluency." *PNAS* 103, no. 24 (2006): 9369–72. https://doi.org/10.1073/pnas.0601071103.

Anderson, Janna, and Lee Rainie. "The Future of Digital Spaces and Their Role in Democracy." Pew Research Center, November 22, 2021. https://www.pewresearch.org/internet/2021/11/22/the-future-of-digital-spaces-and-their-role-in-democracy.

Angwin, Julia. "The Challenge of Regulating Algorithms." Revue, October 23, 2021. https://www.getrevue.co/profile/themarkup/issues/the-challenge-of-regulating-algorithms-813783.

Applebaum, Anne, and Peter Pomerantsev. "How To Put Out Democracy's Dumpster Fire." *The Atlantic* (April 2021). https://www.theatlantic.com/magazine/archive/2021/04/the-internet-you're-your-have-to-be-awful/618079.

Ardia, David, Evan Ringel, Victoria Smith Ekstrand, and Ashley Fox. *Addressing the Decline of Local News, Rise of Platforms, and Spread of Mis- and Disinformation Online.* Chapel Hill: UNC [University of North Carolina] Center for Media Law and Policy, December 2020. https://citap.unc.edu/local-news-platforms-mis-disinformation.

Arguedas, Amy Ross, Craig T. Robertson, Richard Fletcher, and Rasmus Kleis Neilsen. "Echo Chambers, Filter Bubbles, and Polarisation: A Literature Review." Reuters, January 19, 2022. https://reutersinstitute.politics.ox.ac.uk/echo -chambers-filter-bubbles-and-polarisation-literature-review.

Asch, Solomon E. "Studies of Independence and Conformity: A Minority of One against a Unanimous Majority." *Psychological Monographs: General and Applied* 70, no. 9 (1956): 1–70. https://doi.org/10.1037/h0093718.

Aspen Digital. "Experts Weigh In on Scope of Commission on Information Disorder." *Commission on Information Disorder* (blog), April 20, 2021. https://www.aspenin-stitute.org/blog-posts/experts-weigh-in-on-scope-of-commission-on-information -disorder.

Bago, Bence, David G. Rand, and Gordon Pennycook. "Fake News, Fast and Slow: Deliberation Reduces Belief in False (but Not True) News Headlines." *Journal of Experimental Psychology: General* 149, no. 8 (2020): 1608–13. https://doi.org/10 .1037/xge0000729.

Balkin, Jack M. "How to Regulate (and Not Regulate) Social Media." Knight First Amendment Institute at Columbia University, Occasional Papers, March 25, 2020. https://knightcolumbia.org/content/how-to-regulate-and-not-regulate -social-media.

———. "Information Fiduciaries and the First Amendment." *UC Davis Law Review* 49, no. 4 (April 2016): 1183–234. https://lawreview.law.ucdavis.edu/issues/49/4/ Lecture/49-4_Balkin.pdf.

Ballantyne, Nathan, Jared Celniker, and Peter Ditto. "Can Shocking Images Persuade Doubters of COVID's Dangers?" *Scientific American*, January 25, 2021. https://www .scientificamerican.com/article/can-shocking-images-persuade-doubters-of-covids -dangers.

Barzilai, Sarit, and Clark A. Chinn. "On the Goals of Epistemic Education: Promoting Epistemic Performance." *Journal of the Learning Sciences* 27, no. 3 (2018): 353–89. https://doi.org/10.1080/10508406.2017.1392968.

Bauder, David. "Detailed 'Open Source' News Investigations Are Catching On." *Boston Globe*, May 8, 2022. https://www.bostonglobe.com/2022/05/08/business/ detailed-open-source-news-investigations-are-catching.

Bechmann, Anja, and Ben O'Loughlin. *Democracy & Disinformation: A Turn in the Debate*. Brussels, Belgium: Koninklijke Vlaamse Academie van België voor Weten-schappen en Kunsten Paleis der Academiën, n.d. https://www.kvab.be/sites/de-fault/rest/blobs/2557/Final%20Report%20Dem%20&%20Desinfo.pdf.

Beers, Andrew, Melinda McClure Haughey, Ahmer Arif, and Kate Starbird. "Examining the Digital Toolsets of Journalists Reporting on Disinformation." In *Proceedings of Computation + Journalism 2020*. New York: ACM, 2020. https://doi.org/10 .1145/1122445.1122456.

Benkelman, Susan. "The Sound of Silence: Strategic Amplification," American Press Institute, December 11, 2019. https://www.americanpressinstitute.org/publica-tions/reports/strategy-studies/the-sound-of-silence-strategic-amplification.

"Biden Rows Back on Facebook 'Killing People' Comment." BBC, July 20, 2021. https://www.bbc.com/news/technology-57901710.

Bode, Leticia, and Emily K. Vraga. "See Something, Say Something: Correction of Global Health Misinformation on Social Media." *Health Communication* 33, no. 9 (2018): 1131–40. https://doi.org/10.1080/10410236.2017.1331312.

Bode, Leticia, Emily K. Vraga, and Melissa Tully. "Do the Right Thing: Tone May Not Affect Correction of Misinformation on Social Media." *Harvard Kennedy School Misinformation Review*, June 11, 2020. https://misinforeview.hks.harvard.edu/article/do-the-right-thing-tone-may-not-affect-correction-of-misinformation-on-social-media.

Bontcheva, Kalina, and Julie Posetti, eds., *Balancing Act: Countering Digital Disinformation While Respecting Freedom of Expression.* Geneva, Switzerland, and Paris, France: International Telecommunication Union and UNESCO, for the Broadband Commission for Sustainable Development, September 2020. https://www.broadbandcommission.org//wp-content/uploads/2021/02/WGFoEDisinfo_Report2020.pdf.

Born, Kelly. "The Future of Truth: Can Philanthropy Help Mitigate Misinformation?" Hewlett Foundation, June 8, 2017. https://hewlett.org/future-truth-can-philanthropy-help-mitigate-misinformation.

Bowles, Nellie. "The Complex Debate over Silicon Valley's Embrace of Content Moderation." *New York Times.* June 5, 2020. https://www.nytimes.com/2020/06/05/technology/twitter-trump-facebook-moderation.html.

Boyatzis, Richard, Melvin L. Smith, and Ellen Van Oosten. *Helping People Change: Coaching with Compassion for Lifelong Learning and Growth.* Boston: Harvard Business Review Press, 2019.

boyd, danah. "Did Media Literacy Backfire?" *Points* (blog), January 5, 2017. https://points.datasociety.net/did-media-literacy-backfire-7418c084d88d.

———. "Knitting a Healthy Social Fabric." Medium, May 20, 2021. https://zephoria.medium.com/knitting-a-healthy-social-fabric-86105cb92c1c.

———. "You Think You Want Media Literacy . . . Do You?" *Points* (blog), March 8, 2018. https://points.datasociety.net/you-think-you-want-medialiteracy-do-you-7cad6af18ec2.

Bozarth, Lia, and Ceren Budak. "An Analysis of the Partnership between Retailers and Low-Credibility News Publishers." *Journal of Quantitative Description: Digital Media* 1 (April 2021). https://doi.org/10.51685/jqd.2021.010.

———. "Market Forces: Quantifying the Role of Top Credible Ad Servers in the Fake News Ecosystem." In *Proceedings of the Fifteenth International AAAI Conference on Web and Social Media,* edited by Ceren Budak, Meeyoung Cha, Daniele Quercia, and Lexing Xie (2021). https://ojs.aaai.org/index.php/ICWSM/article/view/18043/17846.

Bras, Andrea. "How Platforms Curate and Elevate Reliable Information during Emergencies." *NewsQ* (blog), August 14, 2020. https://newsq.net/2020/08/14/how-platforms-curate-and-elevate-reliable-information-during-emergencies.

Braun, Joshua A., and Jessica L. Eklund. "Fake News, Real Money: Ad Tech Platforms, Profit-Driven Hoaxes, and the Business of Journalism." *Digital Journalism* 7, no.1 (January 2019): 1–21. https://doi.org/10.1080/21670811.2018.1556314.

Breakstone, Joel, Mark Smith, Sam Wineburg, Amie Rapaport, Jill Carle, M. Garland, and Anna Saavedra. "Students' Civic Online Reasoning: A National Portrait." Stan-

ford History Education Group & Gibson Consulting, 2019. https://purl.stanford
.edu/gf151tb4868.

Brenan, Megan. "Americans Remain Distrustful of Mass Media." Gallup, September
30, 2020. https://news.gallup.com/poll/321116/americans-remain-distrustful-mass
-media.aspx.

Brignull, Harry. "Types of Deceptive Design." Deceptive Design, accessed May 2022.
https://www.deceptive.design/types.

Brock, André, Jr. *Distributed Blackness: African American Cybercultures*. New York: New
York University Press, 2020.

Bronstein, Michael V., Gordon Pennycook, Adam Bear, David G. Rand, and Tyrone
D. Cannon. "Belief in Fake News Is Associated with Delusionality, Dogmatism,
Religious Fundamentalism, and Reduced Analytic Thinking." *Journal of Applied
Research in Memory and Cognition* 8, no. 1 (March 2019): 108–17. https://doi.org/
10.1016/j.jarmac.2018.09.005.

Brown, Sara. "The Case for New Social Media Business Models." MIT Management,
September 22, 2021. https://mitsloan.mit.edu/ideas-made-to-matter/case-new
-social-media-business-models.

Buckingham, David. "Media Theory 101: Agency." *Journal of Media Literacy* 64, nos.
1 and 2, (2017): 12–15. https://aml.ca/wp-content/uploads/2019/09/jml-agency
.pdf.

Bulger, Monica, and Patrick Davison. "The Promises, Challenges and Futures of
Media Literacy." *Journal of Media Literacy Education* 10, no. 1 (2018): 1–21. https://
digitalcommons.uri.edu/cgi/viewcontent.cgi?article=1365&context=jmle.

Byford, Jovan. "I've Been Talking to Conspiracy Theorists for 20 Years: Here Are
My Six Rules of Engagement." The Conversation, July 22, 2020. https://thecon-
versation.com/ive-been-talking-to-conspiracy-theorists-for-20-years-here-are-my
-six-rules-of-engagement-143132.

Carlson, Nicholas. "Googlers Say Larry Page Is a 'Rude' 'Egomaniacal' 'Jerk,' Who
Is an 'Intellectually Honest Visionary.'" Insider, January 24, 2011. https://www
.businessinsider.com/googlers-say-larry-page-is-a-rude-egomanical-jerk-who-is-an
-intellectually-honest-visionary-2011-1.

Case Western Reserve University. "Why Some People Are So Sure They're Right,
Even When They Are Not: Insight Suggests Ways to Communicate with People
Who Ignore Evidence that Contradicts Cherished Beliefs." ScienceDaily, July 26,
2017. https://www.sciencedaily.com/releases/2017/07/170726103017.htm.

CBS. "Mark Zuckerberg Says Facebook Has Removed 18 Million Posts with COVID
Misinformation, but Won't Say How Many People Viewed Them." CBS News,
August 18, 2021. https://www.cbsnews.com/news/mark-zuckerberg-facebook
-covid-misinformation-post.

Chan, Man-pui Sally, Christopher R. Jones, Kathleen Hall Jamieson, and Dolores
Albarracín. "Debunking: A Meta-Analysis of the Psychological Efficacy of Messages
Countering Misinformation." *Psychological Science* 28, no. 11 (September 2017):
1531–46. https://doi.org/10.1177/0956797617714579.

Chayka, Kyle. "What Google Search Isn't Showing You." *New Yorker*, March 10, 2022. https://www.newyorker.com/culture/infinite-scroll/what-google-search-isnt-showing-you.

Cialdini, Robert B. *Influence: Science and Practice*. Boston: Pearson Education, 1984.

Cinelli, Matteo, Gianmarco De Francisci Morales, Alessandro Galeazzi, Walter Quattrociocchi, and Michele Starnini. "The Echo Chamber Effect on Social Media." *Computer Sciences* 118, no. 9 (2021): 1–8. https://www.pnas.org/doi/10.1073/pnas.2023301118.

Clayton, Katherine, Spencer Blair, Jonathan A. Busam, Samuel Forstner, John Glance, Guy Green, Anna Kawata et al. "Real Solutions for Fake News? Measuring the Effectiveness of General Warnings and Fact-Check Tags in Reducing Belief in False Stories on Social Media." *Political Behavior* 42 (February 2019): 1073–95. https://doi.org/10.1007/s11109-019-09533-0.

CMU Ambassadors. "Many Twitter Accounts Spreading COVID-19 Falsehoods May Be Bots." Carnegie Mellon University, July 2020. https://www.cmu.edu/ambassadors/july-2020/covid-falsehoods.html.

Colliander, Jonas. "This Is Fake News: Investigating the Role of Conformity to Other Users' Views When Commenting on and Spreading Disinformation in Social Media." *Computers in Human Behavior* 97 (August 2019): 202–15. https://doi.org/10.1016/j.chb.2019.03.032.

Collins, Cory. "The Miseducation of Dylann Roof: How Does a Kid Become a Killer?" *Learning for Justice Magazine* 57 (Fall 2017). https://www.learningforjustice.org/magazine/fall-2017/the-miseducation-of-dylann-roof.

Confessore, Nicholas. "How Tucker Carlson Stoked White Fear to Conquer Cable." *New York Times*, April 30, 2022. https://www.nytimes.com/2022/04/30/us/tucker-carlson-gop-republican-party.html.

Cook, John. "Understanding and Countering Misinformation about Climate Change." In *Research Anthology on Environmental and Societal Impacts of Climate Change*, edited by Management Association, Information Resources, 1633–58. Hershey, PA: IGI Global, 2022. https://doi.org/10.4018/978-1-6684-3686-8.ch081.

Cook, John, Stephan Lewandowsky, and Ullrich K. H. Ecker. "Neutralizing Misinformation through Inoculation: Exposing Misleading Argumentation Techniques Reduces Their Influence." *PLoS ONE* 12, no. 5 (2017). https://doi.org/10.1371/journal.pone.0175799.

Cook, Katy. *The Psychology of Silicon Valley: Ethical Threats and Emotional Unintelligence in the Tech Industry*. London: Palgrave Macmillan, 2020. https://doi.org/10.1007/978-3-030-27364-4.

Corbu, Nicoleta, Denisa-Adriana Oprea, Elena Negrea-Busuioc, and Loredana Radu. "They Can't Fool Me, but They Can Fool the Others!: Third Person Effect and Fake News Detection." *European Journal of Communication* 35, no. 2 (February 2020): 165–80. https://doi.org/10.1177/0267323120903686.

Corriveau, Kathleen H., Maria Fusaro, and Paul L. Harris. "Going with the Flow: Preschoolers Prefer Non-Dissenters as Informants." *Psychological Science* 20, no. 3 (March 2009): 372–77. https://doi.org/10.1111/j.1467-9280.2009.02291.x.

Cox, Kate. "Facebook's Latest 'Groups' Disaster Will Only Make It More Toxic." arsTechnica, October 6, 2020. https://arstechnica.com/tech-policy/2020/10/facebooks-endless-quest-for-engagement-is-dangerous-for-us-all.

Cox, Kate, Theodora Ogden, Victoria Jordan, and Pauline Paille. *COVID-19, Disinformation and Hateful Extremism: Literature Review Report.* Cambridge, UK: RAND Europe for the Commission for Countering Extremism, March 2021. https://assets.publishing.service.gov.uk/government/uploads/system/uploads/attachment_data/file/993841/RAND_Europe_Final_Report_Hateful_Extremism_During_COVID-19_Final_accessible.pdf.

Cullen, Karen A., Andrea S. Gentzke, Michael D. Sawdey, Joanne T. Chang, Gabriella M. Anic, Teresa W. Wang, MeLisa R. Creamer, et al. "E-Cigarette Use among Youth in the United States." *JAMA* 21 (2019): 2095–103. https://doi.org/doi:10.1001/jama.2019.18387.

Culliford, Elizabeth. "Facebook Suspends Trump until 2023, Shifts Rules for World Leaders." Reuters, June 5, 2021. https://www.reuters.com/world/us/facebook-suspends-former-us-president-trumps-account-two-years-2021-06-04.

Culliford, Elizabeth, Dawn Chmielewski, and Supantha Mukherjee. "Spotify's Joe Rogan Saga Spotlights Podcast Moderation Challenges." Reuters, February 22, 2022. https://www.reuters.com/business/media-telecom/spotifys-joe-rogan-saga-spotlights-podcast-moderation-challenges-2022-02-22.

Davis, Pete. *Dedicated: The Case for Commitment in an Age of Infinite Browsing.* New York: Avid Reader/Simon & Schuster, 2021.

———. "Open Book: The Case for Commitment: Pete Davis Expands on His Commencement Address." *Harvard Magazine,* July–August 2021. https://www.harvardmagazine.com/2021/06/montage-pete-davis.

Dayen, David. "What's Up with Twitter's Content Moderation Policies?" *American Prospect* (blog), March 5, 2021. https://prospect.org/power/whats-up-with-twitters-content-moderation-policies.

Degraeve, Alessia, and Lucy Hodgman. "Anonymous App Librex Abruptly Shuts Down after Nearly Three Years of Operation." *Yale Daily News,* February 21, 2022. https://yaledailynews.com/blog/2022/02/21/anonymous-app-librex-abruptly-shuts-down-after-nearly-three-years-of-operation.

De Moya Correa, Jesenia. "Community Media Keeps Outpacing Mainstream Media." NiemanLab, 2021. https://www.niemanlab.org/2021/12/community-media-keeps-outpacing-mainstream-media.

Department of Justice, US Attorney's Office, Southern District of Florida. "Florida Family Indicted for Selling Toxic Bleach as Fake 'Miracle' Cure for Covid-19 and Other Serious Diseases, and for Violating Court Orders." Press release, April 23, 2021. https://www.justice.gov/usao-sdfl/pr/florida-family-indicted-selling-toxic-bleach-fake-miracle-cure-covid-19-and-other.

"Design a Program or App to Prevent Bullying," Smithsonian Teacher, Teacher Resources, n.d. Accessed May 24, 2022. https://www.tweentribune.com/teacher/lessonplans/design-program-or-app-prevent-bullying.

Disinformation Research Group. "Disinformation Reports." Federation of American Scientists, last modified 2022. https://fas.org/ncov/disinformation-reports.

Doctorow, Cory. "alt.interoperability.adversarial." Electronic Frontier Foundation, November 13, 2019. https://www.eff.org/deeplinks/2019/11/altinteroperability-adversarial.

Donovan, Joan. "How Civil Society Can Combat Misinformation and Hate Speech without Making It Worse." Medium, September 28, 2020. https://medium.com/political-pandemonium-2020/how-civil-society-can-combat-misinformation-and-hate-speech-without-making-it-worse-887a16b8b9b6.

Donovan, Joan, and danah boyd. "Stop the Presses? Moving from Strategic Silence to Strategic Amplification in a Networked Media Ecosystem." *American Behavioral Scientist* 65, no. 2 (September 2019): 333–50. https://doi.org/10.1177/0002764219878229.

Donovan, Joan, Emily Dreyfuss, Gabrielle Lim, and Brian Friedberg. "Disinformation at Scale Threatens Freedom of Expression Worldwide." Shorenstein Center on Media, Politics and Public Policy, February 15, 2021. https://www.ohchr.org/sites/default/files/Documents/Issues/Expression/disinformation/3-Academics/Harvard-Shorenstein-Center.pdf.

Dwoskin, Elizabeth, Will Oremus, Craig Timberg, and Nitasha Tiku, the *Washington Post*. "Racists and Taliban Supporters Have Flocked to Twitter's New Audio Service after Executives Ignored Warnings." *Anchorage Daily News*, December 10, 2021. https://www.adn.com/nation-world/2021/12/10/racists-and-taliban-supporters-have-flocked-to-twitters-new-audio-service-after-executives-ignored-warnings.

Ecker, Ullrich K. H., and Luke M. Antonio. "Can You Believe It? An Investigation into the Impact of Retraction Source Credibility on the Continued Influence Effect." *Memory and Cognition* 49 (January 2021): 631–44. https://doi.org/10.3758/s13421-020-01129-y.

Ecker, Ullrich K. H., Stephan Lewandowsky, Briony Swire, and Darren Chang. "Correcting False Information in Memory: Manipulating the Strength of Misinformation Encoding and Its Retraction." *Psychonomic Bulletin & Review* 18 (February 2011): 570–78. https://doi.org/10.3758/s13423-011-0065-1.

Epstein, Robert, and Ronald E. Robertson. "The Search Engine Manipulation Effect (SEME) and Its Possible Impact on the Outcomes of Elections." *PNAS* 112, no. 33 (August 2015): E4512–21. https://doi.org/10.1073/pnas.1419828112.

Ferreira, Rodrigo, and Moshe Y. Vardi. "Deep Tech Ethics: An Approach to Teaching Social Justice in Computer Science." *Proceedings of the 52nd ACM Technical Symposium on Computer Science Education* (March 2021): 1041–47. https://doi.org/10.1145/3408877.3432449.

Fister, Barbara. "Lizard People in the Library." Project Information Literacy: Provocation Series, February 3, 2021. https://projectinfolit.org/pubs/provocation-series/essays/lizard-people-in-the-library.html.

Forman, Craig I. "Solutions to America's Local Journalism Crisis: Consolidated Literature Review." Harvard Kennedy School: Shorenstein Center on Media, Politics and Public Policy, October 12, 2021. https://shorensteincenter.org/solutions-americas-local-journalism-crisis-consolidated-literature-review/#_ftn2.

Fox, Craig R., and Martin Weber. "Ambiguity Aversion, Comparative Ignorance, and Decision Context." *Organizational Behavior and Human Decision Processes* 88, no. 1 (May 2022): 476–98. https://doi.org/10.1006/obhd.2001.2990.

Frenkel, Sheera, and Katie Benner. "To Stir Discord in 2016, Russians Turned Most Often to Facebook." *New York Times*, February 17, 2018. https://www.nytimes.com/2018/02/17/technology/indictment-russian-tech-facebook.html.

Friesem, Yonty, Diane Quaglia, and Ed Crane. "Media Now: A Historical Review of a Media Literacy Curriculum." *Journal of Media Literacy Education* 6, no. 2 (2014): 35–55. https://digitalcommons.uri.edu/cgi/viewcontent.cgi?article=1162&context=jmle.

Galef, Julia. *The Scout Mindset: Why Some People See Things Clearly and Others Don't.* New York: Penguin, 2021.

Gallo, Jason A., and Clare Y. Cho. *Social Media: Misinformation and Content Moderation Issues for Congress.* Washington, DC: Congressional Research Service, 2021. https://crsreports.congress.gov/product/pdf/R/R46662.

Garrett, R. Kelly. "The 'Echo Chamber' Distraction: Disinformation Campaigns Are the Problem, Not Audience Fragmentation." *Journal of Applied Research in Memory and Cognition* 6, no. 4 (2017): 370–76. https://doi.org/10.1016/j.jarmac.2017.09.011.

Gavet, Maelle. *Trampled by Unicorns: Big Tech's Empathy Problem and How to Fix It.* Hoboken, NJ: Wiley, 2020.

Gehrman, Elizabeth. "The Isolation of Social Media: Social Media Should Promote Conversation and Exchange, yet Increasingly It Doesn't." *Harvard Medicine* (Spring 2022). https://hms.harvard.edu/magazine/viral-world/isolation-social-media.

Geiger, Nathaniel. "Do People Actually 'Listen to the Experts'? A Cautionary Note on Assuming Expert Credibility and Persuasiveness on Public Health Policy Advocacy." *Health Communication* 37, no. 6 (December 2020): 677–84. https://doi.org/10.1080/10410236.2020.1862449.

Gerstein, Julie. "Fox News Pundit Steve Hilton Pushed a Ridiculous Conspiracy Theory That Dr. Fauci Is behind the Coronavirus." *Insider*, January 26, 2021. https://www.businessinsider.com/fox-news-pushing-conspiracy-that-fauci-created-coronavirus-2021-1.

Gharib, Malaka. "WHO Is Fighting False COVID Info on Social Media. How's That Going?" NPR, February 9, 2021. https://www.npr.org/sections/goatsandsoda/2021/02/09/963973675/who-is-fighting-false-covid-info-on-social-media-hows-that-going.

Ghosh, Dipayan. "It's All in the Business Model: The Internet's Economic Logic and the Instigation of Disinformation, Hate, and Discrimination." *Georgetown Journal of International Affairs* 21 (Fall 2020): 129–35. https://doi.org/10.1353/gia.2020.0012.

Gigerenzer, Gerd. "Towards a Rational Theory of Heuristics." In *Minds, Models and Milieux: Archival Insights into the Evolution of Economics,* edited by Roger Frantz and Leslie Marsh, 34–59. London: Palgrave Macmillan, 2016. https://doi.org/10.1057/9781137442505_3.

Giussani, Alessio. "Competing over Truth: A Critical Analysis of EU Initiatives to Counter Disinformation (2015–2019)." Master's diss., Aristotle University of Thessaloniki: Department of Digital Media, Communication and Journalism, January 2020.

Glastris, Paul. "Introduction: Can Journalism Be Saved?" *Washington Monthly*, October 25, 2020. https://washingtonmonthly.com/magazine/november-december-2020/can-journalism-be-saved-2.

Gogarty, Kayla. "Trump Used Facebook to Amplify Fox News and Its Personalities. Of Course the Network Wants Him Reinstated." Media Matters for America, May 11, 2021. https://www.mediamatters.org/fox-news/trump-used-facebook-amplify-fox-news-and-its-personalities-course-network-wants-him.

Goleman, Daniel. *Emotional Intelligence: Why It Can Matter More Than IQ*. New York: Bantam Dell, 1994.

Gordon, Eric, and Paul Mihailidis, eds. *Civic Media: Technology, Design, Practice*. Cambridge, MA: MIT Press, 2016.

Graham, Megan, and Jennifer Elias. "How Google's $150 Billion Advertising Business Works." CNBC, May 18, 2021. https://www.cnbc.com/2021/05/18/how-does-google-make-money-advertising-business-breakdown-.html.

Grassmuck, Volker Ralf. "Towards an Infrastructure for a Democratic Digital Public Sphere." In *European Public Spheres, Digitisation and Public Welfare Orientation, iRights*, edited by Alexander Baratsits. October 2021. https://papers.ssrn.com/sol3/papers.cfm?abstract_id=3937500.

Graves, Lucas. "Boundaries Not Drawn: Mapping the Institutional Roots of the Global Fact-Checking Movement." *Journalism Studies* 19, no. 5 (June 2016): 613–31. https://doi.org/10.1080/1461670X.2016.1196602.

Gray, Colin M., Yuno Kou, Byran Battles, Joseph Hoggatt, and Austin L. Toombs. "The Dark (Patterns) Side of UX Design." *Proceedings of the 2018 CHI Conference on Human Factors in Computing Systems—CHI '18*. New York: ACM Press, 2018. https://doi.org/10.1145/3173574.3174108.

Gregory, Sam. "Deepfakes, Misinformation and Disinformation and Authenticity Infrastructure Responses: Impacts on Frontline Witnessing, Distant Witnessing, and Civic Journalism." *Journalism*, December 11, 2021. https://doi.org/10.1177/14648849211060644.

Greifeneder, Rainer, Mariela Jaffe, Eryn Newman, and Norbert Schwarz, eds. *The Psychology of Fake News: Accepting, Sharing, and Correcting Misinformation*. New York: Routledge, 2021.

Grind, Kirsten, Sam Schechner, Robert McMillan, and John West. "How Google Interferes with Its Search Algorithms and Changes Your Results." *Wall Street Journal*, November 15, 2019. https://www.wsj.com/articles/how-google-interferes-with-its-search-algorithms-and-changes-your-results-11573823753.

Grzesiak-Feldman, Monica. "The Effect of High-Anxiety Situations on Conspiracy Thinking." *Current Psychology* 32, no. 1 (January 2013): 100–18. https://doi.org/10.1007/s12144-013-9165-6.

Guiao, Jordan, and Peter Lewis. *The Public Square Project*. Australia Institute: Centre for Responsible Technology, n.d. https://australiainstitute.org.au/wp-content/uploads/2021/04/210428-public-square-paper-WEB.pdf.

Hagey, Keach, Lukas I. Alpert, and Yaryna Serkez. "In News Industry, a Stark Divide between Haves and Have-Nots." *Wall Street Journal*, May 4, 2019. https://www.wsj .com/graphics/local-newspapers-stark-divide.

Hameleers, Michael, Thomas E. Powell, Toni G. L. A. Van Der Meer, and Lieke Bos. "A Picture Paints a Thousand Lies? The Effects and Mechanisms of Multimodal Disinformation and Rebuttals Disseminated via Social Media." *Political Communication* 37, no. 2 (February 2020): 281–301. https://doi.org/10.1080/10584609.2019 .1674979.

Harbach, Marian, Markus Hettig, Susanne Weber, and Matthew Smith. "Using Personal Examples to Improve Risk Communication for Security and Privacy Decisions." *Proceedings of the SIGCHI Conference on Human Factors in Computing Systems*, 2647–56. New York: ACM, 2014. https://doi.org/10.1145/2556288.2556978.

Harris, Adam J. L., and Ulrike Hahn. "Bayesian Rationality in Evaluating Multiple Testimonies: Incorporating the Role of Coherence." *Journal of Experimental Psychology: Learning, Memory, and Cognition* 35, no. 5 (September 2009): 1366–72. https:// doi.org/10.1037/a0016567.

Harris, Tristan. "Our Brains Are No Match for Technology." *New York Times*, December 5, 2019. https://www.nytimes.com/2019/12/05/opinion/digital -technology-brain.html.

Hart, Joshua, and Molly Graether. "Something's Going On Here: Psychological Predictors of Belief in Conspiracy Theories." *Journal of Individual Differences* 39, no. 4 (2018): 229–37. https://doi.org/10.1027/1614-0001/a000268.

Hart, William, Dolores Albarracín, Alice H. Eagly, Inge Brechan, Matthew J. Lindberg, and Lisa Merrill. "Feeling Validated versus Being Correct: A Meta-Analysis of Selective Exposure to Information." *Psychological Bulletin* 135, no. 4 (2009): 555–88. https://doi.org/10.1037/a0015701.

Hatmaker, Taylor. "Yik Yak Returns from the Dead." TechCrunch, August 16, 2021. https://techcrunch.com/2021/08/16/yik-yak-is-back.

Haugen, Frances. "Europe Is Making Social Media Better without Curtailing Free Speech. The U.S. Should, Too." *New York Times*, April 28, 2022. https://www .nytimes.com/2022/04/28/opinion/social-media-facebook-transparency.html.

Head, Alison J., Barbara Fister, and Margy MacMillan. *Information Literacy in the Age of Algorithms: Student Experiences with News and Information, and the Need for Change.* Project Information Research Institute, January 2020. https://projectinfolit.org/ publications/algorithm-study.

Heilweil, Rebecca. "Why Algorithms Can Be Racist and Sexist." Vox, February 18, 2020. https://www.vox.com/recode/2020/2/18/21121286/algorithms-bias -discrimination-facial-recognition-transparency.

Hertwig, Ralph, and Till Grüne-Yanoff. "Nudging and Boosting: Steering or Empowering Good Decisions." *Perspectives on Psychological Science* 12, no. 6 (2017): 973–86. https://journals.sagepub.com/doi/10.1177/1745691617702496.

Hill, Kashmir, and Jeremy White. "Designed to Deceive: Do These People Look Real to You?" *New York Times*, November 21, 2020. https://www.nytimes.com/inter- active/2020/11/21/science/artificial-intelligence-fake-people-faces.html.

Hobbs, Renee. "Propaganda in an Age of Algorithmic Personalization: Expanding Literacy Research and Practice." *Reading Research Quarterly* 55, no. 3 (February 2020): 521–33. https://doi.org/10.1002/rrq.301.

Horta Ribeiro, Manoel, Shagun Jhaver, Savvas Zannettou, Jeremy Blackburn, Gianluca Stringhini, Emiliano de Cristofaro, and Robert West. "Do Platform Migrations Compromise Content Moderation? Evidence from r/The_Donald and r/Incels." CSCW 2021 (2021). https://arxiv.org/pdf/2010.10397.pdf.

Horwitz, Jeff. "The Facebook Files." *Wall Street Journal*, September 13, 2021. https://www.wsj.com/articles/the-facebook-files-11631713039.

Hsu, Tiffany, and Gillian Friedman. "CVS, Dunkin', Lego: The Brands Pulling Ads from Facebook over Hate Speech." *New York Times*, July 7, 2020. https://www.nytimes.com/2020/06/26/business/media/Facebook-advertising-boycott.html.

Hwang, Tim. "Subprime Attention Crisis." Interview by Ethan Zuckerman. *Reimagining the Internet*, December 2, 2020. Podcast, 28:16. https://publicinfrastructure.org/podcast/07-tim-hwang.

———. *Subprime Attention Crisis*. New York: Farrar, Straus and Giroux, 2020.

Imhoff, Roland, and Martin Bruder. "Speaking (Un-)Truth to Power: Conspiracy Mentality as a Generalised Political Attitude." *European Journal of Personality* 28, no. 1 (January 2014): 25–43. https://doi.org/10.1002/per.1930.

Ingraham, Christopher. "What's a Urinal Fly and What Does It Have to Do with Winning a Nobel Prize?" *Washington Post*, October 9, 2017. https://www.washingtonpost.com/news/wonk/wp/2017/10/09/whats-a-urinal-fly-and-what-does-it-have-to-with-winning-a-nobel-prize.

Jarrett, Caitlin, Rose Wilson, Maureen O'Leary, Elisabeth Eckersberger, and Heidi J. Larson. "Strategies for Addressing Vaccine Hesitancy: A Systematic Review." *Vaccine* 33, no. 34 (August 2015): 4180–90. https://doi.org/10.1016/j.vaccine.2015.04.040.

Jeffries, Adrianne, and Leon Yin. "Google's Top Search Result? Surprise, It's Google." The Markup, July 28, 2020. https://themarkup.org/google-the-giant/2020/07/28/google-search-results-prioritize-google-products-over-competitors.

Johnson, Eric. "Tristan Harris Says Tech Is 'Downgrading' Humanity—But We Can Fix It." Vox, May 6, 2019. https://www.vox.com/recode/2019/5/6/18530860/tristan-harris-human-downgrading-time-well-spent-kara-swisher-recode-decode-podcast-interview.

Johnson-Laird, P. N. "Mental Models and Consistency." In *Cognitive Consistency: A Unifying Concept in Social Psychology,* edited by Bertram Gawronski and Fritz Strack, 225–44. New York: Guilford Press, 2012.

Kahneman, Daniel. *Thinking, Fast and Slow*. New York: Farrar, Straus and Giroux, 2011.

Kamerer, David. "Media Literacy." *Communication Research Trends* 32, no. 1 (2013).

Kaplan, Sheila. "Juul to Pay $40 Million to Settle N.C. Vaping Case." *New York Times*, June 28, 2021. https://www.nytimes.com/2021/06/28/health/juul-vaping-settlement-north-carolina.html.

Karr, Timothy, and Craig Aaron. *Beyond Fixing Facebook.* Free Press, February 2019. https://www.freepress.net/sites/default/files/2019-02/Beyond-Fixing-Facebook-Final_0.pdf.

Kavanagh, Jennifer, and Michael D. Rich. *Truth Decay: An Initial Exploration of the Diminishing Role of Facts and Analysis in American Public Life.* Santa Monica, CA: RAND Corporation, 2018. https://www.rand.org/pubs/research_reports/RR2314.html.

Kearns, Michael, and Aaron Roth. *The Ethical Algorithm: The Science of Socially Aware Algorithm Design.* New York: Oxford University Press, 2020.

Kendal, Rachel L., Neeltje J. Boogert, Luke Rendell, Kevin N. Laland, Mike Webster, and Patricia L. Jones. "Social Learning Strategies: Bridge-Building between Fields." *Trends in Cognitive Sciences* 22, no. 7 (July 2018): 651–65. https://doi.org/10.1016/j.tics.2018.04.003.

Kendall, Tim. "Testimony of Tim Kendall." House Committee on Energy and Commerce, September 24, 2020. https://energycommerce.house.gov/sites/democrats.energycommerce.house.gov/files/documents/09.24.20%20CPC%20Witness%20Testimony_Kendall.pdf.

Kertysova, Katarina. "Artificial Intelligence and Disinformation: How AI Changes the Way Disinformation Is Produced, Disseminated, and Can Be Countered." *Security and Human Rights* 29, nos. 1–4 (2018): 55–81. https://doi.org/10.1163/18750230-02901005.

Khan, Israr. "How Can States Effectively Regulate Social Media Platforms?" *Oxford Business Law Blog,* January 13, 2021. https://www.law.ox.ac.uk/business-law-blog/blog/2021/01/how-can-states-effectively-regulate-social-media-platforms.

Kim, Jooyeon, Behzad Tabibian, Alice Oh, Bernhard Schölkopf, and Manuel Gomez-Rodriguez. "Leveraging the Crowd to Detect and Reduce the Spread of Fake News and Misinformation." In *WSDM 2018: The Eleventh ACM International Conference on Web Search and Data Mining: Marina Del Rey, CA, USA, February 05–09, 2018,* 324–32. New York: Association for Computing Machinery, 2018. https://doi.org/10.1145/3159652.3159734.

Kleinberg, Jon, Jens Ludwig, Sendhil Mullainathan, and Cass R. Sunstein. "Discrimination in the Age of Algorithms." SSRN, February 5, 2019. http://dx.doi.org/10.2139/ssrn.3329669.

Knight Foundation. "Disinformation, 'Fake News' and Influence Campaigns on Twitter." Knight Foundation, October 4, 2018. https://knightfoundation.org/reports/disinformation-fake-news-and-influence-campaigns-on-twitter.

Kozyreva, Anastasia, Stephan Lewandowsky, and Ralph Hertswig. "Citizens versus the Internet: Confronting Digital Challenges with Cognitive Tools." *Psychological Science in the Public Interest* 21, no. 3 (December 2020): 103–56. https://doi.org/10.1177/1529100620946707.

Kreps, Sarah, and Miles McCain. "Not Your Father's Bots: AI Is Making Fake News Look Real." *Foreign Affairs,* August 2, 2019. https://www.foreignaffairs.com/articles/2019-08-02/not-your-fathers-bots.

Kublin, Nathaniel. "The [BLEEP] You Can't Say on TV: A History of Swearing in Television." *Brown Political Review,* August 13, 2018. https://brownpoliticalreview.org/2018/08/the-bleep-you-cant-say-on-tv-a-history-of-swearing-in-television.

LaCour, Mark, and Tyler Davis. "Vaccine Skepticism Reflects Basic Cognitive Differences in Mortality-Related Event Frequency Estimation." *Vaccine* 38, no. 21 (May 2020): 3790–99. https://doi.org/10.1016/j.vaccine.2020.02.052.

Lauer, Dave. "You Cannot Have AI Ethics without Ethics." *AI and Ethics* 1 (February 2021): 21–25. https://doi.org/10.1007/s43681-020-00013-4.

Lawrence, Regina G., Eric Gordon, Andrew DeVigal, Caroline Mellor, and Jonathan Elbaz. *Building Engagement: Supporting the Practice of Relational Journalism.* Agora Journalism Center, April 2019. https://agorajournalism.center/wp-content/uploads/2019/04/201904-Agora-Report-Building-Engagement.pdf.

Lee, Taeyoung, Claudia Wilhelm, Gina M. Masullo, Martin J. Riedl, João Gonçalves, and Natalie (Talia) Jomini Stroud. "How to Signal Trust in a Google Search." Center for Media Engagement, January 2021. https://mediaengagement.org/research/how-to-signal-trust-in-a-google-search.

Legg, Heidi, and Joe Kerwin. "The Fight against Disinformation in the U.S.: A Landscape Analysis." Shorenstein Center on Media, Politics and Public Policy (November 2018). https://shorensteincenter.org/the-fight-against-disinformation-in-the-u-s-a-landscape-analysis.

Lewandowsky, Stephan, John Cook, Nicolas Fay, and Gilles E. Gignac. "Science by Social Media: Attitudes towards Climate Change Are Mediated by Perceived Social Consensus." *Memory & Cognition* 47, no. 18 (June 2019): 1445–56. https://doi.org/10.3758/s13421-019-00948-y.

Lewandowsky, Stephan, Ullrich K. H. Ecker, Colleen M. Seifert, Norbert Schwarz, and John Cook. "Misinformation and Its Correction: Continued Influence and Successful Debiasing." *Psychological Science in the Public Interest* 13 (September 2012): 106–13. https://doi.org/10.1177/1529100612451018.

Lewandowsky, Stephan, Werner G. K. Stritzke, Klaus Oberauer, and Michael Morales. "Memory for Fact, Fiction, and Misinformation: The Iraq War 2003." *Psychological Science* 16, no. 3 (March 2005): 190–95. https://doi.org/10.1111/j.0956-7976.2005.00802.x.

Lim, Chloe. "Checking How Fact Checkers Check." *Research and Politics* 5, no. 3 (July 2018). https://doi.org/10.1177/2053168018786848.

Lorenz-Spreen, Philip, Stephan Lewandowsky, Cass R. Sunstein, and Ralph Hertwig. "How Behavioural Sciences Can Promote Truth, Autonomy and Democratic Discourse Online." *Nature Human Behaviour* 4 (June 2020): 1102–9. https://doi.org/10.1038/s41562-020-0889-7.

Lozano, Marianela Garcia, Joel Brynielsson, Ulrik Franke, Magnus Rosell, Edward Tjörnhammar, Stefan Varga, and Vladimir Vlassov. "Veracity Assessment of Online Data." *Decision Support Systems* 129 (2020). https://doi.org/10.1016/j.dss.2019.113132.

Lynn. "New Survey in Vermont Reveals More Trust among Neighbors." *Front Porch Forum: Ghost of Midnight* (blog), February 14, 2018. https://blog.frontporchforum.com/2018/02/14/new-survey-in-vermont-reveals-more-trust-among-neighbors.

Mac, Ryan, Cade Metz, and Kate Conger. "'I Don't Really Have a Business Plan': How Elon Musk Wings It." *New York Times*, May 3, 2022. https://www.nytimes.com/2022/05/03/technology/elon-musk-twitter-plan.html.

Marchese, David. "Yale's Happiness Professor Says Anxiety Is Destroying Her Students" *New York Times*, February 18, 2022. https://www.nytimes.com/interactive/2022/02/21/magazine/laurie-santos-interview.html.

Marcin, Tim, and Rachel Kraus. "Here Are the (Many) Companies Pulling Their Ads from Facebook." Mashable, June 27, 2020. https://mashable.com/article/list-facebook-advertisers-pulled-out.

Marietta, Morgan, and David C. Barker. *One Nation, Two Realities: Dueling Facts in American Democracy*. New York: Oxford University Press, 2019.

Marshall, Lisa. "How Black Twitter Has Become the New 'Green Book'—and More." CU Boulder Today, October 27, 2021. https://www.colorado.edu/today/2021/10/27/how-black-twitter-has-become-new-green-book-and-more.

Martin, Erik Nikolaus. "Can Public Service Broadcasting Survive Silicon Valley? Synthesizing Leadership Perspectives at the BBC, PBS, NPR, CPB and Local U.S. Stations." *Technology in Society* 64 (February 2021): 1–11. https://doi.org/10.1016/j.techsoc.2020.101451.

Marwick, Alice, Rachel Kuo, Shanice Jones Cameron, and Moira Weigel. *Critical Disinformation Studies: A Syllabus*. Chapel Hill: Center for Information, Technology, & Public Life (CITAP), University of North Carolina, 2021. https://citap.unc.edu/critical-disinfo.

Massachi, Sahar. "How to Save Our Social Media by Treating It Like a City." *MIT Technology Review*, December 20, 2021. https://www.technologyreview.com/2021/12/20/1042709/how-to-save-social-media-treat-it-like-a city.

Matamoros-Fernández, Ariadna. "Platformed Racism: The Mediation and Circulation of an Australian Race-Based Controversy on Twitter, Facebook and YouTube." *Information, Communication & Society* 20 no. 6 (February 2017): 930–46. https://doi.org/10.1080/1369118X.2017.1293130.

Matz, S. C., M. Kosinski, G. Nave, and D. J. Stillwell. "Psychological Targeting in Digital Mass Persuasion." *PNAS* 114, no. 48 (November 2017): 12714–19. https://doi.org/10.1073/pnas.1710966114.

McDermott, Rose. "Psychological Underpinnings of Post-Truth in Political Beliefs." *PS: Political Science & Politics* 52, no. 2 (January 2019): 218–22. https://doi.org/10.1017/S104909651800207X.

McDowell, Zachary J., and Matthew A. Vetter. *Wikipedia and the Representation of Reality*. New York: Taylor and Francis, 2022. https://library.oapen.org/handle/20.500.12657/50520.

"Media Manipulation Casebook." Technology and Social Change Project, last modified 2022. https://mediamanipulation.org.

Menczer, Filippo, and Thomas Hills. "Information Overload Helps Fake News Spread, and Social Media Knows It: Understanding How Algorithm Manipulators Exploit Our Cognitive Vulnerabilities Empowers Us to Fight Back." *Scientific American*, December 1, 2020. https://www.scientificamerican.com/article/information-overload-helps-fake-news-spread-and-social-media-knows-it.

Mihailidis, Paul. "Civic Media Literacies: Re-Imagining Engagement for Civic Intentionality." *Learning, Media and Technology* 43, no. 2 (2018): 152–64. https://doi.org/10.1080/17439884.2018.1428623.

Mihailidis, Paul, and Adam Gamwell. "Designing Engagement in Local News: Using FOIA Requests to Create Inclusive Participatory Journalism Practices." *Journalism Practice*, September 16, 2020, 1–20. https://doi.org/10.1080/17512786.2020 .1819381.

Milan, Stephania. "Liberated Technology: Inside Emancipatory Communication Activism." In *Civic Media: Technology, Design, and Practice*, edited by Eric Gordon and Paul Mihailidis, 107–24. Cambridge, MA: MIT Press, 2016.

Miles, Tom. "U.N. Investigators Cite Facebook Role in Myanmar Crisis." Reuters, March 12, 2018. https://www.reuters.com/article/us-myanmar-rohingya-facebook -idUKKCN1GO2PN.

Miller, Greg. "As U.S. Election Nears, Researchers Are Following the Trail of Fake News." Science, October 26, 2020. https://www.science.org/content/article/us -election-nears-researchers-are-following-trail-fake-news.

Miller, Joanne M., Kyle L. Saunders, and Christine E. Farhart. "Conspiracy Endorsement as Motivated Reasoning: The Moderating Roles of Political Knowledge and Trust." *American Journal of Political Science* 60, no. 4 (November 2015): 824–44. https//doi.org/10.1111/ajps.12234.

Miller, Katherine. "Radical Proposal: Middleware Could Give Consumers Choices over What They See Online," HAI Stanford University, October 20, 2021. https:// hai.stanford.edu/news/radical-proposal-middleware-could-give-consumers-choices -over-what-they-see-online.

Mims, Christopher. "Without Humans, Artificial Intelligence Is Still Pretty Stupid." *Wall Street Journal*, November 12, 2017. https://www.wsj.com/articles/without -humans-artificial-intelligence-is-still-pretty-stupid-1510488000.

Minow, Martha. *Saving the News*. New York: Oxford University Press, 2021.

Mitra, Mallika. "Nike Won Its First 'Outstanding Commercial' Emmy in 17 Years for an Ad Featuring Colin Kaepernick." CNBC, September 16, 2019. https://www .cnbc.com/2019/09/16/nike-wins-emmy-for-ad-featuring-colin-kaepernick.html.

Muthukrishna, Michael, Thomas J. H. Morgan, and Joseph Henrich. "The When and Who of Social Learning and Conformist Transmission." *Evolution and Human Behavior* 37, no. 1 (January 2016): 10–20. https://doi.org/10.1016/j.evolhumbe-hav.2015.05.004.

Myers, Steven Lee, and Cecilia Kang. "Barack Obama Takes on a New Role: Fighting Disinformation." *New York Times*, April 20, 2022. https://www.nytimes.com/ 2022/04/20/technology/barack-obama-disinformation.html.

Napoli, Philip M. *Social Media and the Public Interest: Media Regulation in the Disinformation Age*. New York: Columbia University Press, 2019.

———. "What If More Speech Is No Longer the Solution? First Amendment Theory Meets Fake News and the Filter Bubble." *Federal Communications Law Journal* 70, no. 1 (2018): 55–104. http://www.fclj.org/wp-content/uploads/2018/04/70.1 -Napoli.pdf.

Napoli, Philip M., and Fabienne Graf. "Social Media Platforms as Public Trustees: An Approach to the Disinformation Problem." *TPRC48: The 48th Research Conference on Communication, Information and Internet Policy*. SSRN, December 14, 2020. http:// dx.doi.org/10.2139/ssrn.3748544.

National Highway Traffic Safety Administration. "Seat Belt Use in 2016: Use Rates in the States and Territories." US Department of Transportation, May 2017. https://crashstats.nhtsa.dot.gov/Api/Public/ViewPublication/812417.

———. "Seat Belts." US Department of Transportation, n.d. https://www.nhtsa.gov/risky-driving/seat-belts.

New_ Public. "The Case for Integrity Workers." New_ Public, last modified February 27, 2022. https://newpublic.substack.com/p/-the-case-for-integrity-workers.

———. "Reintroducing The Signals: A Quick Primer on Our Research about Flourishing Digital Public Spaces." New_ Public, June 27, 2021. https://newpublic.substack.com/p/-reintroducing-the-signals?

———. "The Signals Research." New_ Public, last modified March 7, 2022. https://newpublic.org/signals.

Nieminen, Sakari, and Lauri Rapeli. "Fighting Misperceptions and Doubting Journalists' Objectivity: A Review of Fact Checking Literature." *Political Studies Review* 17, no. 3 (July 2018): 296–309. https://doi.org/10.1177/1478929918786852.

Nitzberg, Mark, and Camille Carlton. "Technology Solutions for Disinformation." BRIE Working Paper 2021-7. Berkeley Roundtable on the International Economy (August 2021). https://brie.berkeley.edu/sites/default/files/brie_wp_2021_7_tech_solutions_for_disinformation.pdf.

Noble, Safiya Umoja. *Algorithms of Oppression: How Search Engines Reinforce Racism.* New York: New York University Press, 2018.

Nordheim, Lena V., Malene W. Gundersen, Birgitte Espehaug, Øystein Guttersrud, and Signe Flottorp. "Effects of School-Based Educational Interventions for Enhancing Adolescents Abilities in Critical Appraisal of Health Claims: A Systematic Review," *PLoS ONE* 11, no. 8 (2016). https://doi.org/10.1371/journal.pone.0161485.

Novemsky, Nathan, Ravi Dhar, Norbert Schwarz, and Itamar Simonson. "Preference Fluency in Choice." *Journal of Marketing Research* 44 (August 2007): 347–56. https://doi.org/10.1509/jmkr.44.3.347.

Nugent, Ciara. "WhatsApp's Fake News Problem Has Turned Deadly in India. Here's How to Stop It." *Time*, August 1, 2018. https://time.com/5352516/india-whatsapp-fake-news.

O'Connor, Cailin, and James Owen Weatherall. *The Misinformation Age: How False Beliefs Spread.* New Haven, CT: Yale University Press, 2019.

O'Hara, Amy, and Jodi Nelson. "Combatting Digital Disinformation: An Evaluation of the William and Flora Hewlett Foundation's Disinformation Strategy." Hewlett Foundation, October 2020. https://hewlett.org/wp-content/uploads/2020/10/Final-Hewlett-evaluation-report-on-disinformation-.pdf.

O'Kane, Sean. "New Study Will Show Misinformation on Facebook Gets Way More Engagement Than News." The Verge, September 3, 2021. https://www.theverge.com/2021/9/3/22656036/nyu-researchers-study-facebook-misinformation-engagement-election.

One Earth Future. "Taming the Wild West: How Better Governance Leads to Peace." *One Earth Future Foundation.* 2021. https://www.oneearthfuture.org/opinion-insights/taming-wild-west-how-better-governance-leads-peace.

Oppenheimer, Daniel M. "Consequences of Erudite Vernacular Utilized Irrespective of Necessity: Problems with Using Long Words Needlessly." *Applied Cognitive Psychology* 20 (October 2005): 139–56. https://doi.org/10.1002/acp.1178.

Orenstein, Peggy. "If You Ignore Porn, You Aren't Teaching Sex Ed." *New York Times*, June 14, 2021. https://www.nytimes.com/2021/06/14/opinion/sex-ed -curriculum-pornography.html.

Ostrom, Elinor. *Governing the Commons: The Evolution of Institutions for Collective Action.* Cambridge: Cambridge University Press, 1990.

O'Sullivan, Donie. "Doctored Videos Shared to Make Pelosi Sound Drunk Viewed Millions of Times on Social Media." CNN, May 24, 2019. https://www.cnn.com/ 2019/05/23/politics/doctored-video-pelosi/index.html.

Overly, Steven, and Alexandra S. Levine. "Facebook Announces First 20 Picks for Global Oversight Board." *Politico*, May 6, 2020. https://www.politico.com/news/ 2020/05/06/facebook-global-oversight-board-picks-240150.

Pan, Deanna. "Boston Officials Reach Out to Chinatown to Quell Coronavirus Fears, Misinformation." *Boston Globe*, February 13, 2020. https://www.bostonglobe .com/2020/02/13/metro/boston-officials-reaching-out-elderly-chinatown-quell -coronavirus-fears-misinformation.

Patterson, Thomas E. "Election Beat 2020: How News Outlets Become Misinformation Spreaders," Journalist's Resource, October 27, 2020. https://journalistsresource.org/politics-and-government/news-misinformation-superspreaders.

Pazzanese, Christina. "Their Assignment? Design a More Equitable Future." *Harvard Gazette*, February 17, 2022. https://edib.harvard.edu/news/their-assignment -design-more-equitable-future.

Pennycook, Gordon, Adam Bear, Evan T. Collins, and David G. Rand. "The Implied Truth Effect: Attaching Warnings to a Subset of Fake News Stories Increases Perceived Accuracy of Stories without Warnings." *Management Science* 66, no. 11 (February 2020). https://doi.org/10.1287/mnsc.2019.3478.

Pennycook, Gordon, and David G. Rand. "Lazy, Not Biased: Susceptibility to Partisan Fake News Is Better Explained by Lack of Reasoning Than by Motivated Reasoning." *Cognition* 188 (July 2019): 39–50. https://doi.org/10.1016/j.cognition.2018.06.011.

———. "Who Falls for Fake News? The Roles of Bullshit Receptivity, Overclaiming, Familiarity, and Analytic Thinking." *Journal of Personality* 88, no. 2 (March 2019): 1–16. https://doi.org/10.1111/jopy.12476.

Pennycook, Gordon, Jonathon McPhetres, Yunhao Zhang, Jackson G. Lu, and David G. Rand. "Fighting COVID-19 Misinformation on Social Media: Experimental Evidence for a Scalable Accuracy Nudge Intervention." *Association for Psychological Science* 31, no. 7 (2020): 770–80. https://doi.org/10.1177/0956797620939054.

Pennycook, Gordon, Tyrone D. Cannon, and David G. Rand. "Prior Exposure Increases Perceived Accuracy of Fake News." *Journal of Experimental Psychology-General* 147, no. 12 (December 2018): 1865–80. https://doi.org/10.1037/xge0000465.

Pennycook, Gordon, Robert M. Ross, Derek J. Koehler, and Jonathan A. Fugelsang. "Correction: Atheists and Agnostics Are More Reflective Than Religious Believers:

Four Empirical Studies and a Meta-Analysis." *PLoS ONE* 12, no. 4 (2017). https://doi.org/10.1371/journal.pone.0176586.

Petticrew, Mark, Nason Maani, Luisa Pettigrew, Harry Rutter, and May Ci Van Schalkwyk. "Dark Nudges and Sludge in Big Alcohol: Behavioral Economics, Cognitive Biases, and Alcohol Industry Corporate Social Responsibility," *Millbank Quarterly* 98, no. 4 (September 15, 2020). https://doi.org/10.1111/1468-0009.12475.

"The Philippines Social Network Has Been Weaponized by Bots to Spread Fake News." *Networks* (blog), November 12, 2020. https://blogs.cornell.edu/info2040/2020/11/12/the-philippines-social-network-has-been-weaponized-by-bots-to-spread-fake-news.

Phillips, Whitney, and Ryan Milner. *You Are Here: A Field Guide for Navigating Polarized Speech, Conspiracy Theories, and Our Polluted Media Landscape.* Cambridge, MA: MIT Press, 2021.

Pickard, Victor. *Democracy without Journalism? Confronting the Misinformation Society.* New York: Oxford, 2020.

———. "Restructuring Democratic Infrastructures: A Policy Approach to the Journalism Crisis." *Digital Journalism* 8, no. 1 (2020): 704–19. https://doi.org/10.1080/21670811.2020.1733433.

Popli, Nik. "The 5 Most Important Revelations from the 'Facebook Papers.'" *Time*, October 26, 2021. https://time.com/6110234/facebook-papers-testimony-explained.

Porterfield, Carlie. "Twitter Begins Asking Users to Actually Read Articles before Sharing Them." *Forbes*, June 10, 2020. https://www.forbes.com/sites/carlieporterfield/2020/06/10/twitter-begins-asking-users-to-actually-read-articles-before-sharing-them.

Preston, Stephanie, Anthony Anderson, David J. Robertson, Mark P. Shepard, and Narisong Huhe. "Detecting Fake News on Facebook: The Role of Emotional Intelligence." *PLoS ONE* 16, no. 3 (March 2021). https://doi.org/10.1371/journal.pone.0246757.

Pundyk, Jeff. "Fake News: Awareness, Attitudes, and Actions of Advertisers." Conference Board, February 23, 2018. https://conference-board.org/publications/Advertiser-Fake-News-Awareness.

Rahman, K. Sabeel. "The New Utilities: Private Power, Social Infrastructure, and the Revival of the Public Utility Concept." *Cardoza Law Review* 39, no. 5 (2018): 1621–89.

———. "Regulating Informational Infrastructure: Internet Platforms as the New Public Utilities." *Georgetown Law and Technology Review* 2, no. 2 (February 23, 2018): 234–51. https://ssrn.com/abstract=3220737.

Rajendra-Nicolucci, Chand, and Ethan Zuckerman. "Local Logic: It's Not Always a Beautiful Day in the Neighborhood." *Toward a Better Internet* (blog), November 30, 2020. https://knightcolumbia.org/blog/local-logic-its-not-always-a-beautiful-day-in-the-neighborhood.

Rasi, Päivi, Hanna Vuojärvi, and Susanna Rivinen. "Promoting Media Literacy among Older People: A Systematic Review." *Adult Education Quarterly* 71, no. 1 (2021): 37–54. https://doi.org/10.1177/0741713620923755.

Reader, Ruth. "Google Is Placing Ads Next to COVID-19 Misinformation on Conspiracy Sites." *Fast Company*, June 11, 2020. https://www.fastcompany.com/90514329/google-is-placing-ads-next-to-health-misinformation-on-conspiracy-sites.

Reagan, Gillian. "The Evolution of Facebook's Mission Statement." *Observer*, July 13, 2009. https://observer.com/2009/07/the-evolution-of-facebooks-mission-statement.

Reber, Rolf, and Norbert Schwarz. "Effects of Perceptual Fluency on Judgments of Truth." *Consciousness and Cognition* 8, no. 3 (September 1999): 338–42. https://doi.org/10.1006/ccog.1999.0386.

Reeves, Richard V. "Lies and Honest Mistakes." AEON, July 5, 2021. https://aeon.co/essays/our-epistemic-crisis-is-essentially-ethical-and-so-are-its-solutions.

Reuters Fact Check. "Fact Check: Indiana Doctor Makes False Claims in Viral Video." Reuters, August 12, 2021. https://www.reuters.com/article/fact-check-indiana-doctor/fact-check-indiana-doctor-makes-false-claims-in-viral-video-idUSL1N2PJ1KR.

Robinson, Michael D., and Gerald Clore. "Belief and Feeling: Evidence for an Accessibility Model of Emotional Self-Report." *Psychological Bulletin* 128, no. 6 (December 2002): 934–60. https://doi.org/10.1037//0033-2909.128.6.934.

Roose, Kevin. "Inside Facebook's Data Wars." *New York Times*, July 14, 2021. https://www.nytimes.com/2021/07/14/technology/facebook-data.html.

Rose, Joel, and Liz Baker, "6 in 10 Americans Say U.S. Democracy Is in Crisis as the 'Big Lie' Takes Root," NPR, January 3, 2022. https://www.npr.org/2022/01/03/1069764164/american-democracy-poll-jan-6.

Rosenbaum, Judith E., and Jennifer Bonnet, "Looking Inward in an Era of 'Fake News': Addressing Cognitive Bias." Young Leaders of the Americas Initiative, June 10, 2019. https://ylai.state.gov/looking-inward-in-an-era-of-fake-news-addressing-cognitive-bias.

Ross, Lee, David Greene, and Pamela House. "The 'False Consensus Effect': An Egocentric Bias in Social Perception and Attribution Processes." *Journal of Experimental Social Psychology* 13, no. 3 (2004): 279–301. https://doi.org/10.1016/0022-1031(77)90049-X.

Ross, Robert M., David G. Rand, and Gordon Pennycook. "Beyond 'Fake News': Analytic Thinking in the Detection of Inaccuracy and Partisan Bias in News Headlines." *Judgment and Decision Making* 16, no. 2 (March 2021): 484–504. https://doi.org/10.31234/osf.io/cgsx6.

Rossi, Rosemary. "What the Zuck? Mark Zuckerberg Goes Full Cringe with Flag-Waving Surfing Video." *The Wrap*, July 4, 2021. https://www.thewrap.com/zuckerberg-july-fourth-surfboard-flag-john-denver.

Rotenberg, Marc. "Regulating Privacy." *New York Times*, May 6, 2018. https://www.nytimes.com/2018/05/06/opinion/letters/regulating-privacy.html.

Ryan, Padraic. "Who's Your 4chan Correspondent? (And Other Questions Storyful Thinks Newsrooms Should Be Asking after the French Election)." NiemanLab, May 22, 2017. https://www.niemanlab.org/2017/05/whos-your-4chan-correspondent -and-other-questions-storyful-thinks-newsrooms-should-be-asking-after-the -french-election.

Salganik, Matthew J., and Duncan J. Watts. "Leading the Herd Astray: An Experimental Study of Self-Fulfilling Prophecies in an Artificial Cultural Market." *Social Psychology Quarterly* 71, no. 4 (December 2008): 338–55. https://doi.org/10.1177/019027250807100404.

Salvi, Carola, Paola Iannello, Alice Cancer, Mason McClay, Sabrina Rago, Joseph E. Dunsmoor, and Alessandro Antonietti. "Going Viral: How Fear, Socio-Cognitive Polarization and Problem-Solving Influence Fake News Detection and Proliferation during COVID-19 Pandemic." *Frontiers in Communication* 5 (January 2021). https://doi.org/10.3389/fcomm.2020.562588.

Scales, David, Jack Gorman, Cody Leff, and Sara Gorman. "Effective Ways to Combat Online Medical and Scientific Misinformation: A Hermeneutic Narrative Review and Analysis." *MediArXiv*, February 2021. https://doi.org/10.33767/osf.io/rcugs.

Scalese, Roberto. "What Does It Take to Get Fired from Boston Radio?" *Boston*, July 16, 2014. https://www.boston.com/news/local-news/2014/07/16/what-does-it -take-to-get-fired-from-boston-radio.

Schevitz, Tanya, and Sandra Gharib. "New Survey Reveals Teens Get Their News from Social Media and YouTube." *Common Sense Media*, August 12, 2019. https://www.commonsensemedia.org/press-releases/new-survey-reveals-teens-get-their -news-from-social-media-and-youtube.

Schiffrin, Anya, ed. *Media Capture: How Money, Digital Platforms, and Governments Control the News*. New York: Columbia University Press, 2021.

Schmit, Megan. "Providence Students Develop a New Social Media Platform Catered to College Kids." *Providence Monthly*, May 27, 2021. https://providenceonline .com/stories/providence-students-develop-a-new-social-media-platform-catered -to-college-kids,37127.

Schulman, Michael. "Bo Burnham's Age of Anxiety." *New Yorker*, June 25, 2018. https://www.newyorker.com/magazine/2018/07/02/bo-burnhams-age-of -anxiety.

Schwarz, Norbert. "Metacognitive Experiences in Consumer Judgment and Decision Making." *Journal of Consumer Psychology* 14, no. 4 (2004): 332–48. https://doi.org/10.1207/s15327663jcp1404_2.

Schwarz, Norbert, and Madeline Jalbert. "When (Fake) News Feels True: Intuitions of Truth and the Acceptance and Correction of Misinformation." In *The Psychology of Fake News: Accepting, Sharing, and Correcting Misinformation*, edited by Rainer Greifeneder, Mariela Jaffé, Eryn J. Newman, and Norbert Schwarz, 73–89. New York: Routledge, 2021.

Schwarz, Norbert, Eryn Newman, and William D. Leach. "Making the Truth Stick and the Myths Fade: Lessons from Cognitive Psychology." *Behavioral Science & Policy* 2, no. 1 (2016): 85–95.

Seitz, Amanda. "America 'on Fire': Facebook Watched as Trump Ignited Hate." AP News, October 28, 2021. https://apnews.com/article/the-facebook-papers-trump -george-floyd-hate-speech-violence-b0f6f26f3fdf889c090703cc2fa8dce0.

Shane, Tommy. "The Psychology of Misinformation: Why We're Vulnerable." First Draft, June 30, 2020. https://firstdraftnews.org/latest/the-psychology-of -misinformation-why-were-vulnerable.

Sharon, Aviv J., and Ayelet Baram-Tsabari. "Can Science Literacy Help Individuals Identify Misinformation in Everyday Life?" *Science Education* 104, no. 5 (May 2020): 873–94. https://doi.org/10.1002/sce.21581.

Shead, Sam. "Facebook Staff Angry with Zuckerberg for Leaving Up Trump's 'Looting . . . Shooting' Post." CNBC, June 1, 2020. https://www.cnbc.com/2020/06/ 01/facebook-staff-angry--zuckerberg.html.

Shearer, Elisa. "Social Media Outpaces Print Newspapers in the U.S. as a News Source." Pew Research Center, December 10, 2018. https://www.pewresearch .org/fact-tank/2018/12/10/social-media-outpaces-print-newspapers-in-the-u-s-as -a-news-source.

Shu, Kai, Amrita Bhattacharjee, Faisal Alatawi, Tahora H. Nazer, Kaize Ding, Mansooreh Karami, and Huan Liu. "Combating Disinformation in a Social Media Age." *WIREs Data Mining and Knowledge Discovery* 10, no. 6 (August 2020). https://doi .org/10.1002/widm.1385.

Simons, Josh, and Dipayan Ghosh. "Utilities for Democracy: Why and How the Algorithmic Infrastructure of Facebook and Google Must Be Regulated." Brookings Institution, August 2020. https://www.brookings.edu/research/utilities-for -democracy-why-and-how-the-algorithmic-infrastructure-of-facebook-and-google -must-be-regulated.

Singh, Spandana. "How Recommendation Algorithms Shape Your Online Experience." *New America* (blog), March 26, 2020. https://www.newamerica.org/oti/ blog/how-recommendation-algorithms-shape-your-online-experience.

Singularex. "The Black Market for Social Media Manipulation." NATO Strategic Communications Centre of Excellence, 2019. https://www.stratcomcoe.org/black -market-social-media-manipulation.

Sippit, Amy. "The Backfire Effect: Does it Exist? And Does It Matter for Factcheckers?" Full Fact, March 2019. https://fullfact.org/media/uploads/backfire_report_ fullfact.pdf.

Slee, Tom. *What's Yours Is Mine: Against the Sharing Economy.* New York: OR Books, 2017.

Slovic, Paul, Melissa L. Finucane, Ellen Peters, and Donald G. MacGregor. "The Affect Heuristic." *European Journal of Operational Research* 177, no. 3 (March 2007): 1333–52. https://doi.org/10.1016/j.ejor.2005.04.006.

Spartz, James. T., Leona Yi-Fan Su, Robert Griffin, Dominique Brossard, and Sharon Dunwoody. "YouTube, Social Norms and Perceived Salience of Climate Change in the American Mind." *Environmental Communication* 11, no. 1 (2017): 1–16. https://doi.org/10.1080/17524032.2015.1047887.

Stewart, Emily. "Lawmakers Seem Confused about What Facebook Does—and How to Fix It." Vox, April 10, 2018. https://www.vox.com/policy-and-politics/2018/4/10/17222062/mark-zuckerberg-testimony-graham-facebook-regulations.

Stobie, Tristian. "Reflections on the 100th Year Anniversary of John Dewey's 'Democracy and Education.'" *Cambridge Assessment International Education* (blog), September 8, 2016. https://blog.cambridgeinternational.org/reflections-on-the-100th-year-anniversary-of-john-deweys-democracy-and-education.

Suler, John. "The Online Disinhibition Effect." *CyberPsychology & Behavior* 7, no. 3 (June 2004): 321–26. https://doi.org/ 10.1089/1094931041291295.

Sunstein, Cass R. "Hidden Terms, High Cancellation Fees, Complex Disclaimers Should Be Forbidden." *Boston Globe*, March 3, 2022. https://www.bostonglobe.com/2022/03/17/opinion/hidden-terms-high-cancellation-fees-complex-disclaimers-should-be-forbidden.

———. "Nudges.gov: Behavioral Economics and Regulation." In *Oxford Handbook of Behavioral Economics and the Law*, edited by Eyal Zamir and Doron Teichman. February 16, 2013. https://papers.ssrn.com/sol3/papers.cfm?abstract_id=2220022.

Swire, Briony, and Ullrich Ecker. "Misinformation and Its Correction: Cognitive Mechanisms and Recommendations for Mass Communication." In *Misinformation and Mass Audiences*, edited by B. Southwell, E. Thorson, and L. Sheble. Austin: University of Texas Press, 2018. https://brionyswire.files.wordpress.com/2019/03/swireecker2018.pdf.

Swire-Thompson, Briony, Joseph DeGutis, and David Lazer. "Searching for the Backfire Effect: Measurement and Design Considerations." *Journal of Applied Research in Memory and Cognition* 9, no. 3 (September 2020): 286–99. https://doi.org/10.1016/j.jarmac.2020.06.006.

Szeto, Eric, Katie Pedersen, and Asha Tomlinson. "Marketplace Flagged over 800 Social Media Posts with COVID-19 Misinformation. Only a Fraction Were Removed." CBC News, March 30, 2021. https://www.cbc.ca/news/marketplace/marketplace-social-media-posts-1.5968539.

Tan, Andy S. L., Chul-joo Lee, and Jiyoung Chae. "Exposure to Health (Mis)Information: Lagged Effects on Young Adults' Health Behaviors and Potential Pathways." *Journal of Communication* 65, no. 4 (August 2015): 674–98. https://doi.org/ 10.1111/jcom.12163.

Thaler, Richard H., and Cass R. Sunstein. *Nudge: Improving Decisions about Health, Wealth, and Happiness.* New York: Penguin Press, 2009.

Tishman, Shari, and Edward Clapp. "Agency by Design: Exploring Documentation and Assessment Strategies for Maker-Centered Learning." Project Zero, 2020. https://pz.harvard.edu/projects/agency-by-design.

Todd, Chuck, Mark Murray, and Carrie Dann. "Study Finds Nearly One-in-Five Americans Believe Qanon Conspiracy Theories." NBC News, May 27, 2021. https://www.nbcnews.com/politics/meet-the-press/study-finds-nearly-one-five-americans-believe-qanon-conspiracy-theories-n1268722.

"The Top 5 Celebrities Who Love a Vape in 2021." *Chief of Vapes*, March 11, 2021. https://www.chiefofvapes.com/the-top-5-celebrities-who-love-a-vape-in-2021.

Torbert, Preston M. "'Because It Is Wrong': An Essay on the Immorality and Illegality of the Online Service Contracts of Google and Facebook." *Case Western Reserve Journal of Law and Technology and the Internet* 12, no. 1 (2021). https://scholarlycom mons.law.case.edu/jolti/vol12/iss1/2.

Treen, Kathie M. d'I, T. P. Williams Hywel, and Saffron J. O'Neill. "Online Misinformation about Climate Change." *WIREs Climate Change* 11 (May 2020): 1–20. https://wires.onlinelibrary.wiley.com/doi/pdf/10.1002/wcc.665.

"#TrustedJournalism." Trust Project, 2022. https://thetrustproject.org/trusted -journalism.

Turow, Joseph. *The Daily You: How the New Advertising Industry Is Defining Your Identity and Your Worth.* New Haven, CT: Yale University Press, 2011.

Tversky, Amos, and Daniel Kahneman. "Judgment under Uncertainty: Heuristics and Biases." In *Judgment under Uncertainty: Heuristics and Biases,* edited by Daniel Kahneman, Paul Slovic, and Amos Tversky, 3–20. Cambridge: Cambridge University Press, 1982. https://doi.org/10.1017/CBO9780511809477.

UNESCO. "Information as a Public Good." 2021. https://en.unesco.org/sites/default/ files/wpfd_2021_concept_note_en.pdf.

Uscinski, Joseph E., Casey Klofstad, and Matthew Atkinson. "What Drives Conspiratorial Beliefs? The Role of Informational Cues and Predispositions." *Political Research Quarterly* 69 (January 2016). https://doi.org/10.1177/1065912915621621.

Uscinski, Joseph E., and Joseph M. Parent. *American Conspiracy Theories.* New York: Oxford University Press, 2014.

Usher, Nikki. "How Facebook and Google Buy Off the Press." *Washington Monthly,* October 25, 2020. https://washingtonmonthly.com/magazine/november -december-2020/how-facebook-and-google-buy-off-the-press.

Vincent, James. "YouTube Brings Back More Human Moderators after AI Systems Over-Censor." The Verge, September 21, 2020. https://www.theverge .com/2020/9/21/21448916/youtube-automated-moderation-ai-machine-learning -increased-errors-takedowns.

Visser, Penny, and Robert R. Mirabile. "Attitudes in the Social Context: The Impact of Social Network Composition on Individual-Level Attitude Strength." *Journal of Personality and Social Psychology* 87, no. 6 (January 2005): 779–95. https://doi.org/ 10.1037/0022-3514.87.6.779.

Vizoso, Ángel, Martín Vaz-Álvarez, and Xosé López-García. "Fighting Deepfakes: Media and Internet Giants' Converging and Diverging Strategies against Hi-Tech Misinformation." *Media and Communication* 9, no. 1 (2021): 291–300. https://doi .org/10.17645/mac.v9i1.3494.

Vosoughi, Soroush, Deb Roy, and Sinan Aral. "The Spread of True and False News Online." *Science* 359, no. 6380 (March 2018): 1146–51. https://doi.org/10.1126/ science.aap9559.

Waldow, Julia. "George Lakoff Says This Is How Trump Uses Words to Con the Public." CNN Business, June 15, 2018. https://money.cnn.com/2018/06/15/ media/reliable-sources-podcast-george-lakoff/index.html.

Walker, Mason. "U.S. Newsroom Employment Has Fallen 26% Since 2008." Pew Research Center, July 13, 2021. https://www.pewresearch.org/fact-tank/2021/07/13/u-s-newsroom-employment-has-fallen-26-since-2008.

Walker, Mason, and Katerina Eva Matsa. "News Consumption across Social Media in 2021." Pew Research Center, September 20, 2021. https://www.pewresearch.org/journalism/2021/09/20/news-consumption-across-social-media-in-2021.

Walter, Nathan, and Riva Tukachinsky. "A Meta-Analytic Examination of the Continued Influence of Misinformation in the Face of Correction: How Powerful Is It, Why Does It Happen, and How to Stop It?" *Communication Research* 47, no. 2 (June 2019): 155–77.

Walton, Matt. "It's Time That Fox News Is Considered a Political Organization, Not a News Network." Insider, March 28, 2021. https://www.businessinsider.com/fox-news-cable-political-organization-subscription-network-tucker-carlson-hannity-2021-3.

Wardle, Claire, and Hossein Derakhshan. *Information Disorder: Toward an Interdisciplinary Framework for Research and Policymaking.* Strasbourg, France: Council of Europe, September 27, 2017.

Wehsener, Alexa, Vera Zakem, and M. Nina Miller. "Future Digital Threats to Democracy: Trends and Drivers." IST Institute for Security and Technology, 2021. https://securityandtechnology.org/wp-content/uploads/2021/05/IST-RWT_2.0-FDTD-Trends-Drivers_FA_Final.pdf.

Wells, Chris, Justin Reedy, John Gastil, and Carolyn Lee. "Information Distortion and Voting Choices: The Origins and Effects of Factual Beliefs in Initiative Elections." *Political Psychology* 30, no. 6 (December 2009): 953–69. https://doi.org/10.1111/j.1467-9221.2009.00735.x.

Wetmore, Jameson M. "Implementing Restraint: Automobile Safety and the US Debate over Technological and Social Fixes." In *Car Troubles: Critical Studies of Automobility and Auto-Mobility*, edited by Jim Conley and Arlene Tigar McLaren, 111–26. London: Ashgate, 2009.

Wichowski, Alexis. "The U.S. Can't Regulate Big Tech Companies When They Act Like Nations." *Washington Post*, October 29, 2020. https://www.washingtonpost.com/outlook/2020/10/29/antitrust-big-tech-net-states.

Wikipedia. "United States Free Speech Exceptions." Last modified December 13, 2021. https://en.wikipedia.org/wiki/United_States_free_speech_exceptions.

Wood, Thomas, and Ethan Porter. "The Elusive Backfire Effect: Mass Attitudes' Steadfast Factual Adherence." *Political Behavior* 41, no. 1 (March 2019): 135–63. https://doi.org/10.1007/s11109-018-9443-y.

World Health Organization (WHO). "Let's Flatten the Infodemic Curve." n.d. https://www.who.int/news-room/spotlight/let-s-flatten-the-infodemic-curve.

Zakrzewski, Cat, Cristiano Lima, Elizabeth Dwoskin, and Will Oremus. "Facebook Whistleblower Frances Haugen Tells Lawmakers That Meaningful Reform Is Necessary 'For Our Common Good.'" *Washington Post*, October 5, 2021. https://www.washingtonpost.com/technology/2021/10/05/facebook-senate-hearing-frances-haugen.

Zayed, Yago, and John Woodhouse. *TV Licence Fee Statistics.* House of Commons, January 24, 2022. https://commonslibrary.parliament.uk/research-briefings/cbp-8101.

Zhang, Xichen, and Ali A. Ghorbani. "An Overview of Online Fake News: Characterization, Detection, and Discussion." *Information Processing & Management* 57, no. 2 (March 2020). https://doi.org/10.1016/j.ipm.2019.03.004.

Zittrain, Jonathan. "A Jury of Random People Can Do Wonders for Facebook." *The Atlantic,* November 14, 2019. https://www.theatlantic.com/ideas/archive/2019/11/let-juries-review-facebook-ads/601996.

Zuboff, Shoshana. *The Age of Surveillance Capitalism.* New York: Public Affairs, 2019.

Zuckerman, Ethan. "Building a More Honest Internet." *Columbia Journalism Review* (Fall 2019). https://www.cjr.org/special_report/building-honest-internet-public-interest.php.

———. "The Case for Digital Public Infrastructure." Knight First Amendment Institute at Columbia University, January 17, 2020. https://knightcolumbia.org/content/the-case-for-digital-public-infrastructure.

———. "What Is Digital Public Infrastructure?" Center for Journalism and Liberty, November 17, 2020. https://www.journalismliberty.org/publications/what-is-digital-public-infrastructure.

Zuidijk, Daniel. "Misinformation Is Bigger Than Facebook, but Let's Start There." *Bloomberg Business Week,* August 30, 2021. https://www.bloomberg.com/news/articles/2021-08-30/how-to-fix-covid-vaccine-misinformation-on-facebook-fb-social-media.

Index

About the Author

Leslie Stebbins is an independent researcher with more than thirty years of experience in higher education. For twenty years, she helped create and lead information and media literacy programs at Brandeis University. She has a master's in education from the Learning Design, Innovation and Education program at the Harvard Graduate School of Education and a master's in information science from Simmons College.

Currently, she is the director of Research4Ed and also the director for research at Consulting Services for Education (CS4Ed). Her clients at Research4Ed and CS4Ed have included the Harvard University Faculty of Arts and Sciences, the California State University Chancellor's Office, the US Department of Education, Curriculum Associates, Pearson, Facing History and Ourselves, Tufts University, the Joan Ganz Cooney Center, and McGraw-Hill.

Leslie Stebbins is the author of numerous articles and four books, including *Finding Reliable Information Online: Adventures of an Information Sleuth*.

www.ingramcontent.com/pod-product-compliance
Ingram Content Group UK Ltd.
Pitfield, Milton Keynes, MK11 3LW, UK
UKHW041828160725
460857UK00002B/246